D1158359

Antonio Rosmini
Persecuted Prophet

Antonio Rosmini

Persecuted Prophet

John Michael Hill, IC

GRACEWING

First published in 2014

Gracewing
2 Southern Avenue, Leominster
Herefordshire HR6 0QF

All rights reserved. No part of this publication may be reproduced, stored in a retrieval system, or transmitted in any form, or by any means, electronic, mechanical, photocopying, recording or otherwise, without the written permission of the publisher.

© John Michael Hill, 2014

The right of John Michael Hill to be identified as the author of this work has been asserted in accordance with the Copyright, Designs and Patents Act 1988

ISBN 978 0 85244 831 1

Typesetting by
Action Publishing Technology Ltd, Gloucester, GL1 5SR
Printed by
CPI Antony Rowe, Bumpers Farm, Chippenham,
Wiltshire, SN14 6LH

Contents

List of Illustrations

Special thanks are due to graphic artist, Donald Moorhead of Dunedin, who provided the three maps which accompany the text.

Fr Gianni Picenardi, IC, was most generous and helpful in letting me have the use of some of his extensive file of photographs covering Rosmini's life.

Thanks also to two people in Rovereto who kindly sent high-quality photographs of Rosmini's home and the church of San Marco. They are Signora Eleonora Bressa, Librarian of the Palazzo Rosmini, and Signore Federico Baroni, of the church of San Marco.

Cover image: Antonio Rosmini in middle life, about the age of 40. Portrait drawn by Italian artist Vittorio Casetti in 1954 for the centennial of Rosmini's death. Almost certainly taken from a portrait by Giuseppe Andreis of Rovereto, which also shows Rosmini cloaked and holding a book in one hand.

One commentator says of this portrait, 'The is a strong Rosmini, about forty years old, looking into the distance, a bit idealised' (Domenico Mariani, IC). The dating of Andreis' portrait is uncertain, but it was almost certainly posthumous.

Maps
(in the text)

Foreword

Why write a new biography of Blessed Antonio Rosmini? The last full-length biography in English was written by Fr Claude Leetham in the 1950s. It is a very extensive work and a fine piece of scholarship. However, it belongs to its time.

During my years in New Zealand I have spent much time with groups of Ascribed Members of the Institute of Charity, and it was their bidding which first prompted me to write about Blessed Antonio.

Then, some years ago, a friend started to read Fr Claude's book. He said to me, 'This is dated; when are *you* going to write us a modern biography?' This suggestion sowed a seed in me. However, I had to wait for the opportunity and the time, and this came with my retirement in 2010 from being full-time editor of a Catholic magazine.

The main qualification I have, which of course I share with many Rosminians, is that I have lived as a member of the Institute of Charity much longer and have known many more Rosminians than Blessed Antonio himself. This enables me to write confidently about our common inheritance as sons and daughters of our founder. The second source of encouragement has been from my Provincial, Fr David Myers, who said that if I didn't write this biography he did not think anyone else would.

Writing about Rosmini raises one huge problem: how to penetrate to the human being hidden behind the enormous output of words? His printed works and preserved letters represent a vast resource. There are many wise people who have written about him. There is no shortage of written material. But how was I to discover the person behind the holy pictures and the libraries of books? Rosmini is not easy to read. He was not a great stylist and, especially in his earlier days, he adopted a most elaborate, inaccessible form of Italian. He never wrote much about himself – no *Apologia Pro Vita Sua* like his great contemporary, Newman. We have no impressive collection of sermons. It is not difficult, reading Newman's sermons, in one's imagination to hear him speak, to hear his heart beat. That is rarely the case with Rosmini.

What I have tried to do in this biography is, firstly, to put him in context. I believe that you cannot begin to understand someone unless you know something of the times he or she lived in: their family, their nation, their friends, their foes. I have sought comments about him and descriptions of him from those close to him; some of these are very illuminating. I have also tried to evaluate the impact he had on other people, especially his followers in the Institute of Charity and the Sisters of Providence.

What emerges is something of a tragic story. Although he was loved and admired by many people, he was also misunderstood by some and bitterly attacked by his enemies, in international politics and within the Church. While writing this book, I felt a little of the anguish suffered not only by Rosmini himself but by his many friends at the time.

Now he has not only been acclaimed by his fellow Italians but also rehabilitated by the Church. His holiness is affirmed and his person is revered. Yet a biographer is obliged to tell, as best he can, the full story, including those things which may not reflect well on his contemporaries. He was a persecuted prophet, and those who cast the stones need to be named – named and forgiven.

I am grateful to the many people who have helped and inspired me in this work. First, to Frances Skelton who laboured for hours and days reading and researching and commenting. And to Kathleen Doherty who kept a kindly eye on style and meaning. I was fortunate enough to have a little team of readers (peer reviewers) who gave me regular feedback, notably my brethren John Buckner and David Myers, as well as Bishop Charles Drennan, an enthusiast for Rosmini, who found time in a very busy life to send me detailed comments. Finally, our recently retired General, Fr Jim Flynn, kindly read the whole draft and gave me very useful feedback.

Fr John Padberg, SJ, of the Institute of Jesuit Resources, St Louis, USA, has been very helpful in sending material and comments on the unhappy controversies between Rosmini and a group of Italian Jesuits during the 1840s and later. I am grateful to him for his objectivity and candid comments.

As regards my research and preparation, I need to mention encouragement from Fr Antonio Belsito and Br Nigel Cave and the invaluable help given by my lifelong friend and colleague Fr Tony Dewhirst, whose labours to make Rosmini better known are not always appreciated.

To those must be added a delightful group of Italian Rosminians who were generous with time and advice during my research visits to Stresa. Fr Umberto Muratore, Rector of the Centre for Rosminian Studies, deserves pride of place for his generosity with his wisdom and knowledge of the Founder. Alongside him are Frs Gianni Picenardi, Eduino Minestrina and Cyrillo Bergamaschi, and Dottore Samuele Tadini, as well as our newly elected Fr General, Vito Nardin.

My visits to Stresa were in every sense a delight and an inspiration, and I must pay tribute to the hospitality of Fr Umberto as well as to Fr Franco Costaraoss, Rector of the College at Stresa, and their communities, especially the singing poet, Fr Narciso who provided me with the poem to launch the English mission. From the Sisters of Providence, Sr Maria Bruna was generous in allowing me the use of her carefully researched material on many Rosminian topics. Behind these worthy individuals are my brethren at large and the Ascribed Members in New Zealand who have been a spur and an encouragement.

My hope is that you who read this book will find it interesting in content and helpful in your individual journeys of faith. Rosmini was a saint and his example of untiring zeal and unfailing loyalty is an inspiration. His dying testament is spoken to all of us: *adore, be silent, rejoice!*

J.M.H.
Easter 2014

Chapter One

Panegyric of Pope Pius VII

A shaft of early autumn sunlight fell across the packed benches of the magnificent church of St Mark in Rovereto. It was 25 September 1823. The civic leaders and the clergy from the surrounding valleys were present in considerable numbers for the Memorial Mass for Pope Pius VII, whose long life had come to a close four weeks earlier. Rovereto lies in the South Tyrol, some twenty miles from the city of Trent in what is now northeast Italy. For 100 years it had been ruled from Vienna, and was strongly influenced by the culture, art and music of Austria.

The church of St Mark gleams with the rococo decoration more commonly found on the northern side of the mighty Alpine chain. Like many churches of this style it appears to the Anglo-Saxon eye more like a sumptuous ballroom than a house of God – apart from the religious themes in the décor. A casual worshipper could be distracted by the ornate statuary, the cluttered side altars, or the shell-like ornaments and gleaming white corbels holding up a lavishly painted ceiling.

The liturgy for this solemn Memorial Mass was appropriately magnificent, the choir in full voice. On such occasions the *pièce de résistance* was always the panegyric. According to the tradition of the time, panegyrics of distinguished people – and not just popes and prelates – were occasions for a grand show of oratory. The sermon would be in Italian, not in the local dialect, even though Italian would barely have been understood by the majority of the congregation in those days long before Italy was unified. It would, however, be accompanied by gestures and modulations of the voice which would not have been out of place on the stage. Before the age of radio and television, the speaker was expected to entertain as well as to edify and instruct.

And now the eyes of the people were fixed on the slight, youthful figure of the preacher as he processed from the crowded pews flanking the sanctuary to the pulpit, halfway down the body of the church. He was the Abate Antonio Rosmini-Serbati, barely twenty-six years of age and ordained just two years earlier.[1]

Why would such a young and newly ordained priest be chosen to pay tribute to the recently deceased Pope? Rosmini was the eldest son of one of the noblest families in the town. His father, a Count of the Austrian Empire, had died a couple of years earlier, so Antonio had succeeded him as the head of the family and heir to great wealth. He already had a formidable reputation as a highly intelligent and capable young man. He disdained to use his inherited title, preferring to be known simply as 'Roveretan priest'. This too would appeal to the more devout of his townsfolk. They leaned forward in their seats in anticipation of a feast. They were not to be disappointed.

Five months earlier, in April, Rosmini had made his first visit to Rome in the company of the Patriarch of Venice, Msgr Ladislao Pyrker.[2] While there, he had two audiences with the aged Pope. Rosmini was very impressed by the old man, and this recent experience impelled his oratory.

Pius had welcomed the young priest warmly and tried to persuade him to remain in Rome as an Auditor of the Rota,[3] which might have been the springboard for a distinguished career in the Roman Curia. Rosmini declined the honour. But he was much encouraged when the Pope urged him to continue his philosophical writings, which Rosmini had started soon after he was ordained. The Pope also gave him a snuffbox as a mark of esteem!

So, Rosmini spoke this morning with a fervour born out of a recent golden experience. It is frustrating that there is no preserved text of the actual *Panegyric* as delivered. What we have is an edited version, prepared afterwards by Rosmini for publication. It is very long, undoubtedly much longer than what was actually delivered. Its style is dense in what is known as the classical 'Etruscan' Italian style.[4] This is the name given to a literary form of the language which some scholars thought would be closest to the original spoken tongue developed in the centuries prior to Dante. It would be the equivalent of Chaucerian English.

Rosmini favoured this archaic form of writing in his early years. He thought it was the most perfect form of the language. The sentences are often long with the main verb usually placed at the end. It follows the classical Latin grammatical structure. The vocabulary is sometimes obscure. It is not easy to read.

While composing it, he may have been conscious of the famous – and recent – *Panegyric of the Sacred Majesty of Napoleon* composed in praise of the Emperor by the Italian writer and classical scholar, Pietro Giordani. Giordani describes Napoleon in glowing terms, as 'the best of men, for all times the finest of kings . . . the Divine One, Unique Saviour and Rescuer of humanity'.[5]

Rosmini too uses exalted language. He presents the Emperor in stark contrast to the above description. The firmness of the Pope in dealing with Napoleon is depicted as being like 'the pebble striking the Colossus in its feet of clay and causing it to collapse'.[6] Rosmini describes Napoleon as an arrogant man who claims to be 'Roman Emperor, heir to Charlemagne and defender of the Catholic Church'. This, he suggests, is a wolf pretending to be a sheep!

To all the insults and persecution from Napoleon, Pius responds with meekness but with firmness. He returns good for evil. He refuses to take sides in the European wars. In this he is following the tradition of peace and virtue, practised by most popes down the centuries. Pius VII appears as universal Father of all Christians. Although old and weak in secular terms, humiliated, locked up, exiled, Pius nevertheless possesses a spiritual power beyond rival.

On the other hand, Rosmini paints Napoleon as a despot and a bully. Arbitrarily and forcefully he invades the liberties of peoples. It is not difficult to see here a scarcely veiled allusion to the current Austrian Emperor, whose government bound the Church with chains and held in oppression foreign lands, such as his own native Tyrol.

The *Panegyric* concludes with a prayer for Italy, the motherland of the late Pope, (reproduced in part at the end of this chapter). The final words are: 'May Italy find happiness and peace, and before all the world may the name of Italy be not fearsome but gentle.' Rosmini here expresses lyrically his patriotic love of Italy, even though legally he is an Austrian citizen.

The *Panegyric for Pius VII* can be read as a political manifesto. The sacred and the secular in society jockey for rival positions. Where there is reciprocal respect, there will be harmony. But if one seeks to dominate or absorb the other, there will be tension and strife. This was the case between Napoleon and Pius.

There is no record of how the actual sermon was received. But when, later on, Rosmini sought to have his edited version published, he ran into all manner of trouble with the Austrian censors.[7] The work of editing took Rosmini into 1824, when he sought in vain to have it published in Milan. He then tried Venice where initially he had more success, but the law demanded approval by the Governor. Governor Inzaghi refused permission and sent the manuscript on to the censors in Vienna, accusing its author of 'papalism' because of his earlier visit to Rome.

Rosmini attempted to get the Papal Nuncio in Vienna to intervene, but without success. The script seems to have passed through various hands before returning to Italy a year later.[8] In December 1825, he wrote to his friend, Msgr Grasser, Bishop of Treviso: 'They [the Austrian authorities] treat me as if I were a Carbonaro or some other worse devil'.[9] (The *Carbonari* were militant Italian patriots who worked for the unification of Italy and the expulsion of foreign occupying powers, such as Austria.)

The *Panegyric* was finally published anonymously in Modena in 1830. In the original manuscript the Austrian censors amended or struck out some twenty-seven sections, mostly paragraphs referring to Napoleon. The whole of the final page, including the prayer for Italy, was deleted.

∞℘⸰℘∞

Was Rosmini too hard on Napoleon? This was one of the criticisms made by the Austrian censors. The Viennese censor, Canon Ruterstöek, thought Rosmini portrayed Napoleon and the French in tones 'too harsh and biting, exceeding the norms of charity'.[10]

In many respects Napoleon had been kind to the Catholic Church. When he became First Consul and then Emperor, he set about a comprehensive re-ordering of France, giving it laws and structures which survived for a hundred years. The Catholic Church had been ravaged by the Revolution. Napoleon himself was not a religious man although his mother, still alive and well during her son's reign, was a devout Catholic. Napoleon believed that religion, when not corrupt, was a strong bolster to a just society.

So he re-opened the French churches closed by the revolutionaries. Sunday was re-established as the Lord's Day. He set about healing the schism between the so-called revolutionary 'Constitutional' church and the church of tradition, loyal to Rome, which survived in the provinces. And he negotiated a new Concordat with the newly elected Pius VII, a Concordat which lasted until the end of the nineteenth century.

When he made himself Emperor, he invited Pope Pius to the solemn coronation in Notre Dame Cathedral. When Pius arrived in Paris, he discovered that Napoleon and Josephine had undergone only a civil marriage. The Pope insisted that they go through a church wedding before the coronation, and they agreed. At the coronation, however, the Pope's role was to recite prayers and give a blessing. Napoleon placed the crown on his own head first and then on Josephine's. Napoleon was already the autocrat, prepared to patronise the

Pope but insisting always on having the final say! In this respect his conduct was little different from many other rulers of the time.

Joseph II of Austria (1764–1790) had ruled the Church, like everything else in his Empire, as a benevolent despot. He was a practising Catholic, although not as pious and observant as his mother, the redoubtable Empress Maria Theresa. He appointed the bishops; he closed down religious houses he disapproved of; he even decreed how many candles should burn on the altar in church. His so-called policy of *Josephinism* recognised the Pope simply as titular head, but for all practical purposes the Emperor ruled over the Church in Austrian territories – as indeed the Emperor still did in 1823. Napoleon never went as far as that.

However, some years after his coronation, Napoleon and Pius quarrelled over the new French civil marriage laws and over the appointment of bishops. Then, when the Pope refused to apply Napoleon's *Continental System* in the Papal States, Napoleon's army moved in and the Pope was effectively made prisoner.[11]

Later, to ensure his prisoner could not be freed by the English, Napoleon moved him to France, giving him the Chateau de Fontainbleau outside Paris. Pius retaliated by excommunicating the Emperor. Pius always refused to give way to the Emperor's browbeating tactics; yet he retained an affection for Napoleon, saying of him: 'The son is somewhat mutinous, but he remains a son.' It is significant that on his deathbed on St Helena, Napoleon sent for the priest and received the Last Sacraments.

∞∞

In the *Panegyric*, Rosmini makes a lot of the struggle between Pope and Emperor: he sees it as the classic conflict between the religious and the secular power. For Rosmini, the power of the Church must always be paramount. It must enjoy independence from the state. The state has no right to interfere with the appointment of bishops, because this leads to abuse. This brought him into face-to-face conflict with the Austrian government, which claimed absolute authority over the Church.

The final phrases of Rosmini's *Panegyric*, the so-called *Hymn to Italy*, reflect both his affection and loyalty to Pius VII and his own patriotism.[12]

> Because of the unbelievable affection that I bear towards thee,
> O Italy my mother, I will constantly raise this sincere prayer to
> God Eternal:
> all powerful One, who loves Italy, source of undying offspring,
> who from immortal Rome rules the souls of many through your
> Vicars,
> I pray you give us a sense of your high destiny –
> something we fail to perceive.
> Most generous source of all good on earth,
> mirror of faith, make us ambitious to devote ourselves to You freely,
> something You desire of us more than praise or fear.
> Grant that Italy may find happiness and peace;
> before the world, give it a name not fearsome but gentle.[13]

Rosmini's *Panegyric for Pius VII* brought him into disrepute before the Austrian authorities. The Austrian military commander, Marshal Radetzky, noted in his Black Book that the Abate Rosmini was 'a man of dangerous principles'.[14]

Thus this first public action of Antonio Rosmini as a young priest brought a cloud of suspicion over his head, which would always remain with him. It is a presage of a life spent in high endeavour but which so often was to arouse hostility within and outside the Church, and which eventually led to open persecution and disgrace.

Notes

1   'Abate', literally 'abbot', was also used as a courtesy title for priests.
2   Pagani-Rossi, i, 225.

3   The *Sacred Roman Rota* is the highest ecclesiastical court in the Catholic Church, established in Rome by the pope in the thirteenth century.

4   Pagani-Rossi, i, 240.

5   Pietro Giordani (1774–1848) wrote his so-called Panegyric in 1807 when Napoleon was at the height of his power.

6   Pagani-Rossi, i, 235.

7   Pagani-Rossi, i, 241–246.

8   The *Panegyric* was sent to Venice, then to Vienna, to Innsbruck, back over the Alps to Trent; then back to Vienna, again to Innsbruck, where the Imperial Censor finally gave the much mutilated manuscript his *imprimatur* on 9 February 1826, before returning it to Rosmini.

9   *Ep.Compl.,* i, 716.

10   Pagani-Rossi, i, 242.

11   The *Continental System* (1807–1814) was an embargo on English trade with Europe in order to destroy the English economy.

12   *The Panegyric of Pius VII,* final page. The translation is a free one by the author.

13   In quanto a me, per quell'incredibile affeto che a te porto, O Italia, o gran genitrice, inalzerò incessantemente questi devoti prieghi all'Eterno: onnipotente, che prediligi Italia, che concedi a lei immortali figliuoli, che dall'eterna Roma per i tuoi Vicari governi gli spiriti, deh! dona altresi ad essa, benignissimo, il conoscimento de' suoi alti destini, unica cosa che ignora: maestra di virtù alla terra, specchio di religione, rendili avida di liberi voti e d'amore, di cui si degna, più che di tributi e di spavento: e fa che in se stessa ella trovi felicità e riposo, e in tutto il mondo un nome non feroce ma mansueto.

14   Marshal Joseph Radetzky commanded the Austrian armies in Italy from 1834 until 1848. He was made Viceroy of Lombardy and Venice from 1848–1857. The Austrian government had a comprehensive network of spies, so it may be assumed that Rosmini was already known in 1823 to be a loyal papalist and a zealot for Italian nationalism.

Chapter Two

The World into which Rosmini was Born

On 4 September 1796, Napoleon Bonaparte defeated the Austrian army at Rovereto. He entered the town with his victorious troops, commandeering the Palazzo Fedrigotti as his temporary headquarters. This was but one act in Napoleon's astonishing first campaign, which resulted in the comprehensive defeat of the Austrian armies in Italy.[1]

A few months later, on 24 March 1797, Antonio Rosmini was born in the same small north Italian town, the elder son of Pier Modesto Rosmini, a nobleman and wealthy local landowner. The Fedrigottis were cousins of the Rosminis, and it was Pier Modesto's brother Ambrogio who had designed their house, where Napoleon briefly dwelt. Rosmini was to spend most of his early life in the town, his *Panegyric of Pius VII* was preached there, and its text is dominated by the figure of Napoleon.

The Trentino, the Alpine district which includes Rovereto, had been for more than 100 years under Austrian rule and would remain so until 1918. However, much of the rest of north Italy was now ruled by France, following Napoleon's brilliant campaigns. The Cisalpine Republic of 1800, the Italian Republic of 1802 and finally the Kingdom of Italy of 1805 were successive creations of the victorious general.[2] Napoleon had a fondness for Italy, which may have reflected his Corsican origins; so he appointed himself King of Italy, while his stepson Eugène de Beauharnais acted as regent in Milan.

The paramount influence throughout most of Italy during these years, therefore, was French. Any educated person growing up at that time could not but be aware and impressed by the emerging fashions of thought of the eighteenth-century Enlightenment and the explosion of ideas created by the French Revolution, which in 1789 blew the European order apart.

Even after Napoleon was finally defeated at the battle of Waterloo in 1815, the great powers of Europe lived in the shadow of his memory. Led by England and Austria they were determined to prevent any resurgence of French dominance, and that was the achievement of the peace settlement of the Congress of Vienna, imposed by the great powers on France and on Europe.

This was the political world into which Rosmini was born. It was an age of huge swings of political dominance and ideology. Four major factors helped influence him both as a thinker and a priest. The **Age of Enlightenment** was the great ferment of new ideas spreading across Europe during the eighteenth century. This movement culminated in the **French Revolution** of 1789. And then there were the two towering figures who dominated the European scene like Colossi: **Napoleon Bonaparte** and **Prince Metternich**.

The Enlightenment

Literacy was more widespread in France than ever before during the closing years of the eighteenth century. In Europe that period is often called the age of 'Enlightenment' (after the French word *éclaircissement*), because of the literary and philosophical movement, which flourished especially in France. These thinkers broke away from the teachings of Aristotle and Plato, which had dominated the universities and the Church for centuries. Often they were hostile to the Church.

Enlightenment philosophers held that nothing in this world was beyond rational analysis and improvement;

nothing was justifiable which could not be shown as useful to humanity or the promotion of human happiness. They saw themselves as independent thinkers whose principal aim was to improve the lot of their fellow humans. **Voltaire** was the supreme example of this new school. A visit to England in 1728 introduced him to a more religiously tolerant society, to Locke, to Newton and the theoretical empiricism of Francis Bacon. He publicised his discoveries in his *Lettres Philosophique* (*Philosophical Letters*), which enjoyed wide sales in spite of being officially condemned. Voltaire was strongly opposed to religion, especially to the Catholic Church. His ideas provoked the wrath of the French establishment, and he chose to live close to the Swiss frontier, as if poised for a quick getaway.

Another important figure – less controversial – was **Montesquieu**, who also visited England (1729). In 1748 he published his *De l'Esprit des Lois* (*The Spirit of the Law*). In this work he roundly condemns all forms of despotism and asserts that the best buttress against it is the action of 'intermediary powers', such as parliament or the courts. For him, the ideal form of government is that which preserves the liberty of the people. Government should be moderate, and this is best achieved when the executive, the legislature and the judiciary function independently of each other. The book is a highly idealised version of what Montesquieu experienced during his time in England.

What brought the ideas of the Enlightenment thinkers together was the **Encyclopedia**, a compendium of articles issued in successive volumes by editors Diderot and d'Alambert, between 1751 and 1765. The articles were generally sceptical, anti-authoritarian and hostile to religion. Ultimately 25,000 copies of the Encyclopedia were sold, at least half in France. Its influence therefore was immense.

One of its most prolific contributors was Jean-Jacques **Rousseau**. He was a deeply religious man as well as being something of a free thinker. His *Social Contract* (1762) described an ideal in civil government: 'all men,' he said, 'are born free, but are everywhere in chains'. Existing society is depraved. Somehow, political authority must be established without taking away the natural liberty of human beings. This is done by discovering and applying to government the 'general will'. Rousseau became the prophet of popular sovereignty.

There can be no doubt that the ideas of the Enlightenment provided fuel for the French Revolution as well as for other political upheavals across Europe.

The French Revolution

The second half of the eighteenth century in France was a period of increasing unrest. This was fuelled by an unprecedented increase in the distribution of pamphlets and popular journals.[3] There were some attempts at censorship by the state, but that did not prevent new ideas from spreading. Other factors were the increased taxation to pay for the Seven Years War against England (1756–1763); economic hardship brought about by a succession of failed harvests; the example of the successful revolt of the American colonies against the British crown; the unpopularity of the alliance with Austria, which had been cemented by the marriage of Louis XVI to Marie Antoinette, sister of the Emperor Joseph II.

The climax of this period of growing protest was the summoning, in May 1789, of the Estates General, an ancient national representative body in France, which had not met since 1614.[4] This consisted of the elected representatives of the three 'estates': the clergy, the nobility and the people. Lengthy disputes during the preparation period eventually resolved the composition of these three Estates, but the Third Estate was granted a double representation. The meeting took place at the royal palace of Versailles, outside Paris.

The Third Estate soon established its dominance, transforming itself into a National Assembly and demanding the power to legislate. The King, fearing the loss of his absolute authority, attempted to dissolve the Assembly, but at the so-called Tennis Court meeting the members determined on oath to stay put until the King gave way.

Meanwhile in Paris, the mob had begun to assert itself bringing pressure on both the Assembly and the King: much of this disaffection was driven by a shortage of food caused by failing harvests and increasing prices. On July 14 the Bastille prison was stormed and its prisoners released. The army's loyalty could no longer be counted on, and eventually the King gave way to pressure from the National Assembly and withdrew his troops from Paris. It was effectively the end of royal authority.

The National Assembly proceeded to issue a formulation of the *Rights of Man*, which echoes the 1776 American Declaration of Independence.[5] The *Déclaration des Droits de l'Homme et du Citoyen* is the fundamental document of the French Revolution. It affirms:

- the right of all to liberty, property, security and resistance to oppression;
- all sovereignty residing essentially in the nation;
- a citizen's liberty as the freedom to do anything which injures no one else;
- law as the expression of the general will. All citizens are equal before the law;
- all persons to be held as judicially innocent until they are declared guilty;
- the separation of powers (legislature, executive and judiciary).

The French Revolution is regarded as the greatest single upheaval in modern history – with the possible exception of the Russian Revolution of 1917. It changed the face of Europe and much of the rest of the world forever. The call for *Liberty, Equality and Fraternity* echoed round the known world. It prompted movements for political reform and the granting of constitutions right through the nineteenth century. Even in Britain its influence can be seen in Chartism and the Reform Bill of the 1830s.

The democratic achievements of 1789 in France soon degenerated into violence, bloodletting and social chaos. One revolutionary regime succeeded another. The king and queen were first imprisoned, then executed early in 1793 by the new instrument of justice, the guillotine. The revolution had brought about tumultuous change; it had also legitimised violence, making revolution a legal means of getting political change to happen.

The revolutionary government also directed its focus on the power and wealth of the Catholic Church.[6] The Church in France was stripped of much of its wealth. A so-called Constitutional Church was set up, the old aristocratic bishops being thrown out and new more amenable ones appointed. Many priests, religious and bishops were imprisoned or put to death. Monasteries were closed, and their wealth and property expropriated by the new masters, the leaders of the Revolution. The Church largely lost its role in education and in the relief of the poor. Later however, Napoleon was to re-establish Catholicism, although in a much modified form.

There was a backlash. The Popes refused to bow. Pius VI was treated as a prisoner by the French armies. Pius VII was also eventually persecuted by Napoleon. The reaction after 1815 meant the restoration of the *ancien régime*, especially its principle of 'legitimacy', which asserts the rights of sovereigns and dynasties to rule ancestral lands and peoples. Many of the powers of the Church were restored (but not its property). But the true measure of clerical reaction to the French Revolution is to be seen later in the nineteenth century in the clericalism and centralisation of Church power initiated by Pius IX.

Among the long-term effects in France – and later across Europe – were the sweeping away of traditional administrative boundaries and customs barriers. France itself was divided into *departements,* which still exist.[7] The judicial structure was reorganised and the law codified, eventually to become the *Code Napoleon.* The system of weights and measures was metricated, and made universal in France and in conquered territories.[8] Napoleon is even credited with directing Europeans to drive on the right hand side of the road.

Italy at the Beginning of the Nineteenth Century

Prior to 1796 when Napoleon invaded Italy and drove the Austrians out, Italy had been politically divided for centuries. It had been successively fought over by the French, the Spanish and the Austrians. The peninsula was a mosaic of nine separate states.[9]

In the north, Lombardy with its capital Milan had been under the rule of the Austrian Habsburgs for over 100 years. The Bourbons ruled the so-called Kingdom of the Two Sicilies in the south, with Naples as capital. Genoa and Venice had for centuries been independent maritime republics. Piedmont, with its capital Turin, was ruled over by the very traditionalist royal house of Savoy: 'Savoy' encompassed the western end of the Alps, and included places such as Nice, now part of France. There were also smaller independent duchies in middle Italy: Tuscany, Parma and Lucca. The island of Sicily was ruled from Naples and Sardinia from Turin.

Finally there were the Papal States, centred on Rome. The Popes had been the secular rulers of the so-called 'patrimony of Peter' for centuries. The Papal States straddled the middle of Italy, so that no army could move from north to south or vice-versa without passing through territory ruled by the Pope. However, the whole peninsula was fervently and traditionally Catholic, and Catholicism was possibly the strongest unifying factor. Most Italians looked upon the Popes with loyal affection, even though they were often the least effective rulers.

Yet politically, in 1800, Italy was little more than a 'geographical expression' (the contemptuous words of Metternich). It had a glorious distant past as the axis of the Roman Empire and, more recently, it boasted the cultural leadership of Europe during and after the Renaissance. But

Italy in 1815
The northern states of Venezia and Lombardy were both under the control of
Austria after 1815.

during Rosmini's lifetime it was politically weak and culturally dormant.

The invasion of Napoleon began a confusing period of constant political change up to his fall from power after Waterloo. The invaders brought with them the ideals of the Revolution: the pursuit of liberty and the glorification of the nation. The population of many Italian cities welcomed Napoleon and celebrated the departure of the Austrians.

In September 1796, an essay competition was launched in Milan to find which form of free government would be most conducive to the happiness of the Italian people. The winner, a young man called Melchiorre Gioia,[10] proposed a free Italian republic, governed by democratic institutions and united not merely geographically but linguistically, culturally and historically. Gioia also proposed a centralised state, not a federation of separate states.

At first Napoleon supported this surge of nationalism. He recruited many Italians into his armies, and he encouraged these brigades to speak Italian and to salute the tricolour, the new Italian flag. French rule was not, however, an unmixed blessing. The French exacted considerable sums of money out of the various Italian states; they stole works of art to carry off to Paris; the continuous wars and the maintenance of a French army in Italy became burdensome. The Italians soon saw they had simply exchanged dominance by Austria for dominance by France. There eventuated periodic rebellions and massacres of French soldiery – usually put down with equivalent savagery.

Italian Nationalism

But Napoleonic rule did leave a legacy of the experience of an intense patriotism, which had carried the French to total dominance of the European continent. Why should Italians remain inferior? After the return of the Austrians in 1815 there remained an active and steadily flourishing movement among intellectuals looking towards a distant and seemingly unattainable goal of national unity. A good example was the Neapolitan writer Vincenzo Cuoco.[11] As a young man he played a minor part in the revolutionary Neapolitan Republic, which briefly flourished in 1799 before being ruthlessly suppressed by the returning Bourbons supported by Admiral Nelson.[12] Cuoco wrote a history of this revolt, which was widely read. He recognised that a successful movement to create a united Italy would depend on education. Centuries of foreign domination, the influence of priests, political division and ignorance could only be reversed by creating an educated and disciplined population. Cuoco's ideas were later taken up by the greatest nineteenth-century prophet of a united Italy, Giuseppe Mazzini.

However, the most visible sign of awakening Italian nationalism during this period were the *Carbonari,* a network of secret societies similar to Freemasonry, which sprang up in Southern Italy in opposition to French domination.[13] Napoleon was named by them as 'the fat wolf who killed the Republic'.

The word *Carbonari* literally means 'charcoal burners', and their rituals and symbols sprang from that traditional occupation. After 1815 they spread north into the Papal States and into Piedmont. They were instrumental in fomenting unrest against the monarchical governments and were not afraid to use violence. They aimed at a united Italy, preferably a republic, but were implacably opposed to any form of absolutist rule.

They were roundly condemned as being what we would now call 'terrorists' by the Popes as well as by secular rulers; eventually their influence waned and they were gradually replaced by the better-organised *Young Italy* (*Giovine Italia*) movement. Its founder, in 1831, was Giuseppe Mazzini (1805–1872), whose aim was a united Italy to be achieved by Italians, not outsiders.[14] Mazzini spent his whole life as a political agitator; he was imprisoned for a short time by the Piedmontese government and was often in exile in London or in Switzerland. He is regarded as one of the founders of modern Italy.

This was the world in which Antonio Rosmini grew up. The Rosmini household was stable, strongly Catholic and very conservative. His father was a Count of the Austrian Empire. However, the young Rosmini was already open to a much broader world, especially through the influence of his polymath uncle Ambrogio. He read widely and studied the Enlightenment philosophers. He kept abreast of political events. He became a passionate advocate of a united Italy. Rosmini was in every sense a child of the nineteenth century.

Prince Clement Metternich

Prince Metternich was Austrian Chancellor from 1815 until the European 'year of revolutions', 1848 (thus covering most of Rosmini's adult life).[15] Rovereto was under Austrian rule and had been for 100 years before Rosmini's birth, which made Rosmini an Austrian citizen. Few would question the huge influence that Napoleon and the French Revolution had throughout the nineteenth century, whereas most people have even forgotten who Metternich was. Yet in many respects his influence – certainly on Rosmini's life – was no less profound.

Metternich was the principal architect of the 1815 Congress of Vienna, which for Europe ushered in a century of comparative peace and increasing prosperity. He established the so-called 'Concert of Europe', which obliged the main European leaders to come together and consult regularly so as to maintain peace and the status quo. He was himself a skilful diplomat, an art he had learned from the infamous French intriguer, Talleyrand.

History has tended to dismiss him[16] because he was also architect of the return to imperial and autocratic rule, which (except in Britain) was the dominant form of government among the great European powers up to 1914. He himself was an aristocrat and he had little tolerance for any other form of civil government. He was totally loyal to the Austrian Emperor and enjoyed the full trust and confidence of successive Emperors. Even when he fell from grace in 1848 it was largely because he was the chosen 'fall guy', but the system he had uncompromisingly espoused carried on without him.

His principal weapons were extensive censorship of books and papers, and a network of espionage which Vladimir Putin would have been proud of. The powerful forces of the Austrian army and police were at his disposal throughout the Imperial territories, and any sign of radical or revolutionary stirrings was identified and ruthlessly snuffed out. At the same time Austrian administration tended to be efficient and not heavy handed. Citizens are generally more amenable when times are peaceful and prosperous.

During Metternich's time in power Austria ruled much of northern Italy and was the dominant power throughout the peninsula. He had striven for this at the Congress of Vienna and he was successful. There was zero tolerance towards any moves in favour of Italian nationalism. In 1830, a period of insurrection and civil disturbance erupted throughout the peninsula, triggered by the July revolution in Paris (which precipitated the final departure of the Bourbons from Paris). Metternich sent his battalions into northern Italy and order was swiftly restored.

As regards relations with the Catholic Church, the Austria of Metternich simply continued the system which had characterised the rule of Emperor Joseph II. Most of the bishops appointed in the Imperial territories south of the Alps were German-speaking and took their cue from Vienna. This system continued on into Rosmini's lifetime.

It was not only in the matter of the *Panegyric* that Rosmini fell foul of Austrian rule, but also when later he tried to make foundations in the Tyrol and in Verona. Rosmini was an Ultramontane with unquestioning loyalty to the Holy See, so he ran into problems both with the police and with the bishops. This bitter experience caused him to identify the appointment of bishops by secular powers as one of the *Five*

Wounds of the Church, the title of a celebrated book he wrote during the 1830s but was not to publish until 1848.[17]

The Italian state most opposed to Austrian rule in Italy was the kingdom of Piedmont. It was ruled from Turin by the royal house of Savoy, which was no less autocratic than Imperial Austria. However, Italian patriots like Garibaldi and Mazzini tended to gravitate there, and perhaps fed by anti-Austrian sentiment, there grew up the beginnings of a popular movement in favour of eventual Italian unity.

After 1828, Rosmini was to move his centre of operations across the frontier into Piedmont where the culture was much more welcoming to his religious initiatives. He lived the later part of his life in Domodossola, close to the Swiss border, and in Stresa on the western side of Lago Maggiore. Politically, his life was free of the burden of constant political surveillance, even though he still had to travel on an Austrian passport.

Such were the muddied waters of the Italian political scene in the first half of the nineteenth century. The intelligentsia yearned for more enlightened forms of government. Italian nationalism existed as an ideology and was much persecuted. It sowed the seed, but progress was slow and constantly stifled by oppressive governments. In the event, the *Risorgimento,* the process of Italian unification, when finally it did happen, happened more by chance than by design.

Notes

1   It led to the peace of Campo Formio on 17 October 1797, by which much of northern Italy was ceded to French rule.

2   Christopher Duggan, *The Force of Destiny.* London: Allen Lane, 2007, pp. 29–33.

3   William Doyle, *Oxford History of the French Revolution.* Oxford: Clarendon Press, 1989, pp. 45–49.

4   Ibid., pp. 86–111.

5   Ibid., p. 118.

6   Ibid., pp. 259–262.

7   Ibid., p. 125.

8   Ibid., p. 393.

9   Duggan, p. 7, and see map, p. 16. The 'nine' became 'eight' after the Congress of Vienna, which allowed Piedmont to annex the Republic of Genoa.

10 Melchiorre Gioia (1767–1829) was a Milanese economist, intellectual and writer. His writings were strongly criticised by Antonio Rosmini.

11 Ibid., pp. 25–29.

12 The Bourbon dynasty originated in France. Branches spread to Spain, and via Spain to Naples. The Neapolitan Bourbons ruled over Italy from Naples south, together with the island of Sicily.

13 Ibid., pp. 58–60.

14 Ibid., pp. 125–134.

15 Alan Palmer, *Metternich*. London: Weidenfeld and Nicholson, 1972, source of much material in this section.

16 Harry Hearder (*Europe in the Nineteenth Century*, London, Longmans, 1988) dismisses him as 'pusillanimous and cynical', p. 312.

17 *Delle Cinque Piaghe della Santa Chiesa*. Roma: Città Nuova, 1981.

Chapter Three

Daily Life in
Nineteenth-Century Italy

If you were to visit Italy in the early years of the nineteenth century, what would you find? Apart from the Lombardy plain across the north, most of Italy is very mountainous. In 1800 there were none of the road and rail systems that exist today. Therefore, communication and travel would have been difficult and tedious. Napoleon built some major roads in the north, including the one that stretches from Milan to the Simplon Pass and into Switzerland. Rosmini would have been very familiar with this road since it passed right outside the front door of the villa where he spent his final years.

The mountain range, the Apennines, forms the spine of the peninsula, and crossing these mountains from west to east was particularly difficult. It was quicker to go by boat, say, from Rome on the western seaboard to Ancona on the Adriatic coast than to cross directly by road. From Rome south there were only two roads and both of these terminated in Naples. Even as late as 1860, 1,400 villages (out of a total of 1,800) in the mainland south had no proper road access. In the winter the heavy rains would turn mule tracks and sheep runs into glutinous mud, and that would make travel even more hazardous.

At the start of the railway age, construction here was very much slower than elsewhere in Europe.[1] By 1850 Italy had only 620 km of track operating, while Britain had over 10,000 km, Germany 6,000 and France 3,000. This was partly political. The Church under Pope Gregory XVI resisted railway building. In the north, the Austrian overlords were reluctant to support anything that might encourage national unification. Another singular feature of the landscape, which strikes the traveller as much today as in Rosmini's time, are the hill towns.[2] Most small townships appear to cling to mountain summits in a most precipitous fashion, providing the hilltop with a skirt of higgledy-piggledy stone dwellings surrounding a church campanile or the tower of a castle. Access by road is often steep and difficult, and it seems that in the Middle Ages when these settlements began, they were built thus to defend the population against marauding brigands.

Each of these small towns was like a miniature city-state – standing alone with its own special culture, dialect and patron saint. Some of them have since grown into small cities, like Orvieto in Umbria or Bergamo near Milan. 'Bergamo in Alto', the mediaeval town on a hill, is surrounded by a modern industrial city: the ancient Cathedral with other old buildings stand out above the rest like a citadel.

What Napoleon failed to heal was the deep-rooted parochialism of most Italians – the loyalty to the *paese* or the town of one's birth, which transcended any patriotic feeling towards Italy itself. A jargon word used for this is *campanilismo*. The campanile is the bell-tower of the village church: 'my campanile is taller or more impressive than yours!'

There was also a deep-seated antipathy between town and country. The peasants suffered under the burdens of taxes, feudalism and the periodic fluctuation in the price of food. They could see little value in appeals to patriotism if their bellies were empty. They tended to blame the more sophisticated townsfolk for their poverty, often with reason.

After the defeat of Napoleon, most Italian states reverted to adopting protectionist policies – with the exception of Tuscany under Ferdinand III (1790–1824). Tuscany, with its capital, Florence, tended to be the most advanced part of Italy both economically and culturally. Otherwise, the whole peninsula was intersected by customs barriers.[3] For example, travelling 60 km from Mantua to Parma a traveller would pass through seven customs barriers. This severely restricted local trading. The Rosmini family traded in locally produced silk, but much of their produce went across the Brenner Pass for export to northern Europe.

Language

All these factors kept the Italian peninsula very much divided, and this was accentuated by the problem of verbal communication. At the time of unification no more than ten percent of the population spoke Italian as their first language. Some authorities suggest even less. By 1861 twenty-two percent of the population was regarded as literate and presumably had some understanding of Italian, even if many could not write it or speak it well.

So, some eighty percent of the population conversed only in the local dialect and would hardly understand or even recognise Italian. They might struggle to understand people in the neighbouring town. The poet Ugo Foscolo is quoted as saying someone from Milan would need many days of lessons to understand someone from Bologna (less than 200 km distant).[4]

On the other hand, multilingualism was probably more common then than now, especially among educated people. It was quite usual to use one language at home in the house, another at work, and yet another for carrying out official business. Rosmini was a fluent Italian speaker, although at home the family would have spoken dialect.

Dialect was spoken and used every day by nearly everyone, even for sermons and official business.[5] In Piedmont, the king and his ministers generally spoke dialect but wrote in French. Camillo Benso di Cavour, first Prime Minister of Italy, never spoke Italian well and much of his correspondence was in French.

The People

Labourers and farmers (*contadini*, or peasants) formed the largest class of people in nineteenth-century Italy. They were poor with little hope of rising above their status. The peasants could not afford to send their children to school, even when it was available. The children, some as young as five or six, were needed to work and provide income to help support the family.

The typical Italian peasant family lived in a small (possibly only one room) stone, brick, or mud home. Parents, children and often grandparents all lived together under one roof without, of course, running water or electricity. Water for drinking, cooking, and washing had to be carried from the village's central well or fountain. These areas became the meeting place to exchange news or gossip.

Plain clothing, wooden shoes, a wood plank bed with a mattress stuffed with corn stalks, an oil lamp for light (wood and coal were too valuable to be burned just for light: they were used strictly for cooking), a chair or bench and table – such were the comforts of a peasant's home. The main meal would be cabbage soup, boiled potato, pasta and bread. Meat was rarely eaten by the poor, except on Sundays or feast days. Even though most farms had chickens, the eggs were much too valuable to be eaten by the family. They were produced for sale in the towns.

Men who did not have regular jobs would work as day labourers. Employers would come to the town square with a wagon looking for men to spend a day or so hauling stones, picking grapes or clearing land. Evenings were the time for socialising. Children were able to play with their friends; adults could relax and talk with neighbours; young couples could take a walk. On cooler evenings, family and friends would gather in a barn, and the women would knit or spin while they talked, while the men would tell stories or gamble.

Though *family* was a major focus for the peasant, *religion* also played a large role in the life of all nineteenth-century Italians. To them all events were attributed to the will of God or a saint; prayer was a way of possibly swaying events. Each town had a patron saint, whose feast day was celebrated annually with festivities, parades and parties, in the hope that the saint would protect the town throughout the coming year.

Except for feast days and holidays, the peasants had no goals but to survive day to day. As sea travel became easier, thousands of the very poor went overseas. Italian migration was the highest in Europe, many going to America, primarily to South America but increasingly, as the century progressed, to the United States. Some were temporary migratory workers, sending their earnings home to support the family. Family always remained a strong bond.

Travel and Travellers

When there were no wars or civil disturbances, Italy attracted many travellers from northern Europe and from England. They came because of the climate, the history and culture – but also because they found the people attractive. A few, such as John Henry Newman and other Anglo-Catholics, might have been attracted by Catholicism. At one time in the mid-nineteenth century nearly half the British Cabinet spoke Italian. Gladstone would have been one of these.

Stendhal (1783–1842), the great French author, loved Italy. He thought the absence of social constraints and conventions allowed for the spontaneous expression of emotion and passion. However, travelling around Italy in 1816–17, he was struck by

> the fierce and inordinate pride that local people felt towards their town or village. Some aspects of this patriotism were charming; but it was often accompanied by an insularity of outlook and a resistance to any criticism or change ...
>
> As he [Stendhal] travelled southwards from Milan, through Emilia Romagna and Tuscany, he became increasingly disturbed by the levels of prejudice and ignorance he encountered ... Each town, each village, seemed like a closed

universe, impervious to criticism and to the outside world, where the humblest talent and the meanest public building were extolled to the skies. There was also a great deal of superstition, and the emotional life of the poor was dominated by the clergy ... The extent of the cultural gap separating the mass of the population from the educated élite alarmed him.[6]

The celebrated German writer and poet Goethe visited Italy immediately prior to the Napoleonic wars. It was the people who particularly fascinated him. They seemed to live out their lives in public. Here is his description of Venice:

> ... the people is the base upon which everything rests, the spectators are themselves actors, and the multitude is melted into one whole with the stage. All day long the buyer and the seller, the beggar, the sailor, the female gossip, the advocate and his opponent, are living and acting in the square, in the gondolas and in the palaces, and make it their business to talk and to asseverate, to cry and to offer for sale, to sing and to play, to curse and to brawl.
>
> In the evening they go to the theatre, and see and hear the life of the day artificially put together, prettily set off, interwoven with a story. In all this they take a childish delight, and again shout and clap and make a noise ... While I am writing this, they are making a tremendous noise on the canal under my window though it is past midnight. Whether for good or for evil, they are always doing something.[7]

And in Verona:

> The people here jostle one another actively enough; the narrow streets, where shops and workmen's stalls are thickly crowded together, have a particularly cheerful look. There is no such thing as a door in front of the shop or workroom; the whole breadth of the house is open, and one may see all that passes in the interior. Half-way out into the path, the tailors are sewing; and the cobblers are pulling and rapping; indeed the work stalls make a part of the street. In the evening, when the lights are burning, the appearance is most lively.

The squares are very full on market days; there are fruit and vegetables without number, and garlic and onions to the heart's desire. Then again throughout the day there is a ceaseless screaming, bantering, singing, squalling, huzzaing and laughing. The mildness of the air and the cheapness of the food make subsistence easy. Everything possible is done in the open air.[8]

Goethe too was very impressed by Tuscany:

... above all one is struck with the beauty and grandeur which distinguish all the public works, and roads and bridges in Tuscany. Everything here is at once substantial and clean; use and profit not less than elegance are alike kept in view; everywhere we discern traces of the care taken to preserve them.

... it is impossible to find cleaner fields anywhere, not even a lump of earth is to be seen; all is as fine as if it had been sifted. Wheat thrives here most luxuriantly. Every second year beans are planted for the horses, who in this country get no oats. Lupins are also much cultivated which at this season are beautifully green, being ripe in March.[9]

Religion in Italy

Another visitor, during the 1840s, was the novelist Charles Dickens. On his return to England, he wrote his highly entertaining *Pictures of Italy*.[10] Dickens describes sights and experiences more than people, but he has quite a lot to say about Catholicism. In Rome he attended as many religious events as possible, including a Papal Mass; the Easter blessing in St Peter's Square; the Pope washing the 'apostles' feet on Maundy Thursday; the showing of the Bambino in the church of the Ara Coeli; ascending the Scala Sancta on one's knees; and going down the catacombs, which he found unbearably gloomy.

He pays tribute to the genuine devotion of the people, but he is characteristically scathing about superstition, poor singing and dull liturgies. He is not very flattering about the ever-present monks and priests. An exception, however, would be the following description of the Capuchin Friars in Genoa:

> Perhaps the Cappuccini, though not learned, are as an order the best friends of the people. They seem to mingle with them more immediately, as their counsellors and comforters; and to go among them more when they are sick; and to pry less than some other orders into the secrets of families, for the purposes of establishing a baleful ascendency over their weaker members; and to be influenced by a less fierce desire to make converts, and once made, to let them go to ruin, soul and body.
>
> They may be seen in their coarse dress in all parts of the town at all times, and begging in the markets in the early morning. The Jesuits, too, muster strong in the streets, and go slinking noiselessly about, in pairs, like black cats.

The Catholic Church

Dickens' views would be typical of a Protestant Englishman. In fact, Catholicism was almost universal throughout Italy, and it was the one unifying factor. Most people, rich and poor, were devout. Their religion was very devotional. Bells rang out every day calling the people to Mass or to pray the Angelus – as they still do today.

People frequently went on pilgrimage: to visit Rome especially at Easter and for the great feasts was an ambition of rich and poor alike. There were shrines dedicated to the Madonna or the local saints all over Italy. The Pope was generally held in high esteem. If he were an especially holy man like Pius IX, he would become the object of a cult.

Christ in his Passion became an increasingly popular devotion during the late eighteenth and nineteenth centuries. This devotion was specially promoted by new religious Orders such as the Passionists, founded by St Paul of the Cross (1694–1775) at Alessandria near Genoa in 1720, and the Redemptorists, founded by St Alphonsus (1696–1787) at Naples in 1792.[11] Both congregations encouraged the preaching of missions with emphasis on self-denial and the Cross of Christ, and the Redemptorists spread devotion to Our Lady of Perpetual Help.

The practice of making the Stations of the Cross has been a popular devotion in Italy since the time of St Francis of Assisi. An outdoor celebration took place in Rome every year on Good Friday – it still happens – often led by the Pope himself. This devotion was encouraged by Pope Clement XII in 1731 through the erection of 'stations' on the interior walls of churches, and they have become part of the normal furnishings of Catholic churches throughout the world.

Rosmini was to find similar inspiration from the Passion of Christ for his foundation at Monte Calvario (Mount Calvary) at Domodossola, in Piedmont. The road up the mount from the town follows a most elaborate set of Stations of the Cross with life-size figures in separate circular chapels along the route. Rosmini also imbibed a fervent devotion to Mary at the foot of the Cross.

Other popular practices which spread during the eighteenth century in Italy were May devotions: daily public devotion to the Mother of God in parish churches throughout the month. Also the so-called Forty Hours Devotion, which originated probably in Milan about the time of St Charles Borromeo (1538–1584) in the sixteenth century. The Blessed Sacrament was exposed in a parish church for public adoration continuously for forty hours, including throughout the night. The first Rosminian missionaries introduced these Italian practices into England in the 1840s.

The large numbers of clergy, secular and religious, emphasised the central position that Catholicism played in the lives of the Italian people. Not all the priests were engaged in parish ministry. Most education of boys was conducted by priests. Rosmini's teacher in Rovereto, Fr Pietro Orsi, became a lifelong friend. When Pietro died in 1837 Rosmini wrote to his brother Paolo, also a priest:

> I cannot possibly convey to you how deep is my sorrow at the loss ... of the dearest, oldest, and most faithful friend I have

had in the world. You can gauge the greatness of my grief by what you feel yourself. This unexpected happening warns us that we must be resolute in detaching ourselves from everything, and that it is only God whom we never lose.[12]

In his letters Rosmini never misses the opportunity of sharing a pious reflection even in what is primarily a letter of sympathy.

As general education expanded, many new religious congregations were founded whose primary work was the teaching of boys – and, increasingly, of girls as well. Inevitably in a country where there was still a lot of poverty, some young people were attracted to the priestly or religious life primarily because it offered security and status.

This richly devotional Catholicism was part and parcel of daily life in Italy at the time of Rosmini's birth. The secularism of the Enlightenment had made little impact on the mass of people. It was restricted to intellectuals in cities and universities. Rosmini was born into a conventionally devout Catholic family, so from birth he was steeped in this Catholic culture, which had an impact on every aspect of his everyday life. He was a child of his age and heir to a profound and age-old Catholic culture.

Notes

1   C. Duggan, *The Force of Destiny*, p. 103.
2   C. Field and R. Kauffman, *The Hill Towns of Italy*, Chronicle Books, 1996.
3   C. Duggan, p. 104.
4   Ibid., p. 104.
5   Ibid., p. 109.
6   C. Duggan, *Force of Destiny* (quoting Stendhal, *Rome, Naples and Florence*, tr. R. Coe. London: 1959), pp. 110–111.
7   Goethe, *Travels in Italy*, trans. A.J.W. Morrison and C. Nisbet. London: George Bell & Sons, 1892, pp. 66–67.
8   Goethe, p. 40.
9   Goethe, pp. 101–102.
10   Recent edition published by The Echo Press, New York, 1988.
11   Henri Daniel-Rops, *The Church in the Eighteenth Century.* London: J.M. Dent, 1964, pp. 308–312.
12   *Ep.Compl.*, v, 3282.

Chapter Four

Rosmini's Youth, 1797–1816

Antonio Rosmini was born in Rovereto on 24 March 1797. He was baptised the following day, the feast of the Annunciation of Mary, in the parish church of San Marco. Each year Rosmini would remember the anniversary of this event, which he considered the most important day of his life. 'Baptism joins a person to the Word of God,' he wrote to a priest in 1832, '. . . so that he becomes a "new person".'[1]

He regarded the feast day as auspicious since it placed him under the protection of Mary the Mother of God – and 'even more so since on that day the goodness of God who "loved me first" blessed me with rebirth in the saving waters of baptism.'[2]

Rosmini's birthplace is a small town surrounded by the foothills of the Alps in the valley of the River Adige, flowing southward towards its confluence with the Po. Rovereto is barely 20 km from the city of Trent, the provincial centre, residence for centuries of the Prince Bishop and, in the sixteenth century, the site of the famous Ecumenical Council.

The whole area, known as the Trentino or South Tyrol, was once under the rule of Venice – hence the dedication of the parish church to St Mark, but since 1700 it had fallen under Austrian rule. Even though Napoleon battled his way north-wards through Rovereto and Trent towards the Brenner Pass during his 1796 campaign, the Trentino was returned to the rule of Austria by the peace of Campo Formio the next year, and it remained an Austrian possession until 1918.

Rovereto today has a population around 10,000. The streets of the old town are quite narrow with very solid town houses – mostly four-storeyed stone buildings in the dignified Austrian imperial style of the eighteenth century. And such is Rosmini's own home, a large and spacious building with courtyards at the front and rear. The streets are mostly cobbled from wall to wall, with no pavements. It is easy to imagine them on a busy day in 1800 thronged with carts and carriages; normally however there would only be pedestrian traffic. The streets are built straight, and the wider, principal ones, like that where the Palazzo Rosmini is situated, give distant glimpses of the rugged mountains.

The town itself is quite flat with the river Leno, a tributary of the Adige, running through. From Rosmini's house there is a slight rise up to the parish church of San Marco, a magnificent building in the Austrian Baroque style situated in its own small piazza. It has a particularly beautiful ceiling – richly painted with floral motifs scrolled all over it. Its dimensions are pleasing: a wide single nave and a high roof. It holds about 400 people. This church played a major part in Rosmini's early life.

Rosmini's home is a large palazzo. Originally the house was out in the country and surrounded by fields. The family, who came from the district of Bergamo in the thirteenth century, were wealthy landowners – their property would have stretched several kilometres outside the town.

The town grew, and under the Empress Maria Theresa in the 1770s it had attained almost the size of today. The silk trade was booming, and the Rosminis were successful participants. Prior to the Napoleonic wars, Rosmini's father, Pier Modesto, and his unmarried uncle, Ambrogio, travelled widely around Europe, bringing back furniture, pictures and bric-à-brac collected on their journeys. The house was much enlarged and extended in the eighteenth century. There is a spacious reception room near the main entrance. Also on the ground floor are a tiny domestic chapel and an extensive library.

The bedroom on the second floor, where Rosmini was

born, is quite modest. It still contains his cot and baby clothes. Even some of his toys were lovingly preserved by his nurse, who continued to live in the house as part of the family until her death. Upstairs on the third floor are the quarters used by Uncle Ambrogio, which Rosmini eventually made his own. Next to that bedroom is a spacious *salone*, presumably Rosmini's workplace, containing an upright reading desk and prie-dieu.

Many of the rooms have substantial, decorated ceramic stoves in the Austrian style. Since the house was large and the walls were solid, these stoves would have kept it snug and warm in the winters, which can be severe so close to the high Alps. Rosmini was to spend half his life living in this house – from 1797 to 1826. It was a comfortable and homely place, and that is the impression it still gives to visitors today. It is spacious but not grand or in any way overpowering.

Rosmini grew up a small-town boy. Yet he became a patrician who could to some degree hold his own in the sophisticated society of Milan or Turin. It is significant that by choice he naturally gravitated back to the same sort of mountainous ambience along the lakeside at Stresa or at Domodossola, which became the centres of the congregation which he founded.

The Rosmini family crest contains six stars and can already be seen on the portrait of Pietro, one of the early Rosminis, who served as a knight under King Philip II of Spain in the 1500s. This suggests a people who looked above to the heavens rather than below to the land and its herds. The Rosminis were cultivated, intellectual folk. But their bounds were restricted by their beloved mountains.

∞৹৶∞

The Rosminis would have been typical of leading aristocratic families in Rovereto and the district: prosperous, law-abiding, pious, loyal to the Emperor and the Austrian Empire. Antonio's father was a knight of the Holy Roman Empire and was nearly fifty when he settled down to married life. He was a somewhat austere and distant man, keen on poetry but more devoted to hunting than to his books.

His wife, Giovanna, was a kindly religious woman and a capable housekeeper. Rosmini's friend, the poet Tommaseo, wrote to him: 'You have for a mother a woman of rare distinction ... her prudence, modesty and friendliness, her strong religious sense, her devotion to her children and her sweet demeanour never cease to astonish me. I marvel at her and I venerate her.'[3] Rosmini was very attached to her. She outlived her husband by many years and remained a wonderful support to him for the rest of her life.

The Rosminis had four children including one little boy who died in infancy. The eldest was Gioseffa Margherita – usually known by her second name Margherita – two years older than Antonio, and his constant childhood companion. There was a younger brother, Giuseppe, a somewhat morose and difficult child who remained a constant worry to Antonio. It would perhaps not have been easy for Giuseppe, living in the shadow of such a brilliant elder brother. When Pier Modesto died in 1820, Antonio, as eldest son, inherited two-thirds of the estate, something which Giuseppe resented, since his share was only one-sixth.

The two people alongside his mother who had the greatest positive influence on Rosmini as he grew up were his sister Margherita and his uncle, Ambrogio. Margherita was a gifted and beautiful woman. Very intelligent and well educated, she wrote elegant Italian; she knew Latin, French and German very well (she taught German to Antonio); and she was a connoisseur of poetry and music. She is described as a person of great sensibility and rich in Christian virtues. As children, she and Antonio were inseparable.

After she had come back from Innsbruck, where she had attended college, she continued to devote herself to studies, to prayer and to charity. No wonder, therefore, that Margherita and Antonio found themselves on the same wavelength. While Antonio was still a young student in Padua, he often prompted his mother to stay close to Margherita, to encourage and support her with advice and prayer, for he thought that God would require a lot from his sister. He himself also remained very close to Margherita, and he loved her dearly. For example, he wrote to her on 28 May 1825:

My dearest sister,

If I do not write to you as often as I would like, that is due to the occupations that overwhelm me and to my habit of writing only if necessary, even to the dearest persons, though I love them also in my absence and in silence. Therefore never doubt my love, neither judge according to external appearances, but according to my principles. I have always loved you; I have a double reason to love you: blood and your dedication to God, which makes you dearer to me more than any reason of blood. Therefore do accept my treating you so casually, and be sure that I love you all the same, whether I write or I do not write to you ... [4]

Like many pious, wealthy women of that time Margherita devoted herself to charitable work. She visited and looked after the sick in hospital and in their homes, and performed various services for the poor, providing everything they wanted. It was suggested to her she might open an orphanage, very much needed in Rovereto. Margherita saw the will of God in this invitation and, encouraged and assisted by Antonio, dedicated herself to this work of charity.

The orphanage was almost ready in 1819 but the sudden death of Pier Modesto and other unforeseen difficulties delayed its opening. Antonio too wanted things to be done as well as possible, so they decided to consult the Marchesa Maddalena di Canossa. This remarkable woman, before whom even the great Napoleon quailed, had, in 1808, founded the Daughters of Charity, which are still known as the Canossan Sisters, dedicated to the education of girls belonging to very poor families.

They met Maddalena on 24 February 1820 in Verona. She must have made a deep impression on both of them, for that meeting was to change both their lives. Rosmini asked that his sister be allowed to stay with her so as to learn how to run her new orphanage. Maddalena arranged for Margherita to stay in St Joseph's convent, in Verona, to do her training. She remained there a month and learned a lot from Maddalena's example and teaching. When she came back to Rovereto, Margherita was able to devote herself in a more determined way to the orphanage, which was inaugurated on 1 September 1820. Rosmini dedicated his very first published book, *Della Educazione Cristiana* ('Christian Education'), to Margherita, to help her in this work, and he even offered her the manuscript.

Antonio, who knew his sister's brilliant intelligence and culture, often spoke to her about literature. He sent her his works and he dedicated to her one of the volumes of his *Opuscoli Filosofici* (Philosophical Studies), for he was sure that she would appreciate this serious work. Margherita eventually joined the Canossian Sisters and soon became the Foundress's 'right hand'. Sadly, like so many young people in those years, she contracted tuberculosis and died in 1833 aged only thirty-eight. Rosmini was devastated. With Margherita's death he lost the love of his life.

The second great influence on the young Antonio was his Uncle Ambrogio. He was a jovial man, an architect and a profound connoisseur of art. He was a bachelor, and lived in the palazzo as one of the family. Rosmini was strongly attached to him. Early on he encouraged Antonio's interest in art by painting for him, showing him his collection of prints and speaking to him about the beautiful things that were to be seen in other cities. The boy was so interested in these tales and so attentive that when he went to Rome in 1823 as a young priest, he could easily recognize the wonders of art 'that uncle Ambrogio used so vividly to describe. There are only a few things whose history I do not know, such a great influence had on me the words of that man, so dear to me,' as he wrote to his mother from Rome on 22 April 1823.[5]

Certainly his uncle taught him to appreciate and love beauty and art. It is easy to recognize his influence in these words written by young Rosmini to his teacher Fr Pietro Orsi: 'Oh, if I could live two or three hundred lives, I would gladly give one of them to painting! Art delights me greatly, and I can see myself as a Raphael! When I think of his pictures I am enraptured ...'[6]

Ambrogio Rosmini, with his great sensibility and big heart, had recognised Antonio's exceptional gifts and he always tried to encourage them. Since early childhood, Antonio had free access to Ambrogio's library, where he could find a safe refuge and devote himself to reading his favourite books. He knew he could reckon on his uncle's affection and help. Almost certainly, Ambrogio awakened in Antonio his fascination for philosophy, which was to be his principal intellectual pursuit.

When he was a young student, he often wrote to Ambrogio giving him his news and sometimes also asking for money to add to the sum that his father had already given him, in order to buy books.[7] When Ambrogio died on 10 August 1818, Antonio was on holiday, far from home with some of his friends. So as not to spoil his holiday, he was told nothing of his uncle's death until after his return home. He wrote to his cousin Carlo Rosmini: 'I always looked upon him as a father and he treated me as a son ... God did not want me to be at home in the moment of his death; if I had been there, sorrow would certainly have overwhelmed me.'[8]

Today, a visitor to the Rosmini family home can see some of the fruit of Ambrogio's artistic genius hanging on the walls. Outstanding is the extraordinary depiction of the *Deposition of Christ*, a picture which Rosmini particularly loved. There is also a group picture featuring St Francis de Sales. On the right in profile is a figure, which is clearly Rosmini himself as a very young man. So he also acted as an artistic 'model' for his uncle.[9]

∞⁓∞

One of the difficulties in trying to describe Rosmini's youth is that in the early biographies the story is much embellished by pious exaggeration. He was clearly a dutiful and loving child, as one might expect growing up in such a privileged family. He was also highly intelligent and tended to excel in his early schooling.

One amusing anecdote relates to when he was eleven. He appeared to be falling behind in class. He had soon become bored with a diet of Latin grammar. His home tutor, Francesco Guareschi, one day found him reading the *Summa* of St Thomas instead of doing his prescribed homework. Guareschi took the volume from him and smacked Antonio over the head with it.[10] Guareschi reported Rosmini's lack of progress at school to his parents who were not pleased, although his Uncle Ambrogio defended him. Rosmini bore Guareschi no malice. His old teacher also remained part of the Rosmini household until his death in 1841, and Rosmini continued to refer to him respectfully as *Signor Maestro*.

His apparent failure in class caused him to have to repeat that year, but he soon caught up again. One thing that was noted at this time about his method of study is that he was not interested in word-for-word parrot-learning but preferred to make notes of all the ideas he had discovered. He became a voracious reader and note taker, and that stayed with him for life.

Although Rosmini was by nature a quiet child he attracted the friendship of other youngsters. Indeed when he was fifteen he gathered together a group of friends who would meet each month for literary discussion in the Rosmini home. They called themselves the *Accademia dei Vannettiani* after Clementino Vannetti, a local scholar and promoter of the Italian language. Rosmini became its first President. This 'Academy' survived for several years.[11]

When in 1814 Rosmini finished at the local public school, his father decided to engage a priest-teacher from Rovereto, Fr Pietro Orsi, so that Antonio could continue his studies without having to leave town. A school was formed of a dozen or so young men who met together for tuition. Orsi was a good mathematician and also taught philosophy. Sometimes the group would roam the local countryside deep in animated conversation.

Their education is reminiscent of the famous school of Aristotle in Athens. Orsi encouraged his students to debate and to argue. He used a text by a German empiricist philosopher called Franz Samuel Karpe, who had been professor in Vienna some years earlier. Rosmini did not like this man's writing, which he deemed to be 'unfortunate and contrived'. He describes some discussions with Fr Pietro as 'heated tussles'.[12] Orsi was a gracious human being and came to admire Rosmini's mind, even to defer to him in matters philosophical. He allowed Antonio a free rein to discourse on philosophy to the others in the class. He also stimulated him to take an interest in mathematics and physics. Rosmini would summarise his intellectual discoveries or arguments in letters he wrote to Orsi. In one of these he provided a mathematical model for the rotation of the moon. He even dared to correct a mistake he purported to find in a work of the celebrated physicist, Gregorio Fontana, on accelerated motion.[13]

Rosmini's enquiring mind was developing fast and Fr Pietro helped stimulate it. Years later Antonio acknowledged this when he wrote his first great philosophical work, the *New Essay on the Origin of Ideas*. He dedicated the work to Orsi:

> ... my well-beloved teacher who in 1815 and 1816, by his respect for truth and the warmth of his friendship, taught me philosophy but also attracted me to live more virtuously and rejoice in his friendship; I am ever in his debt for the benefits I received from him.[14]

In his *Life of Rosmini*, Fr Pagani notes that the years of youth are often styled ...

> the springtide of life; and such they were in every sense to Antonio Rosmini – a spring without frost, ice or gloom, advancing with even, tranquil and unerring steps. Thanks to the blessing of God, the watchful care of his parents and his firmness of will, he escaped the misfortune so common to the young, of being led astray by error, doubt or the revolt of passion ... Faith and reason grew and throve vigorously side by side in his soul, like two plants grafted upon one another, nourished with the same sap from the same root and soil ... [imparting] to his character a unity and simplicity which become more and more striking.[15]

It was not entirely idyllic, however. Antonio writes complainingly to his cousin Fedrigotti:

> Our life is mean and obscure to the last degree; here we are shut in amongst these mountains, so cut off from the rest of humanity, that we know scarcely anything of the good and beautiful works done by others nor can we enjoy the benefit of them.[16]

This isolation was shortly to be terminated. Rosmini was about to leave his mountain home for the University city of Padua.

Notes

1   *Ep.Compl.*, iv, 1621, to P. Antonio Tommaseo, of Rome.
2   Giovanni Pusineri, *Rosmini.* Stresa: Sodalitas, 1989, p. 10.
3   Ibid., p. 8.
4   *Ep.Compl.*, i, 396, to Signora Margherita De' Rosmini-Serbati.
5   *Ep.Compl.*, i, 248, to Signora Giovanna De' Rosmini.
6   *Ep.Compl.*, i, 37, to don Pietro Orsi, 28 September 1815.
7   *Ep.Compl.*, i, 84, to Signore Zio Ambrogio.
8   *Ep.Compl,.* i, 139, to Signor Cav. Carlo Rosmini.
9   The author is indebted to Rosminian Sister Maria Bruna Ferretti for permission to use material on Rosmini's sister and uncle from her monograph *Rosmini and his Family* (2001).
10   G.B. Pagani, *Life of Antonio Rosmini-Serbati.* London: Routledge & Kegan Paul, 1906, pp. 7–8.
11   Ibid., pp. 14–15.
12   Pagani-Rossi, i, p. 88.
13   Gregorio Fontana (1735–1803), professor of mathematics at the University of Pavia.
14   *Nuovo Saggio sull'Origine delle Idee* in 4 vols. 1828 Introduction.
15   Pagani, *op. cit.,* p. 28.
16   Ibid., p. 26.

Chapter Five

Student at Padua
Vocation

Not far from San Marco in Rovereto there is a very ordinary back street. If you were strolling down this street you would see a small notice underneath a decorated street sign, headed *Contrada della Terra* (District of Terra). The notice reads: 'While walking down this street lost in thought, Antonio Rosmini conceived the "Idea of Being", which became the foundation of his philosophical system'. Wall plaques commemorating where some notable person was born or lived are common enough in European cities, but a notice commemorating someone having a thought is surely unique! Probably most of us would not want our thoughts commemorated.

This thought occurred to Rosmini one day in 1815 when he was a student with Pietro Orsi. He had already studied many contemporary European philosophers and discovered that most of them were preoccupied with the question of how human beings conceive their ideas. Did ideas simply come to them through the senses or were they in some way inborn? Rosmini had already written in his little book of *Thoughts* that this business of the origin of ideas 'must be thought over and reflected upon'.[1] Later he was to describe what happened in the *Contrada della Terra* in these words:

> At the age of 18 I was walking alone wrapt in thought along the street called *Terra*, which as you know lies between the tower and the bridge over the Leno; and while various thoughts were going through my mind, I noticed that the explanation of a mental concept is to be found in a wider concept, and this wider concept in one of still wider application; and thus ascending from concept to concept I found that I arrived at the most universal of all ideas, *being*; and when I tried to take away the idea of being, I found I had nothing left.
>
> I thus became persuaded that the idea of being is the ultimate in every concept, the principle of all thought. The conviction that I had found a truth gave my soul serenity and joy, and I gave praise to the Father of light.[2]

An example may help us understand here what Rosmini is saying. Looking out my window I can see a ginger cat exploring my garden. In my life I have seen lots of other cats. I know they are a species of animal. Animals and plants are quite distinct but both share life: they are 'born' and grow to maturity, they age and they die. Living things depend on inanimate things: we rest on the earth, we breathe air, we fashion things out of minerals such as stone or metal. All animals, including ourselves, share with plants and inanimate objects the fact that we exist, we have being.

But that is as far as I can go in this analysis of my experience. All the data in this sequence come to me via my senses, but the idea of existence does not. It is innate. It is something I am born with. Rosmini asserts that it is unique – it is the only such innate idea that we possess and all intelligent beings have it. Rosmini was to come back to this train of thought and tease it out fully when he wrote his first philosophical work the *New Essay on the Origin of Ideas* (1828). It became the foundation of his philosophical system.

Priesthood

This is by no means the only intuition, or even the most important, that Rosmini describes during his early years. Two years earlier, aged sixteen, he had had what one might describe as a transcendental experience. It was the beginning of his vocation as a priest and religious. In his diary he wrote: '1813. This year was for me a year of grace. God opened my eyes about many things, and I came to understand that there is no other wisdom except in God.'

Such a mystical experience is not uncommon, even among the very young. John Henry Newman, Rosmini's exact contemporary, describes a conversion experience at more or less the same age. He was fifteen, and he writes that it gave him a conviction of closeness to God: 'it made me rest in the thought of two, and two only, absolute and luminously self-evident beings: myself and my Creator'.[3] Newman is more fulsome in the way he describes it, but for both these young men it was to give to their spiritual writings a strong sense of living close to God.

Both of them chose from that early moment to choose a life of service to God. Rosmini conceived a great esteem for the priesthood and desired fervently to become a priest himself. When he revealed this to his parents, they were astounded. This very talented elder son of theirs was destined to inherit the lion's share of the family fortune, property and its titles. His parents were both devout people, but the idea of their son and heir becoming a priest was unacceptable.

The opposition of his parents caused Antonio considerable interior distress, but it did not shake his resolve in the slightest. Eventually, his parents invited a priest friend, the Oratorian Fr Antonio Cesari, to come and stay and try to dissuade their son from his vocation. Cesari was a distinguished scholar in promoting the Italian language; Rosmini admired and respected him greatly. However his parents' plan backfired. Cesari came out of the interview convinced that Rosmini certainly did have a priestly vocation. His parents graciously but reluctantly gave way.

Pier Modesto was determined at least that his son should follow the high road and go to Rome and study at the Academy of Noble Ecclesiastics. This should launch him on a distinguished career, perhaps one day to become a bishop, or higher. Their son would have none of that idea either. He might well have been tempted with the prospect of living in Rome, since Uncle Ambrogio had filled his imagination with stories and descriptions of the wonderful things to be seen in the Eternal City. However, he dug his heels in again. Rome would have to wait.

Rosmini was much more attracted to the idea of following his cousins, Leonardo Rosmini and Antonio Fedrigotti, and studying in Padua. In any case Padua is much closer than Rome to Rovereto, and it had an old and distinguished university. Two hundred years earlier, St Francis de Sales, a saint Rosmini greatly admired, had been a student there. Interestingly, another celebrated alumnus was Galileo! The Rosminis were discovering that their talented son had a mind of his own, so they gave way on this score too.

Padua

So, in November 1816, Rosmini commenced his university studies in Padua. His time there was fairly typical of that of generations of young people down the centuries. University life is often a first experience of freedom, of living away from home. Moreover it introduces enquiring minds to a much wider intellectual horizon than hitherto experienced. In many respects it is an artificial existence free from the responsibilities of later life. It can be a happy and hugely enjoyable time, something to be looked back upon during later life with nostalgia.

Rosmini set up a household with several other young men. He soon attracted many new friends, both students and staff members. He met young men from all over Italy and this certainly broadened his social perspective. One of these was Niccolò Tommaseo, several years younger than Rosmini and later to become a prominent poet and political figure. He remained a life-long friend.

There is an amusing letter to Pier Modesto describing the young men's domestic arrangements, and it reflects on the social status of patrician youths accustomed at home to being waited on hand and foot. 'As for food, we find it cheaper to cook our own. What I thought was the task of women, I discover now that I have started do with manly determination and perseverance. It is a fine sight to see five of us acting as cooks, getting the fire going, washing up, setting the table and preparing the great work ...'[4] Rosmini does not say who did the washing and cleaning.

Like all students he always seemed to be short of money, probably because he was easily tempted to spend liberally on buying books. He wrote to his uncle that he was 'already professed in the order of mendicants'. His interests were very broad – and that meant he felt the need to build up a sizeable library. To achieve this he needed money for books and his allowance was clearly inadequate. In his letters home he would plead for more cash, sometimes directly to his father, at other times to his mother or his uncle, in letters so persuasive that they evidently melted his parents' hearts. He succeeded thus in adding many valuable works to the family library.

However, he did not lose sight of his ambition to prepare himself for a priestly vocation. His description of his daily routine is impressive:

I rise at six, work until eight, after my prayers and breakfast. From eight until midday I go to lectures. Then I go to Mass in the church of St Anthony [the Basilica of St Anthony of Padua was close to their lodgings] and then continue to work until 1.30; then go for a walk with my friends until two: then I eat.

After lunch I play or talk with a friend; sleep for half an hour and amuse myself until 4.30. I then work until seven, and until 9 o'clock I meet with my good friends, who are either University Professors or young men of intelligence. All five of us, including the two young men who live with me, gather in a little room to do our spiritual reading, recite the rosary, then have our meagre meal; after some cheerful conversation we go to our rooms, say our prayers, go to bed where I sleep soundly.[5]

The two companions who Rosmini does not specifically mention here were his cousins Leonardo and Antonio. Antonio also aspired to become a priest, but after the first year he abandoned the idea of a vocation and departed from Padua to study in Innsbruck.

At the end of the year (June 1817) Rosmini was awarded the degree of Bachelor of Theology. As usual, he returned home to Rovereto for the university holidays.

In his first year Rosmini threw himself into his studies with great enthusiasm. He was eclectic in his choice of lectures to attend. In addition to theology lectures he took the opportunity to pursue studies in literature, philosophy and mathematics. He also interested himself in the science of agriculture as well as chemistry, physiology and medicine. The curriculum at Padua allowed him to indulge in this variety of learning – to his delight.[6]

At the beginning of the second year he decided to assume clerical dress, having sought and gained his parents' leave to do so. One interesting fact he notes about this time is that he had completed the reading of the whole Bible in Latin for the second time. It is good to think that he so fully immersed himself in the word of God as he prepared himself for the priesthood.

One severe trial of the second year was the arrival in Padua of his younger brother Giuseppe. The latter's health had taken a turn for the worse: he seemed to be suffering from hypochondria. Their parents therefore persuaded Giuseppe to go and join Antonio in Padua, thinking that that might do the trick. Rosmini put up with him for five months, but it was not easy. His brother's conduct became increasingly erratic. 'one day he was bent on riding, the next on playing the violin. One day he would rise very early, the next he was in bed long after sunrise, and he would do little or no study'.[7]

Rosmini endured all this without complaint. How difficult Giuseppe could be is revealed in a letter that Antonio wrote some years later to his cousin Giuseppe Maria Gentili in which he really bares his soul:

Unfortunately my brother's soul is dominated by the worst of passions: profit and self-interest ... Since my father's death he planned to deprive me of everything. He was always constant in this project and tried everything in order to succeed. He based his strategy on the knowledge he had of my goodness and the great love I have always shown for my brother and his good. He played those cards in every possible way ...

Do you believe, dear cousin, that I have ever had the consolation to receive but one act of friendship from my brother, whom I really love very much? ... It seems that he begins to understand that we need to take care also of others, and not only and exclusively of ourselves. He respects our mother quite well ... He has also understood that walking all over me cannot help him ...

But is all this love? It is of no use that my brother fears me, and acts towards me with some respect and more shrewdness than before. His coldly acting out of self-interest not only distresses me. It frightens me. One of the reasons which made me go far away from home (even if it is not the main one) has been the disgust of seeing my brother's continuous, cool unfeelingness, his tremendous ingratitude to my care, which was more solicitous and loving than a mother's.[8]

Rosmini appears to be at the end of his tether in this letter. However, he persevered in trying to help Giuseppe. When he succeeded to being head of the household, he allowed Giuseppe free use of their house and its garden. But Giuseppe remained a thorn in Antonio's side for many years, as he had been to their parents in early life.

When he decided to get married, Antonio assured him of support, financial if necessary, especially if he had children. Giuseppe even asked Antonio at one stage if he would help him find a suitable wife! Eventually he did find one, and at long last, in 1842, he married the Baroness Adelaide Cristani a Rallo. Antonio performed the ceremony in Rovereto. The marriage seemed to work for a time. But Adelaide later confided in Rosmini that her relationship with Giuseppe was difficult also. The fact is that he found it almost impossible to relate in friendship to anyone, and this seems to have been a defect of character. Adelaide was an intelligent and gentle-humoured lady. The bonus for her was that she became a close friend of Antonio too and was able to confide in him.

∞∾∞

Rosmini's third and final year at Padua is interesting because of the arrival of Niccolò Tommaseo. Rosmini came to admire Tommaseo for his obvious intellectual gifts, even though he found him unpredictable. Rosmini wrote of him:

> His most developed faculty is his imagination . . . He is concentrated within himself, and all the faculties of his mind work with such intensity as to appear to be near madness . . . When melancholic, he gives the impression that he could easily fall into despair and might commit suicide; when he is cheerful he is without restraint and has to jump about and move his body in a comical manner: these contraries are intense but last only a short time, they are almost momentary.[9]

Rosmini offered Tommaseo much better lodgings than his new friend had taken at first. He persuaded him to ground himself in the Italian language, and he also tried to 'improve' him regarding his religious faith. Tommaseo was not at first impressed by this aspect, regarding Rosmini as being too intellectual and too austere. However, their friendship blossomed, and towards the end of Rosmini's life Tommaseo was to become a great support to him.

Tommaseo writes of Rosmini: 'He was a real friend . . . he felt friendship as a natural instinct and as a moral necessity; he cultivated it as a fine art, as a difficult and deep science.' Tommaseo often came and stayed in Rovereto, where Rosmini's parents were very hospitable to their son's companions. But on one occasion Tommaseo simply took off without saying a word, leaving Antonio wondering if he had said the wrong thing.

Later on, when Rosmini was living in Milan, Tommaseo again came to live with him. His stay lasted a couple of months when he again left abruptly, this time finally. Tommaseo was inclined to be temperamental: he could be

exuberant and he could become depressed. Rosmini
continued always to be loyal to him, supporting him with
money and advice. On one occasion he wrote bluntly: 'Stay in
one place; take a job; be controlled by the rules of the job:
perform its duties with constancy and with method (though
you hate method), and put up with resignation with the
labour it involves'.[10]

Tommaseo was a poet and Rosmini a philosopher. Their
temperaments were poles apart. Tommaseo recognised this.
He later wrote of his stay with Rosmini in Milan: 'All that time
the worthy man ... left me full liberty to follow my inclination
and my impulses, as if I were the master of the house and he
the guest: I the more mature in sense and he the less
virtuous.' Tommaseo became one of the great Italian word-
smiths, and his *Dictionary of Synonyms*, published in 1830,
remains to this day an Italian classic.[11]

Later, in Milan, Tommaseo did Rosmini one very great
favour – he introduced him to the novelist Alessandro
Manzoni, who was to become perhaps Rosmini's closest
secular friend. With Manzoni also there was the complemen-
tarity of opposite characters. They seem to have admired in
the other the gifts which they themselves lacked: once again
it was the attraction of poet to philosopher and vice versa.
Manzoni sometimes suffered from scruples, and Rosmini was
for him a calming presence. Their friendship became warm
and constant.

Rosmini had the gift of friendship. He esteemed it. He
loved his friends and he expected them to love him. He
regarded friendship as an aspect of charity, indeed as the
essence of charity. He would make it an important part of the
Rosminian rule, as we shall see. Once he wrote to his brother:
'Nothing gives me greater delight than to love my friends ...
Nothing I may say is more pleasing to me than bearing with
their defects, because I rejoice to know that by doing so I am
fulfilling the law of God.'[12] And another time he writes:

> How can there be anything excessive in a love which leads to
> God, and in whom alone it still burns? And this is consoling;

for it is by loving one another in God that friends, even when they are far apart from one another, are always most close and united together. And this union is not brought about by talk or letters or any other sort of communication: it is entirely internal and spiritual, independent of material circumstances.

What was Rosmini really like and how did he strike people at this time of early manhood? Pagani writes about his physical appearance:

He was rather over middle height, slender and well-proportioned, except that his head was rather large. His massive brow was shaded by an abundance of chestnut hair; he had an aquiline nose, somewhat projecting chin, and large, thoughtful eyes, which sparkled with pleasure at the sight of the good, the beautiful or the true. A sweet and affectionate smile constantly played around his lips, from which no malignant word was ever heard to fall.

In manner, he was extremely gracious and winning; his attire and whole appearance were characterised by a simple and modest dignity. When he spoke of or to God, there was a radiance of grace and supernatural beauty about him which awoke in the listener feelings of love and veneration.[13]

Writing at a much later date in his *History of European Liberalism*, the distinguished historian Guido de Ruggiero calls him 'the gentle Rosmini'.[14] The word 'gentle' is one he often uses himself in his advice to others. He had an attractive personality and therefore made many lasting friendships. Eventually this trait of gentleness as well as his wisdom drew people to seek his advice and spiritual direction, and was probably a powerful factor attracting many to follow him into the religious life.

In July 1819 Rosmini completed his university studies and said goodbye to Padua. He returned home to Rovereto to prepare himself for priesthood. The diocese of Trent had no bishop at that time, so he delayed his ordination as subdeacon. He was content for a time to live a quiet life of prayer and study. Nevertheless his fertile mind was soon full of ideas for writing and schemes for the betterment of society. He was about to enter one of the most fruitful and creative periods of his life.

Notes

1   G.B. Pagani, *The Life of Antonio Rosmini-Serbati* (English translation), p. 21.
2   Related by Rosmini to one of his brethren, Don Francesco Paoli. See Claude Leetham, *Rosmini, Priest, Philosopher and Patriot.* Baltimore: Helicon Press, 1957, p. 15.
3   John Henry Newman, *Apologia Pro Vita Sua.* London: OUP, 1913, p. 108.
4   Leetham, *Rosmini,* p. 18.
5   Ibid.
6   Pagani, *Life,* p. 32.
7   Pagani, *Life,* p. 35.
8   Pagani-Rossi, i, pp. 406–409.
9   Leetham, *Rosmini,* p. 22.
10   Leetham, *Rosmini,* p. 56.
11   Dianne Hales, *La Bella Lingua,* p. 214.
12   Pagani, *Life,* p. 40.
13   Pagani, *Life,* p. 29.
14   Guido De Ruggiero, *The History of European Liberalism.* London: R.G. Collingwood, 1959.

Chapter Six

Rosmini at Rovereto
His Spirituality and Priesthood

In November 1819 Rosmini went to Bressanone, 100 km north of Rovereto, to receive subdiaconate from the bishop, Msgr Carlo Francesco Lodron. That order in those days was the gateway to priesthood. A subdeacon took on the obligation of reciting the Divine Office daily.

At home Rosmini settled down to a somewhat retired life to prepare for becoming a priest. He wrote to his friend Paravia, 'I go to Mass and live the life of a hermit'.[1] At one time he thought of joining the seminary in Trent, but he was sensitive to the wishes of his parents who wanted him to stay near them now that he had finished at Padua. So, for the next six years Rovereto continued to be home for him.

His routine of prayer and an intense regime of study occupied his time. In some respects it can be seen as the most creative period of his life. During these years he developed his principles of spirituality, which were to bear fruit in the founding of the Institute of Charity. Through his studies he laid the foundations of his philosophic system. A special part of this was his study of politics, which equipped him to play a significant part in the movement to unify Italy.

These three aspects of his life – as priest, philosopher and patriot – should not be seen as three totally separate occupations independent of each other. Rosmini saw his vocation to serve God as a single all-embracing calling. Everything he did, everything he wrote was 'for the greater glory of God'. His life was one.

In January 1820 his father died suddenly. Pier Modesto had always enjoyed robust health, so that even though he was seventy-five his death came as a great shock. The immediate consequence was that Antonio, unexpectedly, became the head of the household and main heir to the family fortune. He acquired responsibility for his mother who was to live for another twenty years, his sister and brother.

Of these, as we have seen, the heaviest burden by far was his brother Giuseppe whose bipolar temperament made him a perpetual worry to Antonio and to everyone else. Giuseppe was at once fond of Antonio and also intensely jealous of him. At one stage Antonio became so exasperated that he offered to go halves with him in the family fortune. That did not happen, which was just as well, as Giuseppe would certainly have squandered it. As it was, Antonio gave his brother free access to the house, its garden and stables.

We have noted earlier the close friendship Rosmini had with his older sister, Margherita and his gift to her of his first published work, *Della Educazione Cristiana*. This little book was more religious than pedagogical. Its main objective was to restore to the minds and hearts of youth a sense of God's presence in an integrated life and stressed the need for the educator not only to believe what he teaches, but to love the life that he proposes to his charges.

The book also reflects Rosmini's intense loyalty to Catholic faith and practice, and already bears the stamp of meticulous and detailed scholarship, which became the hallmark of his writing. It includes, for instance, a detailed analysis of the value of reciting the Divine Office. The public recitation of the principal Hours, unusual among secular priests and most apostolic religious congregations, has become common among Rosminian communities where there are sufficient members living together. This echoes the preference and teaching of their Founder. He writes how the hours, days, weeks and seasons of time are made holy by the meaningful praying of the Hours. He notes how the Canticles at Matins are appropriate to the days of the week where they appear. Thus the Canticle of Habakkuk on Friday 'refers to the Cross of Christ,' commemorating the day of the week when Christ died.[2]

His reputation for serious scholarship attracted notice in the town. Local clerics asked his assistance with their studies. He set up philosophy classes in his house each morning, and in the evenings he presided over theological conferences based on the *Summa Theologica* of St Thomas Aquinas. He even made a start in translating the *Summa* into Italian. At that time St Thomas had fallen into disfavour in ecclesiastical circles, so Rosmini was a pioneer in recovering Thomistic studies. This is ironic since later on when his philosophical works were attacked, one canard spread abroad was that Rosmini was opposed to the teachings of St Thomas.

During these first years at Rovereto Rosmini was also engaged in various charitable activities for the benefit of others. First was the *Società degli Amici* (*Society of Friends*), which he set up and which could be seen as a successor to the *Accademia dei Vannettiani* of several years earlier. Its scope however was much broader, no longer primarily literary but aiming to defend religion and promote the interests of the Church. Some friends joined him, but he was careful to keep the activity private for fear of attracting attention from the ever-suspicious Austrian authorities.

Rosmini had ambitions that this sort of religious association might be a powerful means for renewing the Church. During his time at Padua he had already conceived the idea of composing a *Christian Encyclopaedia*, to counter the sort of secular and anti-Christian propaganda being put out by the French Encyclopaedists.

Another initiative was his ambition to set up an Oratory of St Philip Neri in Rovereto for the service of lay people in the town. These oratories were common enough around Italy at that time. It failed to get off the ground, but he kept it in the back of his mind and when he was parish priest in Rovereto fourteen years later he did in fact set up such an Oratory with considerable initial success. He also planned to establish a printing press for producing more wholesome literature than what was being spread about to the detriment of ordinary people. He felt this plan for a publishing house came from God, but he received little support from others. So, once again his ideas failed.

These ambitions, while they were very noble, were somewhat grandiose for a young cleric in an obscure mountain town. Yet their very failure was a pivotal experience for him. It taught the young Rosmini a lesson: to question whether his own plans and good ideas were in fact what Almighty God was asking of him.

He was sure of one thing, that God was calling him to be a priest. Later in 1820 Rosmini took the opportunity of a visit to Rovereto by the bishop of Chioggia on 2 July to be ordained deacon, and on 21 April 1821 (Holy Saturday) he was ordained priest by the same bishop in Chioggia.

Priesthood brought him the responsibility of celebrating Mass daily. His very first Mass was said on Easter Sunday in Venice in the company of his friends. He made his way home to celebrate his first public Mass at San Marco's. His daily Eucharist was for Rosmini of supreme importance and he prepared for it diligently. His preference was to celebrate privately, but he was always available to say a public Mass when needed.

Various people have commented on Rosmini's spirit of recollection when at the altar. Many years later a priest in Naples said this of him: 'I have seen Rosmini celebrate Mass, and I was struck by the great piety manifested in his countenance; it gave me the impression that he was a venerable and profoundly pious priest.'[3]

Rosmini was ordained in his own patrimony so he was not directly under the authority of the local bishop. This may seem strange to us, but there were plenty of priests ordained privately in those days, often from wealthy families. In both France and Italy the secondary education of boys was largely in the hands of such priests. Rosmini's own teacher, Pietro Orsi, was an example.

However, Rosmini was occasionally called upon to perform pastoral duties and he was always available to preach or hear confessions in the local church. We have seen that it fell to him to preach the panegyric for Pius VII in Rovereto. During the Lent of 1822, he was asked by the Vicar General to look after a country parish where the parish priest was mortally ill. For a few weeks he diligently celebrated the sacraments, visited the sick and instructed the village children. When the priest died, Rosmini gave the funeral eulogy.

He was gradually becoming known as a wise person and was invited by the local clergy to preach their retreat in September 1823. People, often clergy, began to seek his spiritual guidance and that was the beginning of an immense correspondence which grew over the years. One early correspondent who became his friend was Msgr Giuseppe Grasser, an Austrian chosen to become bishop of Treviso. Grasser came to stay at Rovereto where Rosmini helped him learn Italian to equip him for this new post, and was present at his Episcopal ordination in Venice.

Rosmini's Spirituality

When Rosmini looked back reflectively over his early months of priesthood he noted that whenever he undertook some good work at the request of another it usually succeeded. Enterprises he launched on his own initiative invariably seemed to fail. Out of this reflection arose his 'principle of passivity'. Briefly it can be summarised in two phrases:

1. Not to undertake any work of charity on my own initiative but to apply myself to putting right my own life;
2. Not to refuse any work of charity when it is offered me by the providence of God and not to prefer one work to another but do them all with equal enthusiasm.

At first sight this might appear a recipe for inertia, but a glance at the immense accomplishments of Rosmini's life soon gives the lie to that.

Some years later, writing to Fr Pietro Rigler in Trent, Rosmini used an amusing and striking series of similes to describe his principle of passivity. 'Our life of contemplation must never be a state of inertia', he insists. 'but a stage of preparation ... We should rest in our retirement like lions poised to spring, or like taut bowstrings, or like the stopper on a bottle of Spumante about to explode ...'[4]

Over the next few years Rosmini built round this principle of passivity the edifice of his personal spirituality, which also became the rule of his religious Institutes.[5] The starting point for Rosmini is a very simple principle, which appears often in his writings, his Rule and letters: 'to seek the salvation and perfection of my own soul is the one thing necessary'.[6] This is the language of his time. At first sight it may seem very self-centred. However, if we reword it and say instead 'it is my bounden duty in life to try to become a better person', then no one would disagree.

But what about my neighbour? The fact is that however much I may worry about the well-being of someone else, the only life I can hope to put right is my own. I may advise, cajole, encourage someone else, but until they decide to make a change off their own bat, little is likely to change. The Twelve Steps programme for Alcoholics Anonymous is a fine example of that principle.

This desire to become a better person is Rosmini's central rule. It is like the axle from which all his other ascetical teachings radiate like spokes. Rosmini sometimes writes that we should 'think big!' (*pensare in grande*). What he means is not that we should have grandiose ideas, but that we should never lose sight of the main aim – to serve God by becoming a better person.

Of course, the context in which we strive to become better people, is social. We live with others; our lives are shaped by them. Behind that there is an even greater truth: we are creatures; we are made by God; our world is made by God; my neighbour too is created by God: 'I am created by God out of love. The law of love permeates everything'. Therefore we love God and all God has made. We love creation, we love all the people in it, and we love all that is good, true and beautiful.

The second half of Rosmini's 'Principle of Passivity' points to the pattern of life Rosmini sought for himself and all those who became his disciples. The aim is personal holiness; the means is universal charity – hence the Institute *of Charity*. Rosmini's foundation is unique in not stipulating any particular charitable work for his followers. They must be prepared to do anything, when it is seen to be the will of God.

Rosmini calls this the principle of indifference. If I am vowed to universal charity I will not pick and choose what I do. 'Indifference' is not an attractive word in English, or in Italian for that matter. It suggests not caring. Another word sometimes used in Italian is *disponabilità* (literally, to be 'disposable'; that sounds even worse!). However, the first term is preferred by Rosmini because indifference implies *understanding* rather than will. I understand the choices before me, but I am indifferent to which way I go. I put aside what would be my own personal preference and instead I rely on the providence of God to guide me; I put myself entirely in God's hands.

This brings us to another of Rosmini's favourite ideas – *providence*. He sees our lives as being wrapped in the providence of God. Nothing happens to us, no encounter we have in daily life, is outside the providence of God. God has a plan for each one of us. This is not an especially original idea. In this respect Rosmini is following the teachings of the seventeenth-century French school.

St Francis de Sales was always a favourite of his. Indeed, Rosmini resembles Francis in his gentleness. Also, during 1821, he read Lorenzo Scupoli's *Spiritual Combat* which reflects a similar spirituality.[7] All these ideas were distilled by Rosmini and became the inspiration for his own spiritual classic, the *Maxims of Christian Perfection*.

∞⤳∞

The text of the *Maxims of Christian Perfection* was largely put together during 1827 and was published in 1830. When asked who was his target audience, Rosmini insisted it was for lay people as well as for vowed Religious. To one enquirer who later joined him, Giovanni Boselli, he wrote: 'I intend the Maxims as much for people living in a regular community as for those living outside and not having vows … The book is so concise it may seem hard to swallow; nevertheless it is worth chewing on as it is!'[8]

The Maxims of Christian Perfection

There are six *Maxims* and they more or less mirror the six stanzas of the *Our Father*.

1.   *To desire only to please God: that is, to be just.*

'Hallowed be your name'. Rosmini starts, as always, with what he sees as the one thing necessary – personal holiness. 'Justice' here means doing what we believe God wishes us to do – doing our duty to God and our fellow humans.

2.   *To delight in Jesus Christ and in his Church.*

'Your kingdom come'. For Rosmini, to serve the Church is a primary duty, because the Church is the means for holiness that Jesus Christ has given us. He specifies loyalty to Pope and bishops. To be a Rosminian is to be a loyal servant of God's Church.

3.   *To desire God's will in all things.*

'Your will be done on earth as in heaven'. The duty of the individual Christian is to seek out what is God's will for her or for him. The Christian banishes anxiety concerning the state of the world, and is content to wait patiently for God's will to be revealed.

4.   *To give myself wholly to God's Providence.*

'Give us today our daily bread'. This is the longest of Rosmini's Maxims, and in it he spells out his teaching on the ruling nature of divine providence in the Christian life. He calls it 'the key to our peace of mind and heart'.

5.   *To regard myself as being of no account.*

'Forgive us our sins as we forgive those who sin against us'. Rosmini looks here at human weakness and sin. We may be full of zeal to do God's work, but the fact is we are fickle, we

make mistakes, and we are constantly in need of forgiveness.
6.   *To be guided in all things by the spirit of wisdom.*
Rosmini parts company with the *Our Father* in his final
Maxim. This notion of the 'spirit of intelligence' as he calls it,
is very dear to Rosmini, and he uses it to round off this
compendium of his spiritual teaching.

Christians, he insists, ought never to walk in darkness but
always in the light. We are ultimately guided in what we do by
the indwelling Spirit of God. This is the source of all human
wisdom. It should also guide us in all our charitable works. It
is this that draws us out of retirement and may propel us into
exhausting activity for God. But, as long as we are guided by
the Spirit, we will have peace of mind. That is the acid test.

∞‿∞

During these years at Rovereto Rosmini was able to formulate
the basis of his ascetical teaching. Another key idea which
gradually grew in his mind was the founding of the Institute
of Charity.

His sister's wish to start an institution for poor girls in
Rovereto had led them to go together to Verona and meet the
Marchesa Maddalena di Canossa to seek her advice and help.
They had been very impressed by her, and Canossa was
equally impressed by Margherita's brother, so when Antonio
was ordained priest she approached him to found an order of
Brothers to do the same sort of work for poor boys that her
Sisters were doing for girls.

This started a correspondence which went on for several
years. Rosmini was unsure whether it was a good idea to
restrict membership to the unordained. He was convinced
that exercising spiritual charity was the highest form of
dedicated life, and this must include the priesthood.

Maddalena di Canossa went on eventually to found her
own order of Brothers of Charity, in 1831, without Rosmini;
nevertheless they continued as good friends. Undoubtedly,
however, her invitation triggered off a line of thought in
Rosmini's mind, the germ of the Rosminian vocation to

universal charity. The education of boys became an important part of Rosminian work, but never as an exclusive work.

His spirituality evolved during his first years of priesthood. Such a unified vision called for a body of people to put it into effect. Thus the idea of founding a Religious congregation began to germinate in his mind. Surrounding this group of vowed Religious he envisaged a group of committed lay people, who would be fully members of the congregation. Such a body of zealous Christians would provide exactly the sort of united force effective in helping build a better world – in a way that his *Società degli Amici* had failed to do.

Rosmini had conceived his dream of a new Religious Congregation. What was now needed was the stimulus, the time and the place for this to happen. In February 1826 he decided to leave Rovereto and move to live in Milan. The opportunity was not long in coming.

Notes

1   *Ep.Compl.,* i, 178.
2   *Della Educazione Cristiana, III,* 18.
3   Pagani, p. 52.
4   *Ep.Compl.,* iv, 1837.
5   See 'Bessero Belti' in *Una Lettura di Rosmini,* by Umberto Muratore, Roma, Città Nuova, 1981.
6   Letter to Luigi Gentili. 'I never cease to recommend to our brethren that they should esteem their own perfection and the practising of the Gospel virtues as the greatest possible good: for this is both the foundation and the one great end of the Institute. Do all you can to attain this perfection yourself . . .' (*Ascetical Letters,* tr. J. Morris, v, 24).
7   First printed in Venice in 1589. It quickly went through some 60 reprints.
8   *Ep.Compl.,* iii, 1343.

Chapter Seven

Rosmini in Milan, 1826–1828

In February 1826 Rosmini set out with three companions to make a new temporary home in the city of Milan. He travelled part of the way with his sister Margherita who was herself moving from Trent to launch a community of the Daughters of Charity in Verona.

What were the reasons for his move? The most important was his need to expand the sources of his research, principally for a book on the philosophy of politics. Milan was a city with abundant access to books and academic resources. His cousin Carlo Rosmini, who was a historian, lived in Milan and he became not only a wise counsellor but also introduced his cousin to people who could be of assistance to him. Antonio also wanted to attend to the publishing of other works he had completed.

Another reason for his move was sensitive and personal. Since Margherita left home in 1825 to become a nun, he had had to deal with his brother Giuseppe by himself. This was a real trial for him. His move away from Rovereto would have the double value of sparing him further daily anxiety and also giving Giuseppe the space to grow up without being overshadowed by a brilliant older brother. Both of them seemed to live more contentedly when out of each other's hair.

Another task he had taken on at the suggestion of the Marchesa di Canossa was the direction in Milan of three possible recruits to the planned Brothers of Charity, one of whom, the deacon Giovanni Boselli, was eventually to become a Rosminian.

Rosmini's three companions on the journey were his friend from Padua days, Niccolò Tommaseo, his secretary and close friend Maurizio Moschini, and his servant, Antonio Bisoffi. They arrived in Milan on 4 March 1826 and took up residence at a hotel, the Croce di Malta, close to where Carlo Rosmini lived and handy to the Ambrosian library.

From the start, the little community lived an orderly and disciplined life. Rise at six. Prayer followed by Mass. Breakfast and then study until noon. A light lunch and more study up to three o'clock. They recited the Divine Office together followed by spiritual reading. Dinner at four. Then they were free to go out walking or visiting. They would return home about nine, say the rosary – and so to bed. Rosmini was already rehearsing the regular way of life which was soon to become his norm.

Milan had been one of the great cities of Europe since Roman times. During the third and fourth centuries it was the capital of the Western Roman Empire. It became a principal bishopric of Mediaeval Europe and for centuries one of the most prosperous cities in the peninsula. Its prosperity continues. Now it is the second city of Italy as well as its commercial and industrial capital.

When Rosmini arrived in Milan it was, like Rovereto, under Austrian government. The city lies on the River Po at the centre of the Lombardy Plain, one of the most fertile areas of Italy. It was already connected to most of northern Italy by a network of functioning canals.

Rosmini was immediately impressed by many aspects of his new home. He wrote enthusiastically to various friends about the city. To his old parish priest in Rovereto, Fr Giambattista Locatelli, he said:

My sojourn in Milan is very pleasing. The state of religion is most impressive and I doubt if there is another city like it. The principal families seem to be really devout. On feast days you see people of every sort paying visits to the churches, reciting prayers out loud and performing various acts of piety and penance.

The charity and generosity of the well-to-do is most impressive. Churches, hospitals and works of piety are set up: it seems one only has to ask and the money rolls in. The clergy do not appear especially learned but they are solid, pious and disciplined – while being quite laid back.[1]

Rosmini thought that the religious spirit of the Milanese people reflected a tradition springing from their great Archbishop of the 1500s, St Charles Borromeo. The people perhaps lacked the refinement of the Venetians, but he liked their courtesy and simplicity. They were welcoming especially towards strangers, even to a 'country bumpkin' like himself.[2]

Rosmini's social horizons expanded dramatically. He was soon introduced to the high society of the city and he made friends with many clergy, such as Fr Luigi Polidori. However, his most significant social contacts were the distinguished politician Count Giacomo Mellerio and the already famous author Alessandro Manzoni, both destined to become his close friends.

Mellerio (like Rosmini himself) was a wealthy patrician, born in 1777 in Domodossola, a mountain town on the main route to Switzerland through the Simplon Pass. He too had moved to live in Milan where he took a prominent part in local politics. He became Vice-Governor of the city under Eugène Beauharnais during the Napoleonic period, and later Grand Chancellor of Lombardy when the Austrians returned to power. He retired from politics in 1816, and spent his life as a patron of charitable works.

Rosmini's cousin Carlo introduced him to Mellerio and Rosmini became a regular visitor to his new friend's house. One biographer says that Mellerio became 'like a brother'.[3] Later he was to become a great benefactor and supporter, especially when Rosmini took up residence in Mellerio's hometown, Domodossola.

But it was Tommaseo who introduced Rosmini to the man destined to be perhaps his closest friend, the famous author Alessandro Manzoni, who already knew Rosmini's writings.

When he read Rosmini's tract on *Christian Education* he said it manifested 'the spirit of the early Fathers of the Church'. On his part, Rosmini was an admirer of Manzoni's writings, especially his poetry. It was a meeting of kindred spirits. From that time on, Rosmini loved to spend time with him. They would discuss language, literature, religion, politics, economics – but especially philosophy. At first Manzoni challenged many of Rosmini's philosophical ideas, but little by little he was totally convinced and became an ardent disciple.

Manzoni discovered in Rosmini the philosopher he had been looking for. On Rosmini's part he found in Manzoni a perceptive critic of his ideas and a literary mentor. He helped Rosmini to develop a much clearer Italian style.

At that time Manzoni was busy completing his literary masterpiece, the novel *I Promessi Sposi*.[4] He allowed Rosmini to read the proofs and his new friend was full of praise. Later, when Rosmini settled in Piedmont, Manzoni moved house to be near him. Manzoni was to attend him faithfully during his final illness.

છ૭ર

Manzoni is responsible for leaving a unique and presumably reliable pen portrait of his new friend. It seems that he decided to use Rosmini as the model for an important character in *I Promessi Sposi*.[5] Federico Borromeo historically was the cousin of St Charles Borromeo, the famous Archbishop of Milan. He succeeded his cousin to the See of Milan and continued the reform policies of his illustrious relative and predecessor.

In Chapter 22 of the novel Manzoni inserts a parenthesis in the narrative to describe the character of Federico Borromeo. Here are some extracts:

> Our story has now brought us into the presence of a man the mention of whose name, the memory of whose character, can never at any time fail to refresh the mind with the calm emotion of reverence, with a happy feeling of affection . . .

Federico Borromeo ... was one of those few men – rare in any age – who devote the resources of an exceptional intellect, of vast wealth and of a privileged position in society to seek out and practice the means of making the world a better place ...

Born in luxury and splendour, he paid due heed from earliest childhood to those words of abnegation and humility, those maxims regarding the vanities of pleasure, the injustices of pride and the nature of true dignity and true values, which are handed down from one generation to another (whether any notice is taken of them or not) in the most elementary religious instruction.

Federico Borromeo *did* take heed of those maxims: he took them seriously, tested them and found that they were true. He realised that certain other words and maxims which contradicted them could consequently only be false, although they had been passed down from generation to generation with equal assurance and often by the same lips. He decided to use those which were true as the standard for his own actions and thoughts.

Convinced that this life is not meant to provide a treadmill for the many and unending holidays for the few, but rather to furnish each one of us with a task to perform of which an account one day must be rendered, he began at an early age to consider how to make his own life holy and useful ...

Towards himself, he was a most frugal and precise administrator of his own resources. For he never threw away a garment until it was really worn out; though his passion for simplicity was accompanied by the most exquisite personal cleanliness ... To ensure that nothing should be lost of what was left over from his frugal table, he allotted the remnant to a hostel for the destitute, one of whose inmates came every day into his dining room, by his order, to collect what remained uneaten ...

The inexhaustible charity of Federico Borromeo showed in everything else he did no less than in his giving. He was easily accessible to everybody, but it was to those of so-called low degree that he felt he owed a special duty to show them a cheerful countenance and a friendly courtesy. The lower they were in the social scale, the more strongly he felt this duty.

On one occasion on a visit to a rough mountain village, Federico was giving instruction to certain poor children; and as he was asking them questions and teaching them the truth he put his arms affectionately around them. At this, one of his companions warned him that he ought to be more careful because they were disgustingly dirty ... But the good bishop replied with some anger: 'They are souls in my care, who will probably never see my face again; and you will tell me not to embrace them?'

He was very rarely moved to anger, however, being admired for the gentleness of his ways and for an imperturbable calmness of manner, which might have been attributed to an extraordinary equanimity of temperament, but was really a triumph of constant self-discipline over a lively and indeed fiery nature. If he sometimes appeared severe, or even hasty, it was with his subordinate priests, when he found them guilty of avarice, of negligence, or any other sins especially contrary to the spirit of their noble calling.

In any matter which involved his own interest or his temporal glory, he never gave any signs of joy, or resentment, or enthusiasm, or agitation. His conduct was admirable if he did not feel any of these passions, and still more admirable if he did.

Modesty and unwillingness to predominate appear no less clearly in the common events of his life. Though he gave his full attention and all his efforts to the arts of planning and administration wherever he considered it to be his duty, he always avoided interfering in other people's affairs; in fact, he made every effort *not* to become involved in them even on request. Such discretion and restraint, as we all know, are not common among men who are zealous for the good, as Federico was.

... Federico, among all his other claims to renown, did enjoy among his contemporaries the reputation of a very learned man ... Someone may ask whether a person of such intellect and such learning has not left any monuments of his scholarship to posterity? Monuments of his scholarship indeed? He left about a hundred separate works behind, some long and some short, some in Latin and some in Italian, some printed and some in manuscript.

'How on earth has it happened', the same reader may inquire, 'that all these works are forgotten, so seldom sought after?' With all that intellectual force, all that scholarship, all that practical experience of men and affairs, all that meditation, all that passion for the good and beautiful, all that honesty of spirit, all those other qualities that go to make up a great writer, how is it that Federico Borromeo, the author of a hundred works, has not left behind him a single book of the sort that are acknowledged as outstanding even by those who do not agree with them, and known by name even by those who have never read them?[6]

Manzoni does not answer this question, but goes on with the narrative of the novel. He describes Borromeo's forgiving attitude to the chief villain and his gentle compassion to Lucia Mondella, this cruel man's victim and heroine of the story, as well as to Agnese, her mother.

There are descriptions of Federico mixing freely with people while on his visitation, going into the houses of the poor and doing what he could to serve them. During the time of famine and a severe outbreak of plague his ministration and generosity to the most destitute is untiring. He comes out of the text as a caring, yet authoritative human being. It is a rare and precious glimpse of the deep impression Rosmini made on the famous novelist, who had become his devoted friend.

∞৲ৎ∞

This sojourn in Milan was a time of steady literary achievement for Rosmini. He set about writing the first volume of his *Philosophy of Politics* during 1826, following on later in the year with a second volume on *Natural Right*. He began also to write a third, on *The Natural Constitution of Civil Society*.

Much of this work provided the subject for long discussions with his literary friends. Tommaseo suggested that he defer publishing these works until he had completed and published his more metaphysical works, since his Politics needed to be founded on these more fundamental ideas. Rosmini took this advice and his political works were not published – and then much revised – until 1837–39. However, he wrote and published some smaller works, particularly a treatise on *Divine Providence*, which pleased Manzoni greatly. Manzoni said about it: 'God has given a great man to Italy and to the Church.'[7]

His correspondence, especially in the area of spiritual direction, continued to expand. Nor did he lose sight of the dream closest to his heart. In a letter to Cardinal Mauro Cappellari whom he had met and befriended in Rome on his visit there in 1824, he explained that his plan for a new Institute might appear ambitious but in fact, 'it sets no limits to doing whatever promotes the glory of God and the good of our neighbour ... this does not mean that it aims to take on everything'.[8] In fact he notes that whereas other societies specify what they propose to do, 'the members of the Institute take on nothing apart from their own sanctification, unless they are asked by their neighbour to take on some charitable work.'

Although the brothers prefer a contemplative life by choice, 'we only change over to activity at the request of our neighbour ... we leave God for God'. Later in the letter he notes: 'the spirit and intention of the Congregation is not one of doing much, but of doing it well.' Rosmini also sent his friend a small manuscript called *A Brief Description of the Society of Charity*. Cappellari was always most encouraging toward Rosmini, and later he was of great assistance on getting the Institute approved in Rome.

While Rosmini was fully occupied with his research and writing, he suffered two painful bereavements. His cousin Carlo died quite unexpectedly in June 1827. Rosmini was out of town when it happened, and he was quite desolated when he received the news on his return. Carlo was his closest relative in Milan, but he was also a good friend, one whom he admired as the model of a true Christian gentleman.

Shortly afterwards, in August, Rosmini went back home to Rovereto to get away from the summer heat, but also because he had been unwell. Moschini, his secretary, accompanied him, and he also fell ill of a serious chest complaint. The disease advanced rapidly and Rosmini scarcely left his bedside. On 22 October Rosmini had to pay a visit to nearby Trent. When he was about to get back into the carriage for the return trip he suddenly turned to his companion and said: 'Maurizio has just died.' On their return they found that Moschini had passed away at that time. It was another acutely painful blow.

Rosmini immediately engaged a young priest, Andrea Fenner, to be his new secretary. He returned to Milan but continued to be unwell. He had a troublesome cough, suffered sleeplessness and used to bring up blood. His doctor diagnosed a liver complaint, quite likely brought on by overwork.

∞∞∞

About the time of his move to Milan, Rosmini wrote to the Marchesa Maddalena di Canossa re-exploring their joint dream of founding a religious congregation for men. It seems that towards the end of 1825 Rosmini had a flash of inspiration concerning the future Institute of Charity. He shared this with Maddalena: he had undergone a change of mind and now saw it as a society of priests rather than simply of brothers.

In two letters he spelt out in some detail what he had in mind: a society of priests devoted to love of God and neighbour. They would first 'desire to contemplate and praise God in tranquillity and spiritual joy'. They would have no specific works of charity, but respond to requests from outside according to the order of charity, determined by their Superiors.[9]

The Marchesa voiced a fear that undertaking pastoral responsibilities outside the community might lead the religious to become lax. Rosmini counters this (26 January 1826) by using the example of the Good Shepherd who gives his life for his sheep. Jesus 'places in the pastoral ministry the seeds of all perfection,' he says. The members must never aspire to positions of honour, yet may be bidden by their Superiors to undertake them. Rosmini notes that St Augustine, St Eusebius and St Charles Borromeo were all happy for the religious state to be combined with pastoral ministry.[10]

Rosmini insists that it isn't sufficient for religious simply to be involved in the formation of the pastoral clergy. Otherwise, he says, 'we run the risk that these good religious may think themselves a cut above mere parish priests and pastors ... These things are not got from books: what is needed is the actual experience of the duties of ministry'. You cannot exercise charity towards the world without becoming involved in it.

He also hints at something which became for him a very important principle in his future Congregation: to avoid acquiring an *esprit de corps*, tending towards exclusivism or collective pride. The new Society must be humble, and Rosmini concludes his letter by reminding the Marchesa of her own desire that it should be founded 'on Calvary between the crucified Jesus and Our Lady of Sorrows'.

The spark which was to bring all these ideas and dreams into decisive action, came about in Count Mellerio's house on 8 June 1827. Rosmini met for the first time a French priest, named Jean-Baptiste Loewenbruck. Loewenbruck had just arrived from France. He was about thirty years of age, of robust build and florid complexion.[11] He came from Lorraine in northwestern France and had already had quite a turbulent career as a missionary and preacher in Paris and other parts of France.

Loewenbruck could not have been more unlike Rosmini: he spoke animatedly in rapid French; he was dynamic and extrovert; his enthusiasms frequently got him into trouble and he was inclined to run up debts. But Rosmini was immediately fascinated, especially when he spoke of his ambition to found a religious congregation specifically for the improvement of the clergy.

Rosmini told Loewenbruck that he too was interested in making a foundation, and spoke to him about the balance between contemplation and action which was to be its essence. Loewenbruck was attracted, and over the next few days they spent much time in discussion. They even visited together the Certosa of Pavia, a Carthusian monastery near Milan, to pray for light. They then resolved to find a retired place where they could spend time with God and plan their immediate future. It would be an opportunity to discover what God wanted of them.

Fr Luigi Polidori, who lived in Mellerio's household, was party to much of this discussion. A few days later he had an inspiration while saying Mass, which he at once communicated to them. Just outside the town of Domodossola there was a disused sanctuary called Monte Calvario, an ideal place of retreat; he thought it would be available. It was also close to the home of Mellerio, who promised to be supportive.

Loewenbruck was all for starting at once. Typically, Rosmini pleaded caution. They both needed to put their affairs in order first. But he was happy for Loewenbruck to go up to Domodossola on reconnaissance. So Loewenbruck set off, going via Turin to obtain the blessing of the diocesan bishop, Cardinal Morozzo.

The following month Rosmini took the first opportunity to follow him and view the possible site for their enterprise. For the first of many times, he walked up the steep ascent following the route of the Stations of the Cross to Monte Calvario, the place soon destined to become his home. Maddalena di Canossa had predicted that the new foundation would be on Calvary between Christ and Our Lady of Sorrows. And here it was.

Rosmini and Loewenbruck arranged to make a start in Lent the following year (1828). That would give them time to reorganise their lives. Loewenbruck too needed to return to France and settle his affairs. Full of hope, they parted company.

Perhaps the most extraordinary thing about this decision is that all this time Rosmini continued to be far from well physically. In terms of human prudence it was madness for him to embark on such an enterprise in the middle of winter on a bleak and isolated mountain top. But he saw it as providential. In December he wrote to a friend, Count Giovanni Padulli, in Rome:

> ... my infirmity is the clearest proof that the proposed work will succeed. A strong constitution would have made me rely on myself. For here I am, good for nothing ... a block of wood

or marble from which the Lord may carve whatever He pleases. In this state I easily feel my own uselessness. I might otherwise be deluded into thinking I was in some way necessary to the Church of Christ ... [12]

So, in February 1828 Antonio Rosmini was to set out on the most momentous journey of his life.

Notes

1   *Ep.Compl.,* ii, 516.
2   Rosmini's precise words were ' ... di grossa pasta come mi sono io'.
3   Giovanni Pusineri, *Rosmini,* revised by Remo Bessero Belti. Stresa: Sodalitas, 1989, p. 40.
4   First published 1827 in Milan.
5   Niccolò Tommaseo bore witness to this fact in an article, *Antonio Rosmini* in *Rivista Contemporanea*, Turin, 1853. This passage describing the character of Federico Borromeo, from Chapter 22 of *I Promessi Sposi* by Manzoni, is quoted by Tommaseo in full in one of his books, where he calls it *The Life of Antonio Rosmini, by Alessandro Manzoni.*
6   Alessandro Manzoni, *The Betrothed*, tr. by Bruce Penman, Penguin Classics, 1972.
7   Pagani, *Life*, p. 76.
8   *Ep.Compl.,* ii, 611.
9   *Ep.Compl.,* i, 451.
10 *Ascetical Letters,* tr. by J. Morris, I, 13–19.
11 Pagani-Rossi, p. 187.
12 *Ep.Compl.,* ii, 734.

Chapter Eight

Foundation of the Institute of Charity Monte Calvario and Rome, 1828–1830

On 18 February 1828, Rosmini set out with two companions, his secretary Fenner and, once again, the redoubtable Bisoffi, travelling from Milan northwards into the mountains to the town of Domodossola. Even though it is only a journey of some 60 km, he had to leave the Austrian-controlled province of Lombardy and pass into the independent kingdom of Piedmont (ruled from Turin by the House of Savoy). It was still winter and it snowed on the journey. The travellers passed the night in Domodossola, guests of a friend of Count Mellerio.

The following morning the little party made its way up the steep track through the trees to the sanctuary of Monte Calvario.[1] When they arrived at the summit they celebrated Mass in the octagonal chapel, dedicated to the death of Jesus Christ on the Cross.

The date 20 February is regarded by Rosminians as the birthday of Rosmini's foundation, the Institute of Charity.[2] It was Ash Wednesday and Rosmini's declared intention was to spend Lent in prayer in order to discern whether the plan to found a religious congregation was of God or not. The weather was very cold and the house was damp, but the sun was shining. Canon Remigio Capis, the priest in charge of the sanctuary, warmly welcomed Rosmini and his companions.

In the Middle Ages the summit of the hill had been fortified, and the ruins of the mediaeval castle are still to be seen in the garden. Its ancient name was the Hill of Motarella.[3] From behind the house you look down upon the town of Domodossola and towards Alpine peaks and the valley leading to the Simplon Pass. In fine weather it is a delightful situation. But in the winter, because of the proximity of the snow-covered mountains, it can be cold and bleak.

In the early 1600s, two Capuchin Friars resolved to build a sanctuary there dedicated to the Passion of Jesus. With the support of local townsfolk they erected a noble church in honour of the Crucifixion with a small dwelling alongside; later on, more rooms were added for people wanting to make a retreat there.

The Capuchins also planted crosses along the track up from the town commemorating the first eleven Stations of the Cross (the twelfth, the death of Jesus on the Cross, being the sanctuary itself). In the course of time these crosses were replaced by substantial chapels, each depicting an individual Station, with life-size statuary and colourful Baroque decorations. However, the sanctuary on the hill was deserted during the 1700s and many of the buildings fell into ruins. The biographer, Pagani, describes it as a 'refuge for bats, rats and scorpions'.[4]

During his reconnaissance the previous year, Loewenbruck had sought and received the blessing of the local bishop, Cardinal Morozzo of Novara, and had energetically organised a refurbishment of the necessary accommodation, paid for by Rosmini's money. The cells for the new community were small (about nine feet square), sparsely furnished and bare. It was suitably penitential, but Rosmini was exhilarated. The crisp mountain air reminded him of his native Tyrol.

There was only one huge disappointment: no Loewenbruck. The Frenchman failed to appear, so Rosmini wrote to him in France urging him to come at once.

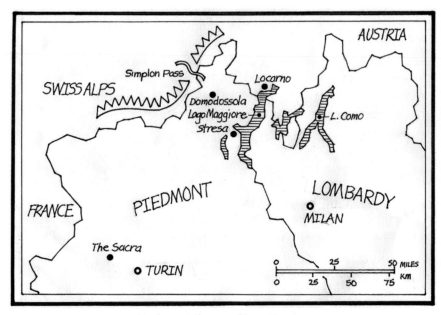

Northwest Italy around Lago Maggiore

Here I am, dear friend and beloved brother in Christ, awaiting you at our rendezvous. I have forestalled you, and am almost pleased with myself for having for once outstripped you in diligence, a virtue in which you are usually so far beyond me. Come! Fly! I am longing to embrace you. We will pass the 40 days in the desert in memory of what was done for us by our Divine Master.[5]

Rosmini wrote again a week later even more urgently. But to no avail. Lent passed, but of his friend and co-founder there was no sign. Rosmini allowed his true feelings to escape in one letter, to his friend Giovanni Padulli in Rome:

Loewenbruck is not here ... I await him anxiously and hope he will soon arrive ... I greatly need him, with his zeal and his active temperament. I myself tend to be inert and undecided even over small matters. That is why I have not yet taken in hand the repair of the fabric here, and am leaving it all to my French friend.

I do not even venture to receive any further companions as yet, because there is no one to impose a proper discipline; I could only give them bad example because of my laziness and slackness. But if the Frenchman comes I will accept more companions ...[6]

If he comes ... Loewenbruck was supposed to be in France settling his affairs. But weeks passed and there was still no sign. There were rumours abroad regarding his hotheadedness and unreliability. Cardinal Morozzo even suggested he had abandoned Rosmini and joined the Jesuits. Rosmini was left alone in his chosen desert retreat.

For Antonio Rosmini, this was the most momentous step he had ever taken, even more radical than becoming a priest. He had exchanged the comfort and security of his beautiful home in Rovereto for a bleak, impoverished hilltop in a strange country. He had turned his back on the civilised and stimulating company of Milan for a few rustic companions in the back of beyond.

Poverty was embraced in place of plenty. He had given up the control of his own life and circumstances to take on a vocation of obedience. That, one might think, was to do no more than anyone else who enters religious life. The difference is that his was a complete step into the unknown. He was going to no established community or rule; there was no spelled-out religious tradition to support him. And his chief chosen companion was absent.

Rosmini's Milanese friends simply could not understand this new venture of his. His mother was aghast, and he had to be quite firm with her that what he was doing was the manifest will of God.[7] Tommaseo thought he was crazy. His reply is illuminating and reminiscent of St Paul: 'The world judges this to be mad, but I am content to be mad with Jesus Christ'.[8]

However, he did receive support from Cardinal Morozzo. The sanctuary of Monte Calvario fell under his jurisdiction, and he was delighted that through Rosmini it would return to being a place of prayer and pilgrimage again. Rosmini confided his intentions fully to the Cardinal.[9]

He also received the blessing of his own local bishop (of Trent) Msgr Luschin: this in spite of the fact that Luschin had hoped to offer Rosmini either a parish or the post of Rector of the Diocesan Seminary.[10] Such an opportunity would have to wait. Of course Maddalena di Canossa and his sister Margherita were most supportive. The important thing was that he himself was at peace. And his health improved.

The Constitutions

In spite of what he had written to Padulli he was certainly not 'inert'. People started visiting the sanctuary again and he ministered to them. After a few days he launched into writing the *Constitutions of the Society of Charity*.[11] He worked assiduously at this task and completed the first draft by 23 April. Although he extensively revised these *Constitutions* up to the time of his death, the substance was composed during that Lent on Monte Calvario. It remains the fundamental text that Rosmini gave to his Institute.

It is an immense work. The English translation runs to nearly 500 pages. It is packed with detail: structures, regulations and ascetical comments. It doesn't make easy reading. For a time it was available only in the original Latin version. It seems as if it were intended as a resource, especially for Religious Superiors and Directors of religious formation. For the brethren at large, they would have Rule Books, some so-called Memorials, and of course they would have Rosmini's *Maxims*. All these were based on his *Constitutions*, but written in a more user-friendly style.

Nevertheless the original *Constitutions* represent Rosmini's vision in fullest detail. Therefore it is very precious to the Rosminian family as his heritage. Rosmini is unique among founders in that he is a philosopher – hence the intricate detail of his prescriptions. At the same time he resembles the first monks of the East in the spirit which pervades the text: his followers were to follow the perfection of the Gospel in its fulness and not any particular, restricted aspect.

As background, Rosmini carefully studied other great Rules. St Ignatius was very influential, especially as regards structure. Like Ignatius, he sketches out a path for his Religious from the noviciate onwards, through the simple vows of profession, to coadjutor vows of final profession, to presbyter vows for a special grouping of senior priests, known as Presbyters. These take a fourth vow of obedience to the Holy See. Rosmini follows Ignatius in binding his Institute to the Holy See through this fourth vow. The Institute seeks to belong to and serve the whole Church, not just a part.

Certain sections are characteristically Rosminian. There is the strong accent on community. Although allowance is made for coadjutors who live outside, they are seen as the exception. Living in community is the essence of the Rosminian vocation, and it demands the daily exercise of charity. Rosmini constantly stresses love among the brethren.[12] For how can a person adequately respond to the call of charity outside if he is incapable of loving his own?

One original aspect is his division of charity into three distinct aspects: Spiritual, Temporal and Intellectual. The three form a continuum, indeed they are like an arch in three distinct sections. At one end is the *temporal*, the sphere of good works. The brethren need to get their hands dirty doing ordinary tasks for others or for the common good. It keeps them grounded.

Central, the keystone of the arch, is the *spiritual* or pastoral aspect, which Rosmini regards as of supreme importance. In essence it means bringing God to people, and nothing can take its place. But Rosmini's originality can also be seen in the way he singles out *intellectual charity* – to which he himself was especially called. To understand and teach the truths of faith is a special call of love for others. This may be seen as the other end of the arch. Rosmini regarded the pastoral care of souls as being the supreme work of his Institute because it embraced all three branches of charity.

As regards religious obedience, the *Constitutions* speak of the 'voluntariness' of obedience.[13] The subject ideally obeys an injunction as if he had willed it himself. Rosmini counsels

Superiors to 'temper the wind to the shorn lamb'. He uses a term *sphere of activity* to describe the sum of a person's talents. The task assigned should ideally fit this sphere of activity but not overstretch it. Rosmini's concept of obedience is very human.

There is a brief section of ascetical comment in the middle of the book, which he entitles the *Foundation of the Society.*[14] It contains themes which he regards as of the highest importance: providence, the grace of Christ, justice and the love of God. It corresponds with Ignatius' *First Principle and Foundation*, regarded as the heart of his *Spiritual Exercises*.

Where Rosmini differs from many contemporary Founders is his minimal emphasis on penances and mortifications. For him, it is sufficient that the members work hard at what Providence assigns to them. For this reason they should be well fed and well housed. At a personal level, Rosmini often urges moderation on his overzealous disciples. The concept of 'burn out' was unknown in those days but that is clearly what he is guarding against.

Whatever one may think about the style and content, it is clear Rosmini was being comprehensive. The Society is to include priests and brothers as well as two other lay categories not under vows but very much part of the whole. There are 'Adopted Sons' who are unable to take vows but live with a Rosminian community. And there are 'Ascribed Members' – men and women who support and share the spirituality of communities, and who strive to live the Rosminian ideal in the everyday world.

In his *Constitutions* Rosmini is catering for widespread growth and for a multitude of possible works. What limitation can be put on what God has intended for the growth of this humble seed? For this reason, the book appears to be very ambitious and many have thought it so. Rosmini in fact was simply being characteristically thorough.

An interesting comment on Rosmini's plan for the Institute was made by one of his early followers, Francesco Paoli. He writes that there are, according to Rosmini, three founders of the Rosminians: St Ignatius for structure and organisation, St Augustine for his emphasis on love, and St Francis de Sales for the gentleness of spirit with which Rosmini imbues his whole vision.

ᖇᖇᘓᘓ

Pagani notes that Rosmini was much at peace during this period of his life. He writes in a playful strain to his mother to reassure her: 'Lent passed off very well. I had not expected so much from my digestion. But I think it is only right to give part of the credit to the cook, who knew so well what to serve it with'.[15] According to Pagani, the cook was none other than Bisoffi, who would certainly 'have let himself be cut to pieces for his master if necessary . . .'[16]

Rosmini also spent time on other works, including making a start on his philosophical masterpiece, *A New Essay on the Origin of Ideas*. In June he travelled to Novara to see the Bishop, and then went on to Turin to meet the Abbé Lamennais, who was visiting the city.[17] Lamennais was at the height of his fame and prestige as a zealous reforming priest, and a party of distinguished French ecclesiastics had formed round him. They were on the point of launching the famous but ill-fated journal *L'Avenir*.

Lamennais had read one of Rosmini's early philosophical works and was anxious to meet him. Their conversation lasted a couple of hours and the discussion revolved round the principle of certainty. Lamennais maintained that certainty is arrived at through 'common sense', i.e. through popular debate. Rosmini, however, saw certainty as something that the individual comes to through correct reasoning and not because an idea receives a majority vote.

They agreed to continue their discussion by correspondence with the possibility that the debate might be published. Rosmini wrote his first sally immediately he returned to Calvario. But Lamennais replied from France that he was too busy to continue the discussion.

On his return journey Rosmini had called in again on

Morozzo and told him about meeting Lamennais. 'That man frightens me,' Rosmini said to the bishop. 'He is consumed by pride. I fear for his fall'.[18] They were prophetic words, because Lamennais fell foul of Rome, and his teachings were condemned by Pope Gregory XVI in the Encyclical *Mirari Vos*, issued in 1832. Later Lamennais left the priesthood and lapsed from the Church.

Rosmini had hardly returned to Calvario when Loewenbruck appeared. Rosmini was overjoyed to have his companion back, and Loewenbruck at once embarked on various apostolic works. Pagani notes: 'News of his return soon spread, and crowds flocked to the Sanctuary for confession'. He applied himself also to improving the house 'mending here, restoring there, or adding a new wall, and readily applying his own muscular arms in the work to make the dwelling fit for future companions or for ecclesiastics, who even now came occasionally to make a quiet retreat'.[19] Loewenbruck manifested aspects of temporal charity which were not Rosmini's gift.

Cardinal Morozzo showed his support by asking Loewenbruck to take on the care of prisoners from Savoy in the gaol at Pallanza, twenty miles away on foot. He also entrusted him with the instruction and supervision of a young cleric, Giacomo Molinari, who was preparing himself for the priesthood. Loewenbruck was as zealous in the active aspect of Rosminian asceticism as Rosmini had been in the contemplative aspect. The little community was beginning to make its mark.

Meanwhile, Rosmini himself had to move away for a time for various reasons: to take the spa waters for his health which had again become precarious, to renew his passport and prepare to go to Rome. His great friend Cardinal Cappellari had urged him to come there in order to get the project for the new Institute approved by the Holy See. Rosmini was also anxious to print some of his most important works – and where better to do this than in the Eternal City?

So he left Calvario barely a month after the arrival of

Loewenbruck, leaving his friend in charge. It was important that the latter took responsibility for the seedling community. Rosmini continued to guide him from afar. He wrote regularly encouraging him to balance his activity with a sound spiritual life. Loewenbruck was ambitious for the future growth of their joint project. Rosmini counselled him to 'be content with the present, in which we can possess Our Lord who is our all, and not to trouble ourselves about the future'.[20]

Rosmini was also concerned that his friend should not overwork. And he sent money to ensure that the house would be adequately heated during the coming winter. New stoves were to be installed. Meanwhile weeks were to pass while he waited in Rovereto for the granting of his passport. The eventual justification was that transferring to the milder climate of Rome would be better for his delicate health.

Second Visit to Rome

Rosmini arrived in Rome with Bisoffi and Fenner on 28 November 1828, and took up residence in apartments adjoining the church of the *Dodici Apostoli* (Twelve Apostles), close to Piazza Venezia, right in the centre of the city.[21] His friend Count Padulli had arranged this accommodation, simple but adequate for their needs.

On his prior visit in 1823, he had come in the company of the Patriarch of Venice – effectively as a tourist. He had explored the art galleries, admired the monuments, visited the churches and had had a memorable audience with Pope Pius VII. This time it was quite different. There was no sightseeing. He had come on business with only his immediate household for company. His main aim was to seek the blessing of the Holy See on his great project, assisted by his friend and patron, Cardinal Cappellari.

Cappellari arranged for him to consult with two experts on Religious Constitutions: Gianluca, a Passionist, and Cesarini, an Oratorian. Rosmini found discussions with them very helpful. Cappellari spoke to the Pope, Leo XII, about his friend and the Pope was eager to meet him. But, early in the New Year and very unexpectedly, Leo XII died.

Rosmini wrote to Loewenbruck: 'The Holy Father is dead. He was very fond of me, more than I can say; but he is dead. It was the will of God'.[22] It was a blow to his hopes, but in a curious way it turned out for the best. The Cardinals gathered in Rome for the Conclave to elect a successor. One was Morozzo, who spoke enthusiastically to others about Rosmini's new venture in his diocese. At the same time Cappellari also was his advocate, promising to talk immediately about Rosmini's project to whoever was elected. The fledgling Institute was receiving useful publicity.

The new Pope, Pius VIII, was a frail old man, a one-time friend of Pius VII. Rosmini had met him earlier, and he awaited a summons. It eventually came on 15 May. Cappellari was on hand to introduce him, and the audience was successful beyond his wildest hopes.[23]

Rosmini arrived armed with some of his books as a gift. The Pope received him kindly and spoke to him of his vocation to write. He took up a book from his desk and pointed out an article which, he said, he regarded as a model of vigorous writing, the sort of arguments which the times needed. Had Rosmini read it? Rosmini blushed. He himself had written it. It was his *Galatea dei Letterati*, published in Milan the previous year.[24] The Pope was delighted to discover this. His words of commendation were so strong that Rosmini includes them as a sort of preface in his *Introduction to Philosophy,* written many years later in 1850. These were the Pope's words, as he recalled them:

> It is the will of God that you employ yourself in writing books: that is your vocation. The Church in these times has a great need for writers – I emphasise this – of really solid writers, of whom we have a real scarcity.
>
> To effectively influence the minds of people, there is no better means than through reason, and that is the path which leads to religious faith. You may be quite certain that you will work more for the advantage of your neighbour by writing than by exercising any other ministry.[25]

They then talked about Rosmini's plans for the *Institute of Charity*. Once again the Pope was warmly encouraging. However, he made one stipulation:

> If you intend to begin in a small way and leave the rest to Our Lord, we give our approval, and are pleased that you should do so. But if you contemplate a great undertaking, we think it would not do. We are not now speaking as Vicar, though unworthy, of Jesus Christ, but solely taking into account the times and circumstances in which we live.[26]

To Loewenbruck Rosmini wrote glowingly: 'The Pope went on at some length to show the need for humility and prudence ... stressing how necessary it is in all such works to begin in a small way and leave the Lord to give the increase ...'[27] Rosmini was keen to pass on the Pope's injunction – 'proceed slowly, step by step' – which might serve to temper Loewenbruck's natural ambition and exuberance.

After the audience Cappellari urged Rosmini to stay on for a while in Rome, in order to 'put together a summary of the *Constitutions*, to present to the Congregation of Bishops and Regulars'.[28]

Rosmini's time in the south was not all work. He took a break from the summer heat by going on holiday with Count Giovanni Padulli and his two sons, first to Albano outside the city, then further south to Naples. There he visited the sights, went bathing in the sea and climbed the famous volcano, Vesuvius. Rosmini writes: 'What a land, what a wonderful sky! It's a shame there isn't only land and sky ...'[29]

In early September Rosmini returned to his desk in Rome. News from the north was generally good. The little community had settled well, and Loewenbruck continued to be a ball of energy. He was asked to preach missions in the neighbourhood. He even gave one to the people of Macugnaga, a town which nestles at the foot of Monte Rosa, Italy's highest mountain, whose dialect was half German.

And then, like a bolt from the blue, came a letter from him announcing his decision to go off to France again in October to settle a debt, with the intention of returning before Easter the following year. Rosmini must have been totally shocked by the possibility of losing his companion at such a vital time. It could throw the whole enterprise into jeopardy. Rosmini's response is a model of diplomacy combined with firmness.

On the whole I approve your project to go to France in October, returning to Calvary before Easter. I agree with your intention (to settle an outstanding debt) as conforming with justice and charity, and then you can come back free from all encumbrance of debt.[30]

Rosmini goes on to reveal his fears of a hidden motive and to remind his companion of his responsibilities. Several times he uses the word *schietto*, meaning 'sincere' or 'honest'. Loewenbruck needed to analyse his motives for such precipitate action. Did he truly intend to come back to Calvario after his trip to France? And what about the little community – who was going to look after them? What about Molinari, whose studies Loewenbruck was supervising? What would he say to Cardinal Morozzo who had entrusted the sanctuary to their care – or to 'our friend in Milan' (presumably he means Mellerio, their principal lay backer)?

Rosmini was worried but perhaps not surprised considering how long he had had to wait for Loewenbruck's arrival in the first place. But this was the companion that Providence had sent him. It may have been this anxiety, but Rosmini was almost immediately smitten by illness, which turned out to be a mild attack of smallpox. Fortunately he quickly got over it. And Loewenbruck seems to have been persuaded by Rosmini's searching letter. He changed his mind and stayed on at Calvario.

While he was still ailing, Rosmini received a visit, which was to open the door to another exciting future prospect. A young Roman lawyer arrived at his door seeking spiritual direction.[31] Luigi Gentili came from a pious Roman family and he was the eldest of twelve children. His father was a lawyer and Luigi, a brilliant student, followed him into the law.

He practised for a couple of years, but became tired of it and shut himself away for a year while he taught himself to be fluent in Spanish, French, and English. He then offered himself to be a guide to the Roman antiquities to aristocratic foreign tourists. This led to a lucrative sideline teaching them to speak Italian. He earned enough money to buy himself a vineyard outside the city, and even got himself a noble title.

He met and fell in love with a young woman, a Miss Anna di Mendoza, of Spanish descent but having an English mother. She was the ward of Bishop Baines, Vicar Apostolic of the Western District in England. The bishop was alarmed at the attentions of the passionate Roman, and Miss Mendoza was swiftly wafted out of harm's way.[32] Gentili was desolated, and sought consolation in religion.

He thought seriously of joining the Jesuits but recurrent bouts of malaria put an end to that idea. So, in January 1830, he came to visit Rosmini. He came a second and third time, and Rosmini became his spiritual director. Gentili was immediately attracted by Rosminian spirituality. Rosmini offered him no overt encouragement, but Gentili became adamant. He wanted to join the fledgling Institute.

The biographer Pusineri comments: 'Gentili was worthy of Rosmini. He had an exuberant and venturesome nature, but he was also the stuff of heroes ... His knocking on Rosmini's door seemed to be the design of Providence'.[33] Rosmini was about to return north, so he arranged for Gentili to be admitted to the Irish College as a student for the priesthood at his expense. Their close collaboration was to continue and bear abundant fruit.

Meanwhile Rosmini had busied himself with the completion and publication of his great philosophical work *A New Essay on the Origin of Ideas*. His most influential ascetical text was also published in Rome at this time, *The Maxims of Christian Perfection*.

The *New Essay* was well received all over Italy. The Cardinal Archbishop of Ancona hailed its author as 'the future teacher of the world'. Many seminaries and universities took it up and the Jesuits at first received it warmly; the Father General Roothaan, himself a philosopher, called it 'a profound and learned work'. Rosmini's friend Niccolò Tommaseo was highly enthusiastic and resolved to become its propagator, a promise he fulfilled. Only Manzoni found it all too difficult to fathom.[34]

In April he had a second audience with Pope Pius. Once again the Pope was all encouragement. He suggested to Rosmini to float his Constitutions before local bishops in the north of Italy first, and then bring them back to him for positive approbation. And he reiterated his insistence that Rosmini should write. This message was music to his ears.

So, having completed his business in Rome, Rosmini set off for the north on 3 May 1830, going via Florence and Genoa and arriving back at Calvario on the twelfth of the month. He had been away a year and a half, but he had accomplished all he had set out to do.

Notes

1   Pagani-Rossi, *Life*, i, 494–495.
2   In recent years, and especially since the Beatification of Rosmini, 20 February has been kept among Rosminians as the 'feast of the cell', to commemorate the Founder's beginning of Lent at Monte Calvario.
3   Pagani-Rossi, ibid., i, 485–487.
4   Pagani-Rossi, ibid., i, 487.
5   *Ep.Compl.,* ii, 766.
6   *Ep.Compl.,* ii, 777; tr. J. Morris.
7   Pagani-Rossi, *Life,* i, 494.
8   *Ep.Compl.,* ii, 798.
9   *Ep.Compl.,* ii, 836, 28 May 1828.
10 Pagani-Rossi, i, 493.
11 *The Constitutions of the Society of Charity* (tr. D. Cleary & T. Watson, Durham).
12 See especially *Rules of the Institute of Charity*, pp. 231–237.
13 *Constitutions,* 692–696.
14 *Constitutions,* 462–468.
15 *Ep.Compl.,* ii, 805.
16 Pagani, *Life*, p. 95.
17 Pagani-Rossi, i, 506–509.

18 Pagani-Rossi, i, p. 509.
19 Pagani, p. 99.
20 *Ep.Compl.*, ii, 878.
21 Pagani-Rossi, i, pp. 523–524.
22 *Ep.Compl.*, iii, 949.
23 Pagani-Rossi, i, 528–553.
24 A critical study of the Milanese writer and economist Melchiorre Gioia.
25 *Degli Studi dell'Autore*, 11.
26 Pagani, *Life*, p. 105.
27 *Ep.Compl.*, iii, 985.
28 Ibid.
29 Pusineri, *Life*, p. 60.
30 *Ep.Compl.*, iii, 1015.
31 Pagani-Rossi, i, 537–539.
32 Gentili was to meet Miss Mendoza many years later in the last year of his life. She had eventually married an Irish nobleman, becoming Lady Bellew of Castle Bellew, Co. Louth, north of Dublin. Gentili spent a few days with the Bellews between missions, which he was preaching in Dublin in 1848.
33 Pusineri, *Life*, p. 62.
34 Pagani, *Life*, pp. 113–114.

Chapter Nine

Monte Calvario
Consolidation, 1830–1831

Returning to Monte Calvario, Rosmini found himself once more breathing the air of his beloved mountains. He was delighted to be back home. He received the warmest of welcomes from the little community there. Writing to Gentili a few days after his return, he says: 'I found things here even better than I expected: everything is well organised, thanks to our dear don Giovanni (Loewenbruck); there is much fervour and humility ... Divine Providence is blessing the works done in the locality, so that great spiritual fruit is to be seen in the valleys round about ... Oh, if only you were here too!'[1]

He was seeing the dream of his little Institute realised before his eyes: a small group of prayerful religious living together contentedly and responding generously to the needs of the local community. Although Calvario was primarily a house of prayer, it was also the wellspring of good works in the service of the people round about. The Religious community consisted of Loewenbruck, the deacon Molinari and two laypeople, Isaiah and a young layman from a good family, Giuseppe Flecchia. And now, of course, himself.

Molinari was ordained priest in June and was immediately able to help share the pastoral load borne by Loewenbruck. Cardinal Morozzo was content for him to continue living there while calling on him to give retreats to young people in the diocese. Molinari was soon to join the other two priests as the nucleus of the Institute, and even to this day you may see at

Monte Calvario the three adjoining cells in the oldest part of the house with the names of the three pioneers inscribed over the doors – along with Gentili who was soon to join them.

Rosmini himself regularly took his turn in the confessional, and a few months after his return he was asked by the clergy of the town to preach a course of Lenten sermons. He consulted Loewenbruck who bade him accept. He chose the *Imitation of Christ* as his theme. Nevertheless, he was always conscious of the Pope's wish that he devote himself to study and writing. At this time he was absorbed in writing his *Principles of Moral Science* and had begun researching for a major work, *A Treatise on Conscience*.

He soon decided the time had come to make the next moves in regularising the situation at Calvario.[2] The community needed a superior, and the three priests needed to make their postulancy and noviciate according to the Constitutions. One day Loewenbruck came to Rosmini's room and, falling on his knees, requested Rosmini to become their superior. A few days later Molinari followed with the same request.

Rosmini protested his great unworthiness, but proposed that they should all spend three days fasting and praying as a process of discernment. We may judge his protestations as no more than a formality of that age, but Rosmini was quite genuine about it. The responsibility appeared to terrify him. The others remained adamant so, reluctantly, Rosmini accepted the position as first superior of the infant Society. He immediately appointed Loewenbruck as his admonitor, with the responsibility of pointing out his faults and errors.

Rosmini commenced his 'first probation' or first trial (his title for what is normally termed 'postulancy') under the direction of Loewenbruck, and then moved on to his noviciate. His two companions soon followed him and, on Christmas Day 1830, they too became novices. A stricter and more regular regime of living was established. Rosmini willingly joined in all the household chores. He was suffering from rheumatism, so Loewenbruck prescribed for him that he should spend time every day sawing firewood.

Another job he regularly undertook was helping the cook. For the cook this was a mixed blessing. One day he lost his temper with his assistant and told him bluntly: 'Go off and preach, hear confessions, or write books. Be off with you; you only make a mess of things here!'[3] However, Rosmini willingly took his turn cleaning and sweeping and acting as porter. It was all a far cry from the palazzo at Rovereto with its flock of servants.

Another situation demanding his attention was to regularise their possession of Monte Calvario. Although the sanctuary was under the jurisdiction of the bishop, the property belonged legally to the Capis family. Rosmini offered to buy it from Capis in exchange for a residence in Domodossola, a disused convent that Mellerio had acquired and had loaned him. Cardinal Morozzo approved of this and the clergy of the town would have been pleased for Capis to return among them.

But Capis took umbrage at the idea of having to move and dug his heels in. Later on, in 1841, the Capis family won a lawsuit against the bishop, so that Monte Calvario continued to be under joint management: the Rosminians using it as their centre and Capis continuing to live there up to the time of his death. Eventually the Piedmontese government stepped in and confiscated it from the Capis family as part of a campaign to suppress the 'chapters' of collegiate churches.[4] In 1861 the Rosminians were at last able to buy it back off the state and secure its future as the mother house of the Institute.

Growth of the Institute

The little family at Calvario started to grow in various directions. The work was beginning to be known throughout that part of Italy, and Rosmini's reputation as a philosopher and an ascetical writer also flourished. Young laymen and clerics began to show interest in joining the fledgling Society. During 1831 a Frenchman, Emilio Belisy, and a local deacon,

Clemente Alvazzi, joined the community, followed gradually by a number of others. The seed was quietly taking root.

At the same time there were requests to undertake new works. The most promising of these came from Rosmini's home territory. Some priests from the diocesan seminary in Trent approached Rosmini with the aim of leading a more regular religious life. This soon developed into a request to become members of the Institute. Meanwhile, Molinari became involved at the school in Domodossola which was part of the charitable outreach of Count Mellerio. This eventually was to lead to the founding of a boys' College in the town.

The most exciting of these new prospects, however, was to come via Luigi Gentili and that was to launch a mission in England. Gentili was busy pursuing his studies at the Irish College in Rome, paid for by Rosmini, and since he had studied theology at the Roman College earlier, he was soon due to receive the diaconate. This happened at Pentecost 1830.

In the letter quoted earlier, Rosmini had expressed his yearning for Gentili to join the little community in Domodossola, but events were not destined to happen quite as fast as Rosmini hoped.[5] All manner of factors intervened to cause delay, and this sparked a fascinating correspondence between the two which bears close examination, since it throws light on the characters of both men.[6]

The first meeting between them had brought about an immediate sense of mutual empathy. They liked and respected each other from the start. It was reminiscent of the first meeting of Rosmini with Loewenbruck. Once again the chemistry of opposites seemed to be generated. Rosmini was immensely impressed by the energy and huge apostolic potential of both these ardent characters. On the other hand the quiet, somewhat introverted Roveretan seemed to fascinate his new friends and draw them inexorably to become his companions. He offered them a pearl of great price, and they could not refuse.

Yet both appeared to falter in the fulfilment of their new

vocations. Loewenbruck, as we have seen, effectively left Rosmini in the lurch for several months wondering if his chosen companion was ever going to arrive at Calvario. With Gentili, it was a succession of what both he and Rosmini referred to as his 'temptations'.

First, however, it was Rosmini's place to apologise. On leaving to return north he had left a little gift for Gentili in the form of a letter. In it he takes Gentili to task for his manner of speaking to others as if he was giving them a lecture. Gentili was quite taken aback. He humbly acknowledged this fault, but expressed his amazement that Rosmini should say it by letter and not to his face.

It was a case of the extrovert chiding the introvert to communicate more directly and freely – and not via a letter delivered by someone else. Rosmini apologised immediately and confessed to his 'pusillanimity'. It arose from a 'sense of unworthiness, to which I did not want to add the temerity of wishing to remove the mote from someone else's eye while I had a beam in my own.'[7]

Gentili went on to urge Rosmini never to hesitate to point out his defects. He little realised what he was letting himself in for. Among all Rosmini's many correspondents no one received the cutting edge of reprimand more than Gentili. This was to continue through the many years of their relationship. Rosmini recognised in his new friend a strong and valiant soul, but one who occasionally would need firm restraint.

The first 'temptations' came soon enough. They arose partly from Gentili's human respect, but also from his marked reluctance to abandon Rome, the centre of his world, for a freezing mountaintop in north Italy. On 22 June, Rosmini wrote to him bluntly, listing his reasons for dithering, and demolishing them one by one.

What will people think? 'You show great apprehension over the gossip of the world. My dear friend, if we are afraid of what the world says, we shall never do anything that makes for the glory of God ... We shall be wretched creatures if we take notice of the world's tittle-tattle.'[8]

People will think I am mad going to the foothills of the Alps in my state of health? 'Is what the world calls madness truly so? If so, then the cross of Christ is madness too; and so is the gospel and so is the action of the Apostles ... I call this judgment senseless even when it comes from our family, our friends, even priests.'

I would be deserting my mother and my family? Rosmini describes at some length what he said to his own mother when she bade him not to leave home. 'I told her that if I acceded to her wishes I should be doing her will, not the will of my Father, who is my God.'

Gentili replied humbly and the apology was accepted. He was coming up to his ordination to the priesthood (at St John Lateran on 18 September), but Rosmini showed great patience by not chivvying him to come away at once: 'I do not want to put any pressure on you to do so, I am quite content for you to stay in Rome until the spring.'

Gentili continued to live a rich social life, meeting various distinguished visitors to the Eternal City, and from these arose further temptations. Bishop John Dubois of New York pressed him to come to his diocese, but Gentili told him of his prior commitment to the Institute of Charity. He was not attracted by the idea of going to America.

More alluring however was a letter from the English Bishop Baines inviting him to come and work at Prior Park, a mansion converted into a college near the city of Bath in southwest England. Ever since his time socialising with English pilgrims and tourists, Gentili had felt a genuine desire to assist in the conversion of England back to Catholicism. So he wrote back to the bishop describing his commitments, but saying that when the Institute of Charity was formally approved, such a mission might be possible.

A few months later he was visited by a young English layman, Ambrose Phillips de Lisle, a recent convert to Catholicism living in Leicestershire in the centre of England. Phillips was anxious to find a priest for the work of evangelisation in that neighbourhood. This time Gentili kept Rosmini fully posted, and Rosmini responded positively and generously. He too was greatly attracted by the thought of the Institute working for the conversion of England. 'The English Catholics are so near to my heart,' he wrote to Gentili, 'that I do not know what I would not do to help them in any way possible.'[9] He was even prepared to cut short Gentili's time of noviciate to just one year and promised him two companions in the English mission. 'I should be prepared to part with my dear Loewenbruck, who is at once my support and my chief advisor and to give him to you as one of your companions.'

He instructed Gentili to reply encouragingly to Phillips. But the next time Gentili saw the Englishman he found him quite cold. Phillips had heard rumours that Rosmini was regarded by some in Rome as being heretical in his teaching. Gentili was able to reassure him that Rosmini was held in the highest esteem and quoted to Phillips what Pope Gregory had said about his evident holiness.

Phillips was happy with this and on his way home he took the trouble to visit Rosmini. They became friends and continued to correspond regularly. Phillips cherished the hope that the Rosminians would one day come to help him in his dream for the conversion of England. Meanwhile, Gentili was much encouraged by all this and wrote to Rosmini that he would shortly be setting out for Calvario, 'walking without staff or purse'. Gentili was nothing if not a Romantic, and perhaps was dreaming of himself as a new Augustine of Canterbury.

However, there was yet one more temptation to lure Gentili away from his resolve. For some time he had been working happily and successfully among young people in Rome, when he was approached by a Canon Muccioli to join his *Opera degli Esercizi* – a mission to poor young people of the city – those who might now be termed 'street kids'. Gentili knew he had a way with young people and was immediately attracted. He saw it as an ideal work for the Institute of Charity. And of course it would keep him in his beloved Rome. But he hesitated to tell Rosmini what he was engaged in, fobbing him off with obscure references to 'grave matters' and 'silence imposed by the highest authority'. In fact, he had even been emboldened to seek an audience with the Pope to get his blessing on this enterprise.

Rosmini was suspicious that Gentili was up to something and might be pulling the wool over his eyes. When at last he learnt the truth he was horrified. He wrote at once to Canon Muccioli and to a Cardinal who was the patron of the work thanking them for the trust they had placed in his little Society but respectfully declining the invitation. He then took up his pen and gave Gentili a thorough dressing down:

> Your last letter gave me great pain. I see from it that you have allowed your imagination to run away with you ... You say you felt an 'inspiration' to act like this. Well, what I want from you is less inspiration and more resolution, and especially more obedience.
>
> ... You speak of doing heroic things, and say that you have decided to come here like a pilgrim, on foot without staff or purse. My dear man, mere words do not impress me: I look at the facts. And the facts are that you have not turned up, and that you have built all sorts of castles in the air, committing a whole mass of imprudences ... [like] blowing your own trumpet on my behalf. It is all totally against the spirit of the Institute which prefers to remain hidden, humble and content within itself.
>
> ... You add also that you asked audience several times of the Holy Father, from the moment he took office, to congratulate him in the name of our Society ... Who made you our ambassador? It was nothing but fantasy which put such ideas into your head.
>
> ... Let me speak plainly to you. I will not accept any more excuses ... I enjoin you, if it is true you have a vocation to the Institute of Charity, to set off immediately for Domodossola, not on foot but comfortably in a carriage ... At present we are in no position to accept the proposed foundation in Rome – it is a mere will o' the wisp. We need to consolidate the two foundations already made, and give no thought to spreading ourselves until we have taken root.[10]

Gentili was duly chastened by this broadside, and wrote back immediately full of apologies. Rosmini graciously accepted these, but did not withdraw one word of what he had said.[11] The fact was that Gentili had been behaving like a prima donna and deserved to receive strong medicine.

He proceeded to pack his bags and leave Rome scarcely informing family or friends. He travelled by boat up to Genoa and then took the coach across the Apennines, arriving in Domodossola on 26 August 1831. He was received by the community, and especially by Rosmini, with great joy.

❦

Gentili soon settled down to the regular life and started his own noviciate. Rosmini was most content with the sincerity and zeal with which his friend threw himself into a new and more rigorous routine of life. Since there were more postulants arriving at Calvario it was only a few months before Rosmini gave him the responsibility of becoming Novice Master while making his own noviciate.

Rosmini himself was occupied during this time getting the Institute approved by local bishops.[12] To facilitate this process he wrote two digests, one a brief description of the Society in its essence and the other a description of the Society as it might become when fully developed. He sent the first to Cardinal Cappellari in Rome who replied that he found the document 'brief, clear and precise' and promised to pass it on to Pope Pius.

Sadly, in November 1830 Pius VIII died. Considering the encouragement and support Rosmini had received from him, this appeared to be a setback, but in the conclave that ensued it was his friend Cappellari who was elected (February 1831), taking the name Gregory XVI. Rosmini was overjoyed, although he was wary of writing too soon to him since it might appear as currying favours. The new Pope forestalled him by sending him a cordial message via Cardinal Morozzo. This prompted an exchange of letters.[13] The Pope sent a commendatory Brief in which, for the first time, the little society was officially named the *Institute of Charity*.

In April 1831, Rosmini sent the bishop of Novara, Cardinal Morozzo, a full copy of the *Constitutions* of the Society. The Cardinal took his time examining them but eventually he fully approved, 'thanking God for conferring such a bonus on his diocese'.[14] He followed this up in 1833 approving the Institute of Charity by solemn decree and officially assigning it the custody of the sanctuary of Monte Calvario.

This was followed by similar approbation from the Archbishop of Genoa and the Patriarch of Venice. Meanwhile the little family at Calvario grew steadily, and in general it seemed that Providence was blessing the new enterprise. Rosmini had complete confidence in the good will and zeal of Loewenbruck as leader of the community, so he was able to turn his main attention to the promising developments in the Tyrol.

Notes

1   *Ep.Compl.*, iii, 1152.
2   Pagani-Rossi, i, p. 569.
3   Pagani, *Life*, p. 121.
4   A collegiate church was a large church staffed by a group of diocesan priests, called canons, who recited the divine office daily even though they were not monks. They were known collectively as a 'chapter'. Common in mediaeval times, by the nineteenth century they were something of an anachronism, hence the decision of the Turin government to get rid of them.
5   *Ep.Compl.*, iii, 1152.
6   See Antonio Belsito, *Witness*, 24 June 2009, pp. 19–37.
7   *Ep.Compl.*, iii, 1165.
8   *Ep.Compl.*, iii, 1175.
9   *Ep.Compl.*, iii, 1333.
10   *Ep.Compl.*, iii, 1460.
11   *Ep.Compl.*, iii, 1476.
12   Pagani, p. 123.
13   *Ep.Compl.*, iii, 1364.
14   Pagani, p. 130.

Chapter Ten

New Foundations in the Tyrol
The Five Wounds, 1831–1835

The city of Trent lies about twenty miles from Rovereto in the South Tyrol (or Trentino) and is the centre of the diocese. It has a long and illustrious history. In the sixteenth century the famous Council of Trent was held there, launching the so-called Counter-Reformation which sought to renew the Catholic Church after the Protestant Reformation.

In 1830, the bishop of Trent was Msgr Saverio Luschin. Rosmini, who belonged to the diocese even though he was not under the bishop, had sought the bishop's blessing to live outside the diocese in Domodossola when he first made the move to test his own vocation as a religious. During 1830, Rosmini was contacted by a priest from the diocesan seminary in Trent, Giulio Todeschi, who had ideas, along with the seminary Rector Pietro Rigler, of forming a society of priests for charitable works. Rosmini went to meet them while visiting Rovereto, and after talking with them about the structure and spirit of his Institute the two priests along with two of their colleagues asked to join it.

The bishop gave his blessing to this plan; indeed he issued a fresh invitation to Rosmini to return to the diocese and set up a house. Rosmini kept in touch by correspondence, and once Gentili had settled in at Calvario and began to exercise responsibility, he was able to go to Trent himself. En route in Milan he met up with Giovanni Boselli, one of three men the Marchesa di Canossa had recommended to his spiritual care.

Boselli too had decided to join the Institute, so he accompanied Rosmini to Trent.

In Trent, Rosmini admitted four priests as postulants, and on 31 July 1831 they started their noviciate. A house was found close to Santa Maria Maggiore, the church where the famous Council had met, and it was adapted to the needs of the new community. Rosmini dedicated it to St Vigilio (first bishop of the diocese). Rigler was appointed superior, and the community soon began to attract recruits. By the end of the year there were ten, including a young man named Francesco Puecher who later became a prominent Rosminian.

At first the project prospered. It seemed that the community at Calvario was being replicated in the Tyrol. However, first signs of opposition appeared in the following year, 1832. Some of the local clergy were critical of these more than zealous priests. The religious impact of their ministry began to attract young people of the city to their various works of charity. There was some local opposition, and the Austrian police became suspicious. Rumours of this disquiet reached the ear of the bishop.

Luschin appeared to take fright and declined to allow his clergy to enter the Institute until it had been 'sanctioned by proper authority'.[1] Rosmini protested that ecclesiastical approval had already been given, quoting the recent Brief from Pope Gregory XVI. But the bishop was talking about the secular authority, and he insisted Rosmini seek the approval of the Emperor of Austria.

Rosmini could not see why the wholly religious activities of his followers should require secular sanction. Nevertheless, he acquiesced and on 25 June 1832 he was granted an audience with Emperor Francis I in Innsbruck. The Emperor had in fact received good reports about Rosmini, and said that as long as the local bishop approved he would protect his little Society. However, Francis was not impressed by the fact that the Holy See had given its blessing. What was important was the approval of local bishops whom he appointed and controlled. Shades of Joseph II!

For the time being Bishop Luschin was satisfied. The new

community undertook various works of charity: an oratory for young people and spiritual direction in a local college (also dedicated to St Vigilio), care of the poor and teaching in the seminary. Rosmini was able to return to Calvario in October with some confidence that all was well again. He continued to supervise progress from afar.

During 1833, numbers in the Trent community grew steadily – as indeed at Calvario. Rosmini returned to Trent in April to find a community of fifteen. There was also an invitation from his friend Msgr Grasser, now bishop of Verona, to extend the Rosminian outreach to that city and establish a mission to German-speaking Catholics. In November Rosmini went to Verona and established a small community of three religious, who would be dependent on Trent. This new mission was later to flourish, when the parish of the ancient church of San Zeno in Verona was offered to the Institute.

It was about this time that Rosmini suffered a terrible personal blow with the mortal sickness of his beloved sister, Margherita.[2] He became aware of her failing health – she had tuberculosis – in November 1832. The Marchesa di Canossa recalled her to Verona, and Rosmini sought the best medical care for her. Her condition steadily grew worse and, in spite of many prayers from the Rosminians and Canossians, she died on 15 June 1833. Rosmini wrote tenderly to his mother:

> We must be ready to accept with Christian resignation the loss of our dearly beloved Giuseppina ... She bid me to seek your pardon for all the wrongs she may have done you, for all the distress or displeasure she may have caused you ... Giuseppina, who never did any harm, cannot die but can only go to eternal life.[3]

∞∿∞

During 1833 the foundation at Trent continued to thrive apart from the vacillating attitude of the bishop. Meanwhile the people of Rovereto presented a petition to the bishop that the Institute should open a house in that town too. He replied he could not accord with this until the Institute had received full ecclesiastical approval. Rosmini went to see the bishop to again seek clarification.

Luschin, who had had a copy of the *Constitutions* for more than a year, eventually gave his formal approval, but hedged it with conditions. There should only be one house of the Institute in the diocese with at most fifteen priests; they were not to have charge of a parish; and they should depend directly on the bishop for the exercise of their ministry.

Having stated that the Rosminians were not to have care of a parish, he proceeded to offer the small parish of St Maria in Rovereto to Fr Giulio Todeschi, and later Rosmini himself was offered the main parish of San Marco. This inconsistency on Luschin's part may have disguised a plan to weaken the Trent community by dispersing some of its key people.[4]

Perhaps a truer idea of the predicament in which the Rosminians found themselves in Austrian territory was given by the civil governor of the Tyrol, Wülzek, who visited Trent in October. He told Rosmini that the main obstacle to approving the presence of the Institute in the Tyrol was that it had other houses outside the Imperial control of Vienna. Rosmini said that if he were to conform to such a restriction it would be the end of the Institute: it would simply become a diocesan organisation and the charism of universal charity would be lost.

It was evident to him that Wülzek was anxious about Mazzini's *Giovine Italia* movement which was beginning to make noises and threaten Austrian power south of the Alps.[5] But Rosmini assured him that 'no citizen could give the state a greater guarantee [of loyalty] than a member of a religious Institute since they were determined to uphold justice and therefore were above suspicion'.[6]

Whatever his personal political views, Rosmini believed that wherever his brethren were they had a duty of loyalty to the bishop and to local authorities. Rosmini was eventually to accept the bishop's desire for him to go to San Marco. He thought that his presence in Rovereto with a small group of brethren might be a support to the house in Trent.

During 1835 the situation in Trent gradually deteriorated.

There was a lot of sickness among the community. Even Rigler himself had to go away for a while leaving Todeschi in charge. On return, Rigler became increasingly agitated – 'disturbed in spirit' were Rosmini's words – and eventually launched a somewhat bitter attack on Rosmini by letter. Rosmini replied at length.[7] He accepted that Rigler's distress might be his (Rosmini's) fault. Rigler accused him of being obsessed with cold logic; of being too attached to his own ideas; of teaching at variance with reputable authors. Rosmini, he said, had a domineering spirit and accepted new candidates too easily; he was ambitious for important posts, and had not submitted his *Constitutions* to the approval of the Holy See.

It seems likely that Rigler too was influenced by the government's and the bishop's judgment that Rosmini was not focussing on the needs of Trent. Rigler belonged to a culture which would see the Institute as serving the diocese exclusively. His vision differed from that of Rosmini, for whom the service of the universal Church took priority. Rosmini replied to him carefully, point by point, but closed by issuing him an ultimatum. Rigler must choose either to behave magnanimously as a good religious subject – or he must leave.

Rigler chose to depart. Eventually Rosmini had to wind up the Trent community and disperse the remaining members. He generously offered Rigler the house in Trent for his personal use. Afterwards Rigler continued to revere Rosmini as a person even if he was unable to accept his teachings. Eventually he joined the Knights of the Imperial Teutonic Order, a mediaeval order of chivalry.

∞∞

Meanwhile Rosmini himself had accepted the Bishop's offer as parish priest of his home parish of San Marco, Rovereto. His year as parish priest requires a chapter on its own (see Chapter 11). Rosmini thought that his appointment there might solve the uncertainties in which the foundation in Trent had found itself. He had been convinced that the Institute was called by God to spread its wings in the Tyrol; in fact his tenure at San Marco spelt its end. He eventually attributed this to his own failings, writing to Luschin's successor in Trent, Bishop Tschiderer:

> God has enabled the Institute to flourish in Piedmont. On the other hand it stands humiliated in the diocese of Trent. It seems that God's will is that we are not wanted here, even though it is my own home patch, which I love and for which I have striven my utmost. This doubt that I feel could be dissolved at once by a word from the bishop of the diocese. Without that word I must presume that the work of the Institute has to cease here forthwith.[8]

That word never came, but on 26 September 1835 the bishop repeated the same restrictive terms as his predecessor had imposed under which the Institute could work in his diocese. Rosmini did not accept these conditions. The bishop of Verona tried to intervene on his behalf, again without success. Therefore, on 15 December Rosmini formally and with sadness withdrew from the Diocese of Trent.

On 16 December he wrote to the remaining members of the Trent community informing them of the final closure of the house and setting them free from any obligations they had to the Institute 'since we have no other house within the Austrian Empire ... I also ask pardon for my bad example and mistakes – perhaps it was because of these things that God has laid His hand heavily upon us.'[9] However, a few members of the Trent community, like Giulio Todeschi, followed Rosmini back to Domodossola and continued their vocation in the Institute of Charity.

Why Rosmini was not supported by the diocesan authorities is mysterious. Perhaps the simplest judgment would be to say that they found themselves in a quandary, caught between what the Austrians demanded and what was pastorally desirable. Msgr Luschin especially had admired the idealism of Rosmini, and could not but be aware of the veneration that the people and clergy of Rovereto felt for him. And it was his pressing invitation which caused Rosmini to become parish priest of Rovereto.

But Luschin depended for his bread and butter on the Imperial power, which had installed him as bishop (and was about to transfer him to an archiepiscopal See). Luschin still aspired, in the See of Trent, to the title of *Prince Bishop*. One commentator remarks that he was 'more prince than bishop'. He was a member of the Imperial hegemony: in his exercise of authority he reflected the autocracy of Vienna.

In a letter to Antonio Mazzetti, President of the Civil Courts in Milan (8 October 1836), Rosmini details a series of steps whereby Bishop Luschin encouraged him in making a foundation in Trent. He then adds:

> ... when he first received a letter from the Governor, he lost heart and began to be afraid that he would clash with the government if he gave too much support to the Institute. Msgr Luschin does not know that I saw his original reports and all the relevant documents. (These came to me from Vienna itself, where they were not approved, as I was told.) If he knew these facts he would understand better my quarrel with him over his lack of sincerity.[10]

The Austrians would accept a new religious congregation only if it was totally under the jurisdiction of the local bishop – and therefore subject to the civil powers. And they were already suspicious of Rosmini because they saw him as a 'papalist' and as pro-Italian. Perhaps one should conclude that Rosmini was naïve to hope that it would ever be any other way, and that a Rosminian foundation in the Tyrol, or in any Austrian territory, was always doomed to fail.

The Five Wounds of the Church

During 1832 Rosmini put pen to paper to write the most widely read and influential of all his books *Delle Cinque Piaghe della Santa Chiesa* (*The Five Wounds of the Church*). It is significant that this book should have been written at this time when he was locked in struggle with a bishop and diocesan authorities totally under the dominance of the Imperial government in Vienna.

In this book Rosmini looks back to the practice of the first six centuries of the Church, before the barbarian invasions threw society into chaos and the Church with it. Rosmini exhibits a somewhat starry-eyed view of the purity and innocence of the first Christians, in preserving much of the spirit of the Apostles. Nevertheless he uses the spirit and the standards of the early Church as a template against which to judge what comes later.

The *Five Wounds* became very much a source text during the time of the Second Vatican Council. Much of what he proposed has influenced the changes in the post-Vatican II Church. The Five Wounds are:

(1) The separation of people from clergy in the liturgy,
(2) The inadequate education of the clergy,
(3) Disunion among the bishops,
(4) The nomination of bishops by the secular power,
(5) The appropriation of church property by the state (aggravated by a loss of a sense of poverty among churchmen).[11]

The First Wound: The separation of people from clergy in the liturgy

Rosmini put a high value on the dignity of the laity, and for him the 'faithful' comprise laity and clergy in union. Their unity in dignity derives from the notion of the 'priesthood of the laity' received at baptism and strengthened at confirmation. The worship of the Church, he writes, should be a single action of priests and people together. 'The people should be actors as well as hearers, while in fact they are mostly present at Mass like the columns and statues of the building.'

Rosmini ascribes the decline in this union of clergy and people to two causes:

(1) Poor teaching: The people need to understand what is happening in the liturgy so that they can participate in it.

(2) Latin: The language of the Latin Rite was no longer understood by most. If a person does not understand what is

going on they cease to participate actively. It is not surprising, therefore, that Rosmini was accused of advocating a vernacular liturgy. He denies this; while he always acknowledges the beauty of the Latin language, yet it is an obvious implication of his suggestion that the use of Latin divides priests from people.

Since the Vatican Council the vernacular has largely replaced the use of Latin; church furnishings have been reorganised to bring the people and the clergy closer together; and in the newly introduced RCIA,[12] instruction and practice in the liturgy go hand in hand with catechesis. The *Constitution on the Sacred Liturgy* states: 'participation by the Christian people ... is their right and duty by reason of their baptism.' Rosmini's ideas are fully vindicated by these changes.

The Second Wound: the inadequate education of the clergy
Rosmini notes that in the early Church the clergy often received their formation and education in the home of the bishop. They were schooled in Scripture and often they were receiving their instruction directly from the Fathers of the Church. Rosmini comments: 'only great men can form great men'.

This closeness of the bishop to his clergy, and especially to those in training, was lost as the Church grew in numbers. The clergy of the Middle Ages were often poorly educated, except perhaps the few attending the new universities. The Council of Trent attempted to improve this situation by setting up seminaries. But Rosmini notes that seminary teachers often lacked experience of parishes and pastoral work.

The clergy of his time suffered especially in their education from the fact that the communities they came from were themselves spiritually impoverished; their teachers were lacking in suitability for the task; the textbooks were poor – he was referring here to the scholastic manuals whose use continued right up to the time of Vatican II; formation in Sacred Scripture was inadequate; the methodology of clerical formation tended to separate theological instruction from moral training.

The Third Wound: Disunion among the bishops
In the first centuries of the Church, numbers were small and bishops kept in touch with each other. Councils were held frequently, and since Latin and Greek were the universal languages of the educated in the Mediterranean world, the bishops were able to communicate easily. That gave bishops a sense of unity.

While the Bishop of Rome did not wield the centralised authority that came later, nevertheless he was generally recognised as the successor of Peter – and Patriarch, at least of the West. He was the centre of unity.[13] Periodically this union was threatened by heresies such as Arianism. But the great Ecumenical Councils of the early centuries sorted out these conflicts, thus restoring the desired unity in faith and practice.

The Middle Ages brought about the rise of petty princes, and the bishops were drawn into the new feudal structure. They too became princes, and often loyalty was directed towards the local Imperial Lord rather than the Pope. This movement towards local autonomy was aggravated by the rise of nation states.

Gallicanism was a principle that evolved primarily in France, claiming that a local church and its bishop owed its prime allegiance not to the Pope but to the prince or king, who claimed authority over the church by divine right. The Austrian version of this – known as Josephinism after the Emperor Joseph II – was a particularly virulent form and was the source of much of Rosmini's troubles with the local bishops in the Tyrol and with the Austrian authorities who supported it.

The Second Vatican Council proposed that the bishops should work together with the Pope in a collegial manner to govern the Church. National hierarchies meet together frequently, and they are free to act independently of the state except in totalitarian states such as China.

Lumen Gentium, the Constitution on the Church, states: 'The Sacred Council earnestly desires that the venerable institutions of synods and councils flourish with new vigour.' However, it would be true to say that the synods which now meet at regular intervals are largely directed by the Roman Curia. The Church has still some distance to travel to reach the status of true collegiality, as was the norm in the early Church.

The Fourth Wound: The nomination of bishops by the secular power

Rosmini opens this section with a series of forthright assertions. 'Every free society has an inherent right to choose its own officers. This right is essential and inalienable ... The Church of Jesus Christ cannot cede her government to others ... Any absolute concession of this kind is invalid, a pact without substance.'[14]

In a long historical section Rosmini gives numerous examples through the early centuries of how the bishops were elected 'by clergy and people'. Once again, the onset of the Middle Ages caused a violation of the Church's freedom, as secular rulers sought to control the Church by making bishops subject to themselves. A struggle for power ensued, and this was won temporarily by the triumph of Pope Gregory VII over the Emperor Henry IV at Canossa.

An author of the time, Florus, asserted that a new bishop must be 'chosen by common consent of the clergy and all the people'.[15] However, the rise of centralised Christian governments meant that bishops became state appointees and continued under the thrall of Imperial powers. It was this fact that gave Rosmini so much trouble dealing with some of the bishops in the Tyrol, under the rule of Austria.

Rosmini always acknowledged the right of the Holy See to approve or deny the choice made by the local church. But he was adamant that the nomination of a new bishop should arise out of the community the bishop belonged to, and the people would then know, esteem and approve the choice. He was highly critical of any imposition from outside.

Rosmini's thinking regarding election seems to have evolved. He was influenced as a young man by the author Karl Ludwig von Haller, a Swiss jurist who spent much of his life in France and Austria. Haller had reacted strongly against the French Revolution and became politically reactionary, as well as being converted to Roman Catholicism. He was especially critical of Rousseau's *Social Contract*.[16] But when Rosmini went to live in Milan, he mixed in a society whose views were much broader and more liberal than von Haller's, and who maintained the universal dignity and equality of all human beings. Manzoni was especially influential. He had travelled widely and spent time in Paris where he had absorbed French liberal ideas, especially those of Rousseau regarding the 'social contract'.

Another widely read contemporary was the Frenchman, Alexis de Tocqueville, a huge admirer of the working American constitution, which explicitly safeguards human rights and equality. De Tocqueville favoured universal suffrage. These ideas are reflected in the arguments and assertions of Rosmini's *Fourth Wound*.

Rosmini understood that the French 'Illuminists' were strongly influenced by the example and experience of England in developing a system of parliamentary democracy. Why had Protestant countries arrived at this more enlightened view earlier than Catholic countries? He speculated that, having lost the sense of the supernatural, they were more open to the needs of the natural – what human beings need for their well-being now. It is a curious bit of reasoning, but explains why he became open to ideas from these eighteenth century sources.

The idea that bishops should in some way be 'elected' provoked consternation when the book was eventually published in 1848, and Rosmini was forced to backtrack and issue a clarification. In the election of a bishop, he said, the clergy and people exercise a 'divine moral right'. However, the Pope, as supreme head of the Church, can for good reasons by-pass this right. He called this a 'divine constitutive right' of the Pope.

The Fifth Wound: The appropriation of church property by the state

Once again Rosmini goes back to the ideal situation of the first centuries of the Church when the first Christian communities arose among the urban poor. Then, the Church itself was poor. But there followed the barbarian invasions, and bishops over time became feudal lords, wielding much power and living surrounded by comparative wealth.

Rosmini's plea is for the Church to go back to the simplicity of the early Church; that is, return to the principles of evangelical poverty. If the Church's goods are responsibly and transparently administered, it will be for the common good. Any surplus would be devoted to the relief of the poor.

Although this book of Rosmini's is by no means a popular tract – it has a sophisticated academic flavour – it has been the widest read of all his works. He was well aware that in the ecclesial and political atmosphere of the 1830s it was dynamite. Gregory XVI, although very kindly disposed and supportive of Rosmini as a religious founder, was himself theologically conservative. It is doubtful that he would have accepted much of what the *Five Wounds* had to say. The book therefore remained in cold storage awaiting the opportunity to launch it upon the world stage at a later date.

Notes

1   Pagani, *Life*, p. 141.
2   See Chapter 4, pp. 36–38.
3   *Ep.Compl.,* iv, 1983, tr. J. Morris.
4   Pagani, *Life*, p. 146.
5   Giuseppe Mazzini was the most prominent and persevering champion of Italian unity and disseminated his ideas throughout Italy via a secret movement he founded known as *Giovine Italia* (see Chapter 2).
6   Pagani-Rossi, i, 628.
7   *Ep.Compl.,* v, 2615 (25 August); v, 2620 (7 September).
8   *Ep.Compl.,* v, 2686.
9   *Ep.Compl.,* v, 2679.
10   *Ep.Compl.,* v, 2921; tr. J. Morris.
11   A. Belsito, IC, *Rosmini for Beginners* (lectures given at Ratcliffe, 2004).

12   RCIA: the *Rite of Christian Initiation of Adults*, introduced by the Catholic Church in 1972 to prepare adults for baptism or admission to the Church.

13   See St Cyprian of Carthage, *De Unitate Ecclesiae*, written about 250 AD.

14   *Five Wounds of the Church*, 4, 74 & 75 (tr. D. Cleary).

15   Ibid., 4, 88.

16   The French Enlightenment thinker Jean Jacques Rousseau is recognised as a founder of the principle of popular sovereignty – government by the people for the people. See Chapter 2.

Chapter Eleven

Rosmini as Parish Priest
Rovereto, 1834–1835

The old parish priest of Rovereto, Fr Giambattista Locatelli, died in February 1834. Rosmini's former teacher, Fr Pietro Orsi, and his brother Paulo, also a priest in the town, organised a petition signed by no fewer than 35 priests and 146 lay people requesting Msgr Luschin to appoint Rosmini as successor at San Marco's.

The bishop agreed and pressed Rosmini to accept. Rosmini replied at some length stating that this invitation had caused him an acute problem of conscience. He pleaded various difficulties: his own incapacity – he felt he lacked the gifts for the job; his physical weakness and lack of strength; his commitments to the Institute of Charity; the obligation placed on him by the Pope to write. He believed that his writing was of greater general benefit to the cause of religion than the more limited work of a parish priest. His obligations to the growing community in Domodossola would take him away for at least two months each year. However, if he were to be given a staff of four assistants (as the petitioners had suggested) and the contract were for two years only, then 'I would abandon myself into your hands and conform myself to whatever conclusion you reach.'[1] The bishop was insistent, so Rosmini accepted.

It took some months for him to make the necessary arrangements including acquiring a suitable community house near San Marco's. Locatelli had had only one assistant, and the parish had become very run down. Rosmini eventually persuaded the diocese to give him three priests and he also brought with him Francesco Puecher as his secretary and three lay brothers. He chose the feast of the Holy Rosary, 5 October, as the day for his inauguration.

Rosmini's time as a parish priest was unique in his life. He threw himself into the work with amazing vigour, which tends to give the lie to his pleas of physical incapacity. It seems that his recurring sickness was largely the result of intense study, whereas the varied tasks of running a big parish seemed to reinvigorate him. It is worthwhile devoting a few pages to describe in detail his apostolic labours during this precious interlude.

'Rosmini felt and lived the care of souls as a total response to his fundamental vocation,' says the late Fr Alfeo Valle, a Rosminian author, 'the summit of his theological and spiritual formation, corresponding to the true spirit of the Institute. No other work could satisfy the energies and aspirations of his soul – as priest and religious founder.'[2]

The parish had 7,000 inhabitants and included a few noble families. There were also factory workers from the silk trade and many poor people, while the deanery over which he was Archpriest comprised 26,000 people in nine parishes, with twenty-five churches and possibly as many as 100 priests. In the parish house Rosmini at once set up a routine of communal prayer characteristic of a religious house.

His first sermon as parish priest, delivered on 5 October 1834, represents the best of his preaching style. The following is the gist of what he said:

My dear people, I have often stood before you, but now I stand before you in a different guise, that of pastor. My pledge is that 'my flock will come to know me, and I shall come to know them'. That is the basis of love.

This task is given to me by Almighty God through the commission of the bishop. It contains the pledge by God to guide the steps and the words of the pastor. I come here, not because I wanted to – I might have preferred a more retired life! – but by divine command.

All this is part of the Providence of God and is contained in the wonderful gift of the Incarnation whereby the divine nature is joined to human nature, fallen but redeemed. Jesus chose his collaborators from among simple fishermen, who became the forerunners of the bishops and priests serving his holy people. The Father sends forth the Son, and we your pastors serve you as the Son served the Father. That is our hope and our boast.

I have to be a man of faith like St Peter on the stormy lake: Jesus calls me, as he did Peter, to pastor His sheep, even if I too am a man of little faith. Nothing is impossible for those who believe ... I am called, firstly, to administer the Sacraments (restoring in humanity the perfection of the first creation lost by sin); to preach the gospel of Christ by word and example; to help form Christian habits in His people; to protect my flock against the wolf and robber.

All this is sufficient to transform even the sinner, and the context is the Church of Christ. The sinner is fed, and just as food transforms us from within, so the word of God will form us as Christian people. Our wills are transformed, our passions controlled, our affections are tempered, our instincts are redirected and our blindest faculties become sensitive to the light of Christ. The fruit of this is seen in the behaviour of Christian people, who become the 'salt of the earth'.

My desire is that you too will work to spread the light among your brothers and sisters. Firstly I address *parents* whose love and care transforms the lives of your children. What can I achieve without your help? What can the church do if the home does not reflect the same values? You *mothers* especially receive your babes from God and return them to Him one day. Your influence lasts for life. And I promise you my fullest assistance.

You *fathers* too influence your grown children. If you educate them well you sanctify yourselves and influence generations to come. The father of the family is like the priest of old, whose responsibility is not usurped today by the priesthood of the Church. You are the lawgiver, the judge, and the support of the whole family. And you must support me in my vocation to become 'father' to the whole parish family.

Regarding the poor families of the parish, I weep tears of compassion. Sadly the plight of those who suffer is caused by the neglect of others, of parents, and of circumstances. You who are fortunate and 'rich' are called upon by heaven to come to the aid of your poor brothers and sisters. You must help me, and in so doing you avert from yourselves the danger of riches.

The predicament of the poor will be my most pressing concern: the care of the orphans and the physical and moral well-being of all. And you must be my assistants in taking on this responsibility, my fellow teachers and carers. We are in good company, supported by the Mother of God herself, our patron St Mark, the patron of the diocese, St Vigilius, and all the angels and saints.[3]

∞◡∞

Rosmini meant what he said about his concern for the poor, and he at once launched a full visitation of the parish, going to see each family in their homes. Much of this visiting he did himself. Within the parish there was a hospital, an orphanage and a convalescent home, as well as agencies which raised funds for the poor. He commissioned a Register of the needs of all the poor families listing age, housing, their condition and possessions. He proposed an annual budget to help supply their needs. The deed of this still exists in the Community Library with Rosmini's signature of 2 October 1835.

Puecher testifies that during this year Rosmini himself gave 3,000 florins of his own money to help the parish poor. He was following a principle spelt out in one of his books with reference to the Early Church: 'The clergy should not use their goods except for their basic sustinence, using the surplus for works of piety, especially the relief of the needy.'[4]

He also initiated a course of catechetical instruction for the adults and the children of the parish. He prepared the course himself, and submitted it for approval to the diocesan authorities. These *Regole della Dottrina Cristiana* (Rules of Christian Teaching) were eventually published in Milan in 1837.

There were over 1,000 children involved, divided into four classes according to age and ability, then subdivided into conveniently-sized groups. He formed a team of twenty-four teachers and four teachers' aides, as well as reserves. A team of seven including himself inspected these classes every month. The laypeople were heavily involved. The classes continued even if Rosmini was absent.

In September 1835, at the end of the first year, there was a prizegiving to reward the most diligent children. Rosmini relied on the support of parents, and he got it. His method included some rote learning initially, followed by explanation. Memorising something without understanding was, in his opinion, useless.

Meanwhile, a course of catechesis was instituted for adults, which Rosmini led himself using a method of dialogue with a selected parishioner. Some remembrance of what was learned as a child formed a basis for this catechesis. But more important was to copy the method of Jesus Christ: mind speaking to minds and heart speaking to hearts. His secretary, Puecher, collected summaries of these instructions for publication.

Rosmini tends to start his catechesis, not with God and working down, but with experience of the world and working upwards. His aim eventually is to give his people a sense of the threefold action of God in the world: through Providence, through laws, and through grace. Later on, he was to sum up his method in his *Catechism according to the Order of Ideas* (published 1837).

A further initiative, this time completely frustrated, was to set up an oratory of St Philip Neri. Such oratories were common enough – and very successful – throughout the southern parts of Italy, but were a novelty in the Tyrol. The members of the oratory would meet regularly on Sundays for an hour of prayer and spiritual reading, and the building would be available at other times, especially on evenings during the week.

At first the oratory thrived. It had an immediate effect on the incidence of drunkenness and the behaviour of the youth of the town.[5] But the Austrian authorities soon accused him of setting up a type of Masonic lodge. They were also suspicious of the apparent foundation of a second Rosminian community (following that of Trent).

The government saw Rosmini as 'a danger ... since his advocacy of the freedom of the Italian nation was well known, also his criticism of state interference in religious and church affairs, as well as his support of Piedmont. His oratory could have become a cauldron of new and dangerous ideas ...'[6]

In April 1835, the diocesan Curia passed on to him a ban placed on the oratory by the Austrian authorities. Rosmini protested but the Curia did not support him, and in spite of his vigorous objections the oratory had to be closed down. The Austrians also attempted to place a ban on the 'Brothers of Charity', ordering him to send away three laymen and Fr Puecher. The Vicar General supported this ban, but fortunately the new bishop, Msgr Tschiderer, arrived at this time and seemed at first to be less vindictive.[7]

In the parish church itself, Tommaseo reports: 'Teaching catechism, visiting the sick and afflicted, being available to those who sought counsel or alms, regular spells in the confessional: all these were dear to Rosmini.'[8] And of course there was the usual round of sacramental occasions: births, marriages, deaths, celebrations.

The keeping of Lent and the course of preparation for First Communion were of particular importance to him. Four hundred more 'kept Easter' that year than previously. In 1835, 72 boys and 55 girls made their first communion. The First Communion Mass was concluded with a firm admonition to parents to care for their children's spiritual welfare.

A parish notary paid abundant tribute to Rosmini's zeal in church. He noted especially his attachment to traditional liturgical actions and to careful catechesis. The vestments, furniture, and decoration of the church were not neglected. Rosmini was devoted to his home town, and he showed this by giving 20,000 florins to set up a charitable fund for a whole range of good works, including books for the library and a stipend for the librarian.

As a preacher, Rosmini stuck closely to the word of God. He esteemed sacred eloquence, but for him its basis was simplicity, which serves to display the truth and not obscure it. Rosmini delivered 'lively and immediate communication: truths which are loved and lived, transmitted not from memory to memory but from one intelligence to another, from one heart to another. It was a communion with God's word in all its fullness.'[9]

Luigi Gentili spent time with him in the parish and wrote to Loewenbrück: 'Here, things are going like a house on fire. Fr Superior [Rosmini] is prodigious, and I have come to the conclusion that he must be a saint. He is wearing himself out for his flock ... God's blessings are multiplied in a wonderful manner: sinners are converted, scandals removed, discords composed.'[10] Coming from an extrovert like Gentili, this is praise indeed!

Then in April 1835, Rosmini's passport to travel to Domodossola was revoked. If he were unable to pass freely to and from Piedmont it would prevent him from effective governance of the Institute. It also became evident to him that he no longer had the confidence of the Bishop and the senior authorities of the diocese. So he decided to resign from the parish after just one year.[11]

One of Rosmini's last tasks was to prepare for execution a poor young man, Felice Robol, who had murdered his girl friend. Rosmini spent time instructing him and preparing him for his final journey – and with success, because Robol died bravely and contritely. He also spent time with Robol's parents. The description of his ministry to this poor man is an admirable example of the way he dealt with individuals in crisis.[12]

During his final weeks in Rovereto Rosmini wrote several times to the new Bishop, Msgr Nepomuceno de Tschiderer, expressing his sadness and dissatisfaction. The bottom line for him was two principles: 'that the Superiors of the religious houses must have appropriate authority to rule and that the "universality" of the Institute must be protected.'[13]

By the second point Rosmini meant that the Institute must, like other Orders in the Church, be able to move its members freely between works of charity in different dioceses. Rosmini received no satisfactory reply so he decided to withdraw the presence of the Institute entirely from the diocese of Trent. Rosmini felt that he was being 'enticed into a noose' (his words), and that for the good of the Institute he must personally resign from the parish.

On 5 October 1835, the first anniversary of his coming back to Rovereto as parish priest of San Marco's, he formally handed back responsibility for the parish. However, he was unable to return at once to Piedmont because his passport had been revoked. He left his home town with many regrets, because he felt an affection for the people and had started many plans which he could not finish.

The clergy were shocked and petitioned the Bishop not to allow him to go. The parishioners also lobbied him to remain with them. But the Bishop took no notice. There was no going back. From this time on, he would return there only occasionally to visit his mother and family and to attend to his affairs.

Notes

1   *Ep.Compl.*, v, 2216; tr. J. Morris.
2   Alfeo Valle, *Rosmini e Rovereto 1834–35.* Rovereto: Longo, 1985, p. 20.
3   Valle, pp. 56–62. Also *Discorsi parrocchiali: opere di AR 44.* These excerpts from Rosmini's first sermon as Parish Priest are translated by the author.
4   Rosmini, *Delle Cinque Piaghe della Chiesa,* ed. 1981, pp. 193,196.
5   Pagani, *Life*, p. 158.
6   Valle, p. 56.
7   Pagani, Life, pp. 162–163.
8   Valle, p. 78.
9   Valle, p. 90.
10 Leetham, *Rosmini*, p. 175.
11 *Ep.Compl.*, v, 2594.
12 F. Puecher, IC, *The Last Days of Felice Robol.* Turin: Marietti, 1837.
13 *Ep.Compl.*, v, 2643.

Chapter Twelve

Growth of the Institute, 1835–1836

If Rosmini was disappointed by the total failure of the Institute in the Tyrol, he showed little sign of it. For him personally, his failure was simply an indication of God's providence that the Rosminians were not wanted in his hometown or province. In fact, failure there was more than compensated by abundant growth elsewhere. His return to Domodossola was the beginning of one of the busiest periods in his life.

Unfortunately he was unable to get back to Piedmont until May 1836 because the Austrians refused to renew his passport. When eventually he received it, it was valid for only six months. However, he occupied himself – as was his custom during any period which might otherwise have been frustrating for him – by his studies and writing. He also prepared the *New Essay on the Origin of Ideas* for a second edition. His philosophical teachings were becoming more widely known and appreciated throughout Italy.

One of the Trent community for whom Rosmini had the highest regard and who had remained faithful to his vocation as a Rosminian was Fr Giulio Todeschi. He too was a Roveretan and, as a young priest teaching theology at the seminary in Trent, it was he who had written the first invitation to Rosmini in 1830, which led to the formation of the Trent Rosminian community. He was an ardent, sensitive young man, whom Rosmini had sometimes to restrain for being overzealous. Todeschi was devastated by the events leading to the closure of the house at Trent and the end of the mission in the Tyrol. He preceded Rosmini to Monte Calvario, but became quite ill and depressed.

However, by the time Rosmini arrived in Piedmont he had cheered up even though physically he was frail. Rosmini resolved to send him to Rome where the milder climate would hopefully lead to a return to full health and where he could represent Rosmini in the process of seeking formal approval of the Institute by the Holy See. He arrived there early in the summer, but his health took a turn for the worse and, to Rosmini's desolation, he died of fever in Rome on 15 September 1836.

Rosmini revered Giulio for his intelligence and his piety. On receiving news of his death Rosmini exclaimed: 'God removes from me all my helpers one by one, that I may learn to rely on Him alone.'[1] In a letter to a member of Giulio's family he called him 'a saint'. 'Giulio was as dear to me as the nearest blood-relation, like a brother. I was greatly obliged to him, and he showed me so much kindness, affection and sympathy.'[2] Although Rosmini treated all his confrères with kindness, he was human enough to warm to some more than others. Giulio had been one of those.

The works of the Institute which had preoccupied Rosmini during the final period he was in the Tyrol and which were now reaching fruition, can be summarised under three headings: the English mission; other new works of the Institute, especially major foundations at the abbeys of the Sacra di San Michele, in Piedmont, and of Tamié, near Albertville in Savoy; and, most important, the foundation of the Sisters of Providence.

The English Mission

From Gregory to Gregory
England with St Benedict rises to heaven
and with Rosmini, transforming an Anglia of the angels,
the land will rediscover Christ to its widest boundaries.
Clemente Rebora[3]

As we saw earlier, the call for Rosminians to go to England began through Luigi Gentili while he was still a student in Rome.[4] The first contact from Bishop Baines, Vicar Apostolic of the Western District, came late in 1830. The following year there was another approach from the young layman Ambrose Phillips, who called on Rosmini in Milan to consolidate his invitation. That invitation was for Gentili to come and establish a mission in Leicestershire in the English Midlands. Finally, an elderly convert nobleman, Sir Harry Trelawney, approached first Bishop Baines and then Rosmini with a project to establish a Rosminian mission based in his home in Cornwall.

In 1833 Bishop Baines reasserted his claim, noting that Rosmini in his *Constitutions* awarded some priority to bishops. Baines persuaded Phillips to withdraw his request. Then Trelawney died, so the bishop's invitation was the only one left on the table. Baines went to Rome the following year on diocesan business and received a glowing commendation of the Institute from Pope Gregory. On his way home he visited Domodossola and a decision was finalised.

Three Rosminians, led by Fr Luigi Gentili, would come in 1835 to Prior Park, in Dorset. Prior Park was (and still is) a Palladian mansion overlooking the city of Bath. The bishop bought it as his headquarters in 1828 and built two colleges flanking the main house: St Peter's for the education of boys, and St Paul's as the diocesan seminary.

Rosmini had long been attracted by the idea of sending priests and brothers to England. Catholic Emancipation, freeing Catholics throughout Britain and Ireland of the disabilities imposed since the Reformation, had been achieved in 1829. The Catholic Relief Act was passed that year by the British parliament largely thanks to the efforts of the great Irish patriot Daniel O'Connell. At the same time there was a revival of interest in Catholic teachings and practices in the Anglican Church through the so-called *Oxford Movement*, led by Edward Pusey and John Henry Newman. The time seemed ripe.

The Catholic Church in England and Wales had been reduced to a remnant by centuries of persecution. Gentili saw the island as fertile soil for conversion back to the old faith. Rosmini's vision was perhaps more global. There were many things he admired about English culture and political institutions, since they combined traditional monarchy with a stable constitutional system. England was becoming a leading world power not only through the Industrial Revolution, in full swing in the 1830s and '40s, but also in the creation of a politically tolerant and enlightened society. The British parliament had, in 1807, made the slave trade illegal, and in 1834 the whole institution of slavery was abolished throughout the British Empire. Many countries soon followed suit. England was in the process of evolving into a liberal democracy, and led Europe in developing and extending parliamentary representation. It is ironic that the Rosminian mission to a predominantly Protestant country encountered far less opposition than Rosmini himself had suffered in the Tyrol at the hands of Catholic Austria.

The prospect of a mission to England was attractive to Rosmini. His dream and ambition was for a renewal of religious practice throughout the Christian world. This vision was prophetic, since from the tiny seed of Gentili's mission Rosminians were to spread first to Ireland, then to the United States of America during the nineteenth century, and to East Africa, India and New Zealand in the twentieth.

Rosmini wrote to Gentili: 'I hold the English Catholics so much in my heart that I am at a loss what to do to be of some help to them even in the slightest way. I will leave no stone unturned to achieve whatever the Providence of God presents to me for their advantage – even to the shedding of my blood.'[5]

Gentili himself did not hold quite such a sanguine view. He was eager indeed to work for 'this unhappy nation', but he laments: 'I should be exposed to continual warfare, not only with heresy, but with its effects, consisting in corruption and low degrading vice.'[6] Later he wrote: 'I think the English mission the most difficult in Europe, for there error and vice are greater than anywhere else.'[7]

His companions were to be two Frenchmen – Emilio Belisy, an unordained cleric, and Antonio Rey, a priest. Rosmini sought the blessing of Pope Gregory on the mission and sent the trio to Rome in May 1835 to have a special audience. The Pope greeted them affectionately, saying to them: 'May the Lord open to you a large field for good, and bless you, help you and prosper you.'[8]

They left Rome at the end of the month and, travelling via Paris, they arrived in London on 16 June. It was the beginning of many trials and many achievements. Rosmini followed their progress with the greatest interest, and showed a very personal concern for every aspect of the new mission.

Once they settled at Prior Park, Gentili was dismayed at the lack of fervour and colour he found in the Catholic life of the college, and he attempted to introduce devotions such as the Forty Hours, Benediction and religious processions. He encountered resistance from some of the English staff and parents. Rosmini counselled caution. He had an instinct for what today would be termed acculturation. A couple of examples demonstrate the discretion and care that he urged on his brethren, especially on Gentili:

> Do not look at things that happen in England with dark spectacles. I say this because I can see that the devil might get a grip on you in this connection and deceive you into a false kind of zeal. Instead, you must try to keep a cool head.[9]

To the trio he writes:

> I recommend all three of you to make yourselves little by little as English as possible in anything which is not sinful, since in this way you will be acting like St Paul: 'I have made myself all things to all people' ... each nation has its own customs, which are good in its eyes. So you ought to see through English eyes, and in your charity approve of what you see.[10]

Again to Gentili:

> I disapprove of your excessive and over-hasty introduction of scapulars, holy pictures and other special devotions. These

are good in themselves certainly, but they better suit countries which have been Catholic for a long time, rather than one where people are new to the faith.

You would have done better to make haste slowly … I have told you many a time to stick to the fundamental principles of our religion, reflecting on and studying what Jesus Christ and the Apostles said and did. The apostles, dealing with people who were still pagan, did not begin by preaching the merits of scapulars of our Lady or anything of that sort … You do not offer a starving man a piece of sugar, but a good slice of bread.[11]

Rosmini's tone here is not unlike a worried schoolteacher dealing with a wayward pupil. Gentili drove himself hard, and he was not always easy on his two subjects. In particular, Antonio Rey found him increasingly difficult. Rosmini attempted to mediate from a distance, but it did not work and eventually Rey withdrew from the Institute. He was not yet in vows, so he was quite free to do so. He continued teaching at Prior Park for some years. Later he went to America, dying there in 1847 while assisting victims of bubonic plague.

Gentili and his companions however soon made an impact, and initially the bishop was delighted with them. He described Gentili in a letter to Rosmini as a 'real treasure'. He wanted to appoint him President of St Paul's College and overcame Rosmini's reluctance in making this happen. Some of the clerical students were attracted to become Rosminians. Two of these, Peter Hutton and Moses Furlong, became the first English recruits and both were destined for fruitful apostolates as Rosminian priests.

Whether it was through a fear of losing his men or simply his own somewhat domineering temperament, Baines soon fell out with Gentili. He withdrew him from Prior Park and in 1838 put him out to grass in a local convent. In spite of this Rosmini used all his slender resources to keep the English mission supplied with reinforcements.

Among these were Frs Fortunato Signini and Angelo Rinolfi who spent most of their lives in England. He also sent the experienced Fr Giovanni Battista Pagani, who succeeded

Gentili at Prior Park, becoming Superior in England and eventually returning to Italy to follow Rosmini as second Provost General of the Society.

Throughout his life Rosmini continued to write frequently and personally to the brethren, endeavouring to promote their spiritual welfare from a distance. In time it became impossible for them to remain under the jurisdiction of the increasingly erratic Baines, so the focus of the mission would eventually shift from the Western to the Midlands district.[12]

Tamié and the Sacra

A wit once said about Rosmini that he certainly had an eye for good real estate. However, in the case of the foundations at Tamié and the Sacra di San Michele, the invitations came from outside without any solicitation on his part.

Tamié is the site of an old Cistercian monastery near Albertville in the Bauges mountains, Savoy (now part of France). The monks had been driven out during the French Revolution. After 1815 that part of Savoy west of the Alps returned to Piedmontese rule. Tamié was then briefly staffed by secular priests, who carried out missions throughout the area. But by 1835 it was deserted.

The Archbishop of Chambéry, Msgr Martinet, in whose diocese it lay, had heard of the missioning activity of Loewenbruck around Aosta (also in Savoy). Early in 1835 he wrote to Rosmini requesting that the Institute might staff the abbey as a centre for mission to the local people. Rosmini was still detained in the Tyrol, so he sent Loewenbruck to have a look at the monastery. He found it well equipped and furnished.

Rosmini hesitated and stalled for time by sending the *Constitutions* to the Archbishop for his perusal. But that made the Archbishop even more determined, and he sought the help of Rome to pressure Rosmini. When Rosmini heard that the Pope himself had given his blessing to the project, he felt obliged to concur and sent Loewenbruck, two other priests, both French, and two lay brothers to make a foundation. It seemed appropriate to staff a new foundation in a French-speaking place with Frenchmen.

In his letters to Loewenbruck Rosmini reveals both confidence in him for his zeal and a certain diffidence regarding his impetuosity. Rosmini recommends prudence and circumspection, the importance of consulting his brethren before acting, and the paramount need to reflect with Almighty God before committing himself to any action. 'My dear Loewenbruck,' he writes, 'I trust you: God and His Holy Spirit will give you the humility, as he has in the past, to profit by my counsels ... it is all the more necessary that you act with gravity and wisdom.'[13]

He also warns Loewenbruck against advertising the Institute more than necessary: 'for its own part the Institute wants to remain as little known as possible ... you must guard against naming it without reasonable cause.'[14] As was his wont, he gives Loewenbruck a series of detailed instructions as to how the house was to be run.

In fact Loewenbruck ran into trouble almost from the start. One of the French priests found the conditions at Tamié too harsh and isolated. One of the problems was that the local people were too busy in the surrounding fields to be available for missions except during the winter months. Inevitably there were going to be long periods when the house would be a purely contemplative one, and that did not suit everyone – and especially the ever-impetuous Loewenbruck.

Later Rosmini himself came to visit and leaves his impressions of the place. Tamié had immediate appeal. He writes from there to Mellerio for the latter's feast day:

> Tomorrow I shall celebrate in this deep solitude the feast of St James ... This vast monastery, these relics of ancient piety lift up one's soul to God in a wonderful way ... I see the shades of many abbots and monks wandering about this holy place where their remains are buried. All this makes me envy that life – more heavenly than earthly – led far from the world by the sons of St Bernard, those daring souls who distanced

themselves from human society in order to find in deserted
valleys the company of angels.[15]

Rosmini is here revealing his romantic streak but also his
own attraction to the monastic life. At a practical level,
however, he found both the French assistant priests waver-
ing in their vocation, and he reproached himself for sending
religious on the mission before they were fully formed.[16]
While he was there he also called on the Archbishop of
Chambéry.

Tamié survived for two years only. Loewenbruck himself
went wandering in France, and Rosmini soon realised that
this foundation was not going to work, so he reluctantly
withdrew his men. Subsequently the Cistercians returned,
and Tamié became a contemplative house. The Rosminian
vocation is one of contemplation *and* action. Perhaps this
was a lesson Rosmini himself had to learn. Sadly,
Loewenbruck from this time onwards began to distance
himself from the Institute. A Rosminian vocation demanded
too much self-discipline for his free spirit.

The Sacra di San Michele

By extraordinary coincidence another invitation to take on an
isolated, deserted monastery arrived at Rosmini's door the
same year. But this time the venture was to be blessed with
success. The Sacra di San Michele sits on the very peak of a
mountain on the southern side of the Val di Susa, a long valley
leading west from the city of Turin to the Mont Cenis pass
into France. It began as a mountaintop hermitage in the tenth
century. The Benedictines came there the following century
and built a large monastery. A great monastic church, which
survives, was built in the twelfth century.

At one time the monastery housed 300 Benedictine monks,
but the numbers declined. By the seventeenth century the
community had all dispersed and the buildings became
derelict. In 1835, King Charles Albert of Savoy, a very pious

Catholic, devised a plan to restore the Sacra as a place of retirement for lay people looking for a life of prayer. He also thought the church would make a fitting mausoleum for his ancestors, the Royal House of Savoy.

The King spoke of his plan to Cardinal Tadini, Archbishop of Genoa, who at once recommended the Rosminians as suitable religious to have charge of the sanctuary. The King then approached Rosmini, who sought the usual blessings of the local bishop and the Holy Father on this scheme. Both were forthcoming. Rosmini was still stuck in Rovereto, but in May 1836 he finally managed to extract a passport from the Austrian government and returned to Domodossola to personally supervise these various new developments.

But first, the noviciate had to be transferred from Monte Calvario to Stresa thirty miles further south on Lago Maggiore. A wealthy widow, Madame Anna Maria Bolongaro, had given the Institute a property there; Rosmini decided to adapt the house, which stood a short distance from the little town and up a hill overlooking the lake; it is where the Collegio Rosmini now stands. The novices were moved from Domodossola because their tenure at Monte Calvario had become uncertain: the house could not be purchased from the Capis family, who were determined to hang on to it.

Rosmini then resolved to go to Turin and negotiate person- ally with King Carlo Alberto over the Sacra. The king welcomed him kindly. He formally conferred the custody of the sanctuary on the Rosminians and undertook to have a guest house built. He also used his personal influence to obtain Rosmini a permit from the Austrian government which would allow him to stay in Piedmont for ten years. That was a huge personal relief.

Early in July 1836 Rosmini paid his first visit to the Sacra. In a letter to his cousin Pietro Rosmini, he gives a vivid descrip- tion:

> The old buildings are very solid, and it must have cost a
> fortune to haul up there the great blocks of stone, well-cut

and variously shaped, which make up what remains of the oldest part of the building . . .

The church itself is situated at the third (uppermost) level of the monastery, where the rocks finish; and to reach the entrance you have to go up a covered stairway. This is both magnificent and tremendously solid: it is perhaps the finest remaining part of the ancient building . . . Today, the pious King Carlo Alberto wants to have the remains of his ancestors translated here, and he wishes to restore the building so that it may serve as a retirement home for some of those who have grown disillusioned with the things of this world . . .

To tell the truth, the ascent up here is rocky and hard, even for the mules (though I think the generosity of the King will remedy this difficulty); but when one actually arrives, two magnificent vistas present themselves: in one direction (eastward) you can see Turin and the Basilica of the Superga, with the whole valley; in the other, (westward) is the area through which the river Susa flows, dotted with small towns.[17]

Rosmini was clearly stunned by this latest acquisition, as is anybody who troubles to visit the Sacra. Some 100,000 pilgrims and tourists now make the arduous ascent every year. A small Rosminian community is still there. It is used for retreats, concerts and conferences. It has, in recent times, been declared a European Heritage Site.

As regards his sojourn in Turin – his first in that city – Rosmini reveals a love-hate relationship with big cities. He always enjoyed meeting people, and during this short sojourn in the capital of Piedmont he made some useful political and social contacts. One with whom he was to have many dealings later was the celebrated Italian priest-philosopher Vincenzo Gioberti. Another was the Marquis Gustavo Cavour, brother to the great Piedmontese and Italian political leader. Gustavo became a close friend to Rosmini for the rest of his life. He also made the acquaintance of Don Bosco, founder of the Salesians, visiting his foundations and assisting the works with money. Yet in the letter to his cousin Pietro quoted above he says: 'When I find myself in big cities I feel like Truffaldino [a harlequin character in a famous Goldoni comedy] who was smothered under 40 or 50 garments. I am swamped by thousands of useless and irritating usages.'[18]

To his mother he is even more frank about his feelings regarding city life. He acknowledges the grace and gentleness of the people of Turin, yet he finds certain aspects of their behaviour 'unbearable to me, a man of simplicity, a "campereccio".' To find so much falsity, mainly in townsfolk, left him longing for the simple life of his early years, which he could now experience in his religious communities.[19]

After his visit to the Sacra, Rosmini visited Tamié before going back to Stresa. There he made preparations for yet another shift of the noviciate, this time to the Sacra at King Carlo Alberto's request. He returned to Turin in time for the ceremony of translation of the royal remains to the abbey church. Eventually twenty-two royal tombs were transferred, and the king had a special vault built under the church to house them. The noviciate was set up in the monastery, and Fr Francesco Puecher, who had been Rosmini's secretary in the parish at Rovereto, continued to be Rector and novice master.

The Rosminian presence at the Sacra di San Michele was to continue down the years. It fitted well with a desire of Rosmini's that there should always be one primarily contemplative community in the Institute. The Sacra is an isolated place, and the community is literally 'up in the clouds'. However, its proximity to a large city means that it is available to priests, religious and lay people as a place for retreat and for religious meetings. It also has had a growing outreach to people of the area in much the same way that Monte Calvario had to the people of the Ossola valley but touching a much larger population.

Notes

1   Pagani, *Life*, p. 199.
2   *Ep.Compl.,* v, 2915.
3   Da Gregorio a Gregorio // l'Inghilterra con Benedetto ascende; // e con Rosmini tornando un Anglia d'angioli, // la terra trovera Cristo in tutti i suoi confini.
    The Rosminian poet, Clemente Rebora, composed this poem in 1935 for the 100th anniversary of the arrival of Gentili and his companions in England. Here is an explanation:
    Just as Pope Gregory the Great (Gregory I) sent the first missionaries, sons of St Benedict, to convert England, so under a new Pope Gregory (Gregory XVI) Rosmini sent his sons to 'England of the angels', that the land might everywhere be won for Christ. 'Anglia of the angels' refers to Gregory the Great's famous punning comment about the blonde Anglo-Saxon slaves in the Rome slave market – 'non Angli sed angeli: not Angles but angels'. (Paraphase by the author)
    The word 'boundaries' (*confini*) is a poetic way of describing the variety of works opened up to the Rosminians in England and Wales, and eventually in Ireland too.
4   See Chapter 10.
5   *Ep.Compl.,* iii, 1333.
6   Leetham, *Rosmini,* p. 157.
7   Leetham, *Rosmini,* p. 159.
8   Pagani, *Life,* p. 181.
9   *Ep.Compl.,* v, 2725.
10 *Ep.Compl.,* v, 2660.
11 *Ep.Compl.,* vii, 3786.
12 See below Chapter 14.
13 *Ep.Compl.,* v, 2623.
14 *Ep.Compl.,* v, 2644.
15 *Ep.Compl.,* v, 2817.
16 *Diario della Carità*, p. 33.
17 *Ep.Compl.,* v, 2809.
18 *Ep.Compl.,* v, 2809.
19 The author is grateful to Fr Luigi Cerana, IC, who, as a fellow Trentino, advised him on Rosmini's feelings towards sophisticated city folk. This aspect may be read about in full in Appendix Three.

Chapter Thirteen

The Sisters of Providence

A most important sphere of Rosmini's activity during this time was the founding of the Sisters of Providence. Rosmini himself had no intention originally of starting another such Institute. The initiative came entirely, and somewhat erratically, from Loewenbruck. However, in time Rosmini embraced the foundation wholeheartedly and at the end of his life he wrote, 'The Sisters of Providence are a branch of the same Institute of Charity, founded by me for the exercise of charitable works towards women, especially for schools and education.'[1] So it truly was for him a second major foundation.

The early apostolate of Loewenbruck had soon spread out from Monte Calvario through the valleys and villages of the Ossola valley and further afield. During his preaching and teaching he was struck by the number of pious young women who came to him, many expressing a sincere desire to consecrate their lives to the service of God. He wrote: 'In these girls from the mountains were gifts and qualities that are hardly to be found among the rich and cultured in the cities, the most important being generosity and complete self-giving.'[2]

Loewenbruck discovered that these girls were not worried what religious congregation they might join, so he sought help from various sources. He tried the Visitation Sisters and the Cannossians who had convents nearby, but drew a blank. He then remembered an Order in Lorraine that he had come across earlier, whose work was among the poor and, in particular, the education of children. This congregation had been founded in France in 1762 and had grown swiftly. By 1830 there were over 1,200 of these 'Sisters of Providence' throughout France. The mother house was in Portieux, near Épinal, and their Superior was the Abbé Feys, parish priest of the town.

Loewenbruck wrote to Feys about the possibility of sending some Italian girls to Portieux to receive training in the religious life. Feys was cautious at first, fearing that the effects of the Revolution might make it unwise for Italians to come to France. However, on reflection, he changed his mind and suggested that some Italian girls be sent, who would learn French and teach the French sisters Italian. Feys' motive was his fear that another revolution in France might cause his Sisters to be expelled. If there were foundations across the border in Piedmont they would then have somewhere to take refuge.

Loewenbruck responded with alacrity, and even though winter was approaching – it was November 1831 – he chose four girls and arranged for them to cross the Simplon Pass and make their way to Portieux. They set out on 26 November and did not get to Portieux until 11 December. Loewenbruck accompanied them as far as the Simplon in a coach he had borrowed from the brother of one of the four postulants. One commentator describes their journey across the high mountains:

> It is hard to imagine how they survived the cold, hunger and fear, in the midst of snow and wind, totally isolated, enduring the nights in temporary shelter. They went on foot for the most part ... or jolted along on their dreadfully slow means of transport, on a road that was steep and frozen, often losing their way because of the inexpertness of their driver or because the snow and ice completely obliterated all traces of the Napoleonic route.[3]

It was madness for Loewenbruck to send this expedition across the Alps in winter, and all the girls suffered in health afterwards. Indeed one had to leave and return home after returning to Italy because she was still enfeebled. However, in spite of such an inauspicious start the girls made a good impression. In March 1832, Feys wrote to Loewenbruck: 'Your good daughters give us great satisfaction by their docility and solid piety ... we wish all our Sisters here were like your four Italians.'

Meanwhile Loewenbruck discovered a disused old hospital in Locarno, and set it up as a convent with four postulants. In July he reinforced the pioneers with thirteen others, and shortly afterwards the four from Portieux returned with two French Sisters to establish a proper noviciate. Their living conditions were spartan. Sometimes they even lacked bread to eat. It was far from ideal, but a start had been made.

The French Superior, Sr Teodora Collin, was at a loss how to improve matters, so she wrote directly to Rosmini seeking help. Rosmini had taken a keen interest in what Loewenbruck in his great zeal and enthusiasm was initiating, but was reluctant to interfere until asked. However, he responded at once to Sr Teodora by sending Fr Giacomo Molinari to Locarno. There was a secular priest in Locarno, Fr Carlo Rusca, whom Rosmini also recruited to help. This move proved very successful. Rusca remained involved with the Sisters for many years as their Director, and himself became a member of the Institute of Charity.

Rosmini instructed Sr Teodora that she should regard Loewenbruck as the spiritual father of this new work since he had created it. But in reply she emphatically begged Rosmini to take it in hand himself. Loewenbruck at last wrote himself, asking for help, admitting he was out of his depth, and threatening to leave the Institute. Rosmini wrote back at once telling him to pull himself together. He was in danger of losing the Sisters of Providence as well as harming the Institute itself.

Rosmini, however, from this point on began to take a more hands-on approach to the Sisters. He actively guided the two French women in the work of forming the postulants and also training them professionally to become teachers. After a year, the French Sisters withdrew and returned to France. Rosmini took pains to look carefully at their Rule, also at the rule of the Cannossians. He modified these for his own Sisters to bring them more into line with Rosminian asceticism.

The bishops required of the Sisters that they should primarily be involved in works of temporal charity such as running elementary schools, orphanages, etc. While this was a limitation, Rosmini was insistent that they too were called to universal charity, and that whatever work divine providence called them to they should do, provided they had the means to do it. In that sense their vocation corresponds entirely to that of the brethren.

Another important decision was his choice of the first Italian Superior. Maria Camilla (Sister Giovanna) Antonietti had been one of the pioneers in Domodossola. Even though she had had little formal education, Rosmini declared he had never met such a wise woman and therefore he chose her to be his collaborator. In 1837 he appointed her Superior of the central house in Domodossola, and it was Rosmini himself who gave her the title of 'Carissima Madre' ('Dearest Mother'), which denoted both her authority and the style of that authority, both spiritual and affectionate. The title is still used by the Sisters.

For these reasons Rosmini is recognised by the Sisters of Providence as their true founder. Their numbers grew rapidly and they soon became known as Rosminian Sisters. The work in which they excelled was teaching in village schools. This demanded that they live in very small communities and had to show a degree of self-reliance. It is interesting to note that a few decades later, in Australia, St Mary McKillop founded her congregation of Josephites with much the same charism to meet a similar need in the Church.

The Sisters began to spread their wings across northern Italy, not only in the diocese of Novara but also further west into the district and diocese of Biella. They also received an invitation to follow their male brethren and make a foundation in England. It is significant that in many parts of the world where the Rosminian fathers have started missions, the Sisters have soon followed. The close bond has continued, and this is as Rosmini would have wished.

For Rosmini, too, it was providential in the sense that it gave an outlet to the maternal side of his own character. He befriended the Sisters, and his correspondence with them is rich and plentiful. He delighted in visiting them in their communities, and there is an abundance of careful spiritual direction in his letters to them. And Sister Giovanna Antonietti became for him a life-long friend.

This had been one of the busiest times of Rosmini's life. The Institute was attracting vocations. The Sisters too were growing fast as a congregation. The Rosminians were becoming known, and that meant many demands from bishops for new foundations. The English mission preoccupied him. It was typical of him that none of these developments was too unimportant not to receive his personal and concentrated attention. The next great milestone was to be the formal approval of the Institute by the Holy See.

Notes

1   *Ep.Compl.*, xii, 7872.
2   Sr Maria Bruna Ferretti, *The Rosminian Sisters of Providence.* Domodossola, 2000.
3   From *The Life of Sr Giovanna Antonietti*, p. 13.

Chapter Fourteen

Approval by the Holy See, 1837–1840

Throughout his life Antonio Rosmini showed an abiding loyalty to the Holy See and to the person of the Pope. It had contributed considerably to his difficulty in relations with the Austrian authorities – and even with the German-speaking bishops. This sense of reverence for one set apart by divine providence to rule the Church was bred into him from birth. For many patriotic Italians of his day, Catholicism was part of their very being, and that implied a love and respect for the person of the Holy Father.

His experience of meeting and conversing with Pius VII during his first visit to Rome in 1823 reinforced this aspect of his faith, and was a major factor in the somewhat dramatic character of his *Panegyric* for Pius when he died shortly afterwards. Rosmini expresses this fidelity to the papacy in the second of his *Maxims of Christian Perfection*:

> The Christian knows through the words of Jesus that the Church on earth is founded on a rock against which the powers of hell cannot prevail: that is, it is founded on the Apostle Peter and on his successors, the Roman pontiffs, who are the supreme Vicars of Christ on earth ...
>
> The See of Peter thus became the essential part of the Church of Christ, whereas other parts of the Church received no infallible promise that, taken singly, they might not for a time perish. The Christian ought therefore to cherish in his heart an affection, an attachment, a respect for the Holy See

... working for her prosperity as the immaculate spouse of Jesus Christ.[1]

So it was very important to Rosmini that the Pope himself should approve and bless this new religious family. From Pius VIII he had received strong encouragement for the embryonic Institute of Charity – along with a caution *festina lente* (hasten slowly!).[2] The popes urged him to seek the approval of local bishops, and he systematically sent a copy of the *Constitutions* to bishops in all the places where the Institute was invited to establish itself.

The present Pope, Gregory XVI, had become a personal friend while still a cardinal. As Pope, he continued to give full support to Rosmini. In fact, he sent one of his closest advisers, Cardinal Castruccio Castracane, to call on the community at Monte Calvario while on visitation to northern Italy. When Luigi Gentili went to Rome in May 1835 to see Pope Gregory and receive his blessing on the English mission, the Pope told Gentili it was high time Rosmini sent the *Constitutions* to Rome for examination and approval. He then instructed Castracane to write directly to Rosmini to that effect.

That was all the stimulus Rosmini needed. When he got back to Monte Calvario from the Tyrol he prepared a compendium of the *Constitutions* with the decrees of approval from nine bishops. This was despatched to Rome in March 1837. The Pope was happy to receive it and at once handed it over to the Congregation of Bishops and Regulars, appointing Castracane to be the promoter of the cause.[3] It is this compendium which was finally approved as the Rule of the Institute of Charity.

Rosmini despatched a young Rosminian priest, Giuseppe Setti, to Rome to facilitate the process. Setti had first joined the Trent community, and had come on to Calvario after its dissolution. Although only 27, 'his gifts of mind, together with his affability, eloquence, easy and gentle bearing, and above all his solid piety and heartfelt devotion to the Institute' equipped him admirably for this role.[4]

There followed a somewhat tortuous process lasting

nearly two years: it appears that there were those in Rome who were determined to frustrate papal approval of the Rosminians.[5] But at first, the process went well. The first consultor to examine the *Constitutions* was Fr Luigi de Luca, OFM, who declared them to be 'entirely in keeping with their title of charity, a charity truly evangelical and wholly conducive to private and public good, spiritually and temporally ...'[6] He recommended that the Constitutions be approved at once; however, the Congregation of Cardinals, whose job it was to examine and approve, advised delay at their meeting of June 16.

Castracane wrote to Rosmini that a sticking point was his concept of religious poverty. Rosmini at once wrote back explaining and defending it. The Congregation then appointed a Jesuit priest, Fr Zecchinelli, to be another consultor. His report was negative. Rosmini read it and replied to the objections, sending his response to Setti to present to the Congregation.

Setti asked for yet another consultor to be appointed: it was a Fr Turco, also Franciscan. Once again, having looked at all the objections and Rosmini's responses, Turco echoed what de Luca had said, stating that the Rosminian Constitutions were 'most holy and worthy of approbation' and that in the Rule 'there was nothing not in strict accordance with the spirit of the Gospel and with Catholic doctrine.'[7]

It is interesting to note that these Franciscans, whose own rule lays such an emphasis on evangelical poverty, found no problems at all with what Rosmini was proposing, namely that the property of the Institute be held in the name of certain senior brethren rather than in the name of the Order as a body (the normal practice). This proviso would protect the Institute from confiscation of land or property by hostile authorities. Private owners are usually protected by the law of the land against such arbitrary confiscations.

The wisdom of this can be easily seen from what happened to many Orders during the time of the French Revolution. Even in Catholic Austria under the Emperor Joseph II, religious Orders were suppressed and their property confiscated at the Imperial whim. The state simply helped itself to lands and buildings of those Orders which were deemed to be not contributing to the public good. In modern times the problem has been largely solved by the development of charitable trusts: a trust can own property in the name of an Order and is regarded as a 'legal entity' protected by the law.

Those in Rome critical of this provision on religious poverty fell into two camps: some thought the Institute was erring on the side of too great a prudence in securing its property against the greed of governments; on the other hand, some suggested a lack of prudence lest a 'Judas' might run off with the Order's goods. Rosmini clearly thought this latter was a risk worth taking.

Rosmini wrote a circular letter to all the brethren in February 1838 prescribing prayers, penance and almsgiving to seek divine help in getting the process of approval completed. But there were further hurdles to negotiate. Rumours were circulating around Rome that Rosmini was guilty of various heresies: quietism, rationalism, and semi-Pelagianism. And his infant Institute was incriminated. Secretly, another consultor was appointed, the Servite Fr Secchi-Muro. When Setti discovered that Secchi-Muro was about to submit a damning report just as the Congregation was about to meet in early August, he intervened and succeeded in getting that meeting postponed.[8]

However, help was imminent and from the highest level. The Pope himself decided to hasten the process, assuring Setti of his personal conviction that the Institute was of God and 'that his eye and hand would watch and protect it from unjust and perverse attacks.'[9] This papal intervention succeeded in breaking the logjam. The mischief-makers ran for cover. Two more consultors were brought in who gave positive approval. The postponed meeting was then convened for 20 December 1838.

There were eight Cardinals present and after a 'stormy session' the Institute was formally approved as a Congregation with the privileges of Regulars.[10] The Holy

Father confirmed the decree as soon as it was presented to him. Rosmini himself received the joyous news on Christmas Day. It was the best of all presents. He at once fixed the Feast of the Annunciation the following year to be the day when the formed brethren would consecrate themselves to God through religious vows.

So, on 25 March 1839, Rosmini and nineteen of the brethren assembled at Monte Calvario. Rosmini's coadjutor vows[11] were received by the senior priest present, Giacomo Molinari. They celebrated Mass, and at Communion the others also pronounced their vows, received by Rosmini himself. Present were five Ascribed Members of the Society, including his great friends Mellerio and Padulli.

A similar ceremony was taking place the same day at two venues in England: four priests made their vows in the presence of Bishop Baines at Prior Park. Pagani and Gentili made theirs at an Augustinian convent at Spettisbury, in Dorset. The Institute now was officially in existence and part of the Catholic Church.

For Rosmini, however, there remained one great sadness. Loewenbruck, who had been preaching missions in France, declined to respond to a pressing invitation to come and be part of the ceremony at Calvario. He wrote that he could not belong to the Institute unless he made his noviciate again. This grieved Rosmini, but he accepted it even though it seemed to be the parting of the ways.

Rosmini and Loewenbruck were both called by God, but their vocations were essentially different. They were brought together for a time providentially to provide the impetus for the founding of the Institute. Loewenbruck, one might say, was a man of faith, decisive and impulsive, moved always by what he felt within his heart. Rosmini was equally a man of faith, but a faith illuminated by reason: always led, as he counsels in the Sixth Maxim, by the spirit of intelligence. They were both saintly men, but different.

Many years later Loewenbruck came to see Rosmini in Rome, calling himself the 'most unworthy and ungrateful of his sons' and begging forgiveness. But he never returned to

Deposition from the Cross by Ambrogio Rosmini

Pier Modesto Rosmini (father)

Giovanna (mother)

Ambrogio Rosmini (uncle)

Antonio Rosmini as a child

S. Francis de Sales by Ambrogio Rosmini (Antonio Rosmini as a young man on the right)

Rosmini's study, Palazzo Rosmini, Rovereto

Palazzo Rosmini, Rovereto

The bedroom where Rosmini was born, Palazzo Rosmini, Rovereto

Reception Room, Palazzo Rosmini, Rovereto

Library, Palazzo Rosmini, Rovereto

S. Marco, Rovereto

Rovereto today

Monte Calvario

Monte Calvario (house and church)

Antonio Rosmini's cell at Monte Calvario

Monte Calvario (Stations of the Cross on the ascent)

Antonio Rosmini as a young man

Antonio Rosmini, portrait with signature

chiari l'aspetto inumano, non i tesori rapiti barbaramente,
non negl'infelici a mille a mille le strida commiserevoli
intristivano e maculavan di colpa quel divin trionfo di Pio;
ma in luogo delle spoglie de' popoli, i beneficii universali
del vincitore sculti ne' cuori lo rallegravano, e in luogo
delle inflitte morti, i proprii patimenti da sè sostenuti
per tutti il santificavano. Onde orsù al concetto t'eleva
della tua pietosa Grandezza, dimentica quello dell'empia e
profana. In quanto a me per quell'incredibile affetto che
a te porto, o Italia, o ~~mia~~ gran genitrice, innalzerò incessantemente per te ~~questi~~ devoti prieghi all'Eterno e
Onnipotente, che prediligi Italia, che concedi a lei immortali figliuoli, che dall'eterna Roma, per li tuoi Vicarj
governi il mondo; deh! dona altresì ad essa, benignissimo, il ~~conoscimento~~ di sè, unica cosa che ignora: ren-
dila avida di liberi voti e d'amore, di cui è degna più
che di tributi e di pavento; fa che in sè stessa ella
trovi felicità e riposo, e in tutto il mondo un nome non
feroce, ma pio.

Manuscript of the Panegyric of Pope Pius VII, showing the concluding Prayer for Italy censored

Gregory XVI

Antonio Rosmini, painting by Luigi Zuccoli

King Carlo Alberto of Savoy

Bas-relief of Alessandro Manzoni and
Antonio Rosmini

Sacra di S. Michele

Sacra di S. Michele, interior of Abbey church

Antonio Rosmini's Room in Villa Bolongaro

Villa Bolongaro, Stresa, where Rosmini spent his final years

Lake Maggiore from behind Stresa

Bust of Antonio Rosmini beside the lake, Stresa

Tomb of Antonio Rosmini, Stresa

the Institute. He survived Rosmini by thirty years, eventually dying suddenly in France while preaching yet another mission.

It is interesting to note the manner of Rosmini's dealings with Loewenbruck. He tended to treat him with kid gloves. He was evidently very fond of him and admired his sincerity and zeal. But he eventually came to accept that Loewenbruck's temperament would always make him an independent operator. Rosmini tempered the wind of criticism to the shorn lamb.

Luigi Gentili, however, was no shorn lamb. Rosmini equally admired him and never doubted Gentili's loyalty and sincerity. It was his impulsiveness and occasional imprudence that needed to be reined in. So, in Gentili's case, the kid gloves were often discarded!

The process of formal approval still had one more act to play. Rosmini needed to receive Apostolic Letters from the Holy See and wished to use the occasion for some senior members to take their Presbyter vows, the fourth vow of special obedience to the Holy Father. So, in July 1840, Gentili, Pagani and Belisy set out from England and joined Rosmini and four others at Stresa. From there the eight brethren travelled together to Rome, where they were received in audience by Pope Gregory XVI.

The Pope asked that the vows ceremony be executed discreetly. Therefore, the following week the party went out to the catacomb of St Sebastian, south of the city, at that time the only catacomb known and visited. (In 1840 the 'Columbus' of the catacombs, Giovanni Battista de Rossi, had not yet begun his epic career of rediscovering and excavating the many miles of underground Roman cemeteries. That was to happen only a few years later.)

St Sebastian's was a place hallowed by the memory of SS Peter and Paul whose bones had, according to tradition, been kept there for a time prior to the building of the great basilicas on the site of their respective martyrdoms. The catacomb became a favourite place of prayer for many holy people: SS Philip Neri and Charles Borromeo among others. It is one of the staging posts of the traditional pilgrimage of the seven churches, initiated by St Philip Neri (the seven churches are the four major basilicas – St Peter's, St Paul's, St Mary Major and St John Lateran – plus St Lawrence, Holy Cross in Jerusalem, and St Sebastian).

On 20 and 21 July the little group made a pilgrimage of visitation to each of these churches, culminating at St Sebastian's on the 22nd. There in the catacomb the eight Rosminians took the fourth vow. The others left shortly afterwards to return north leaving Rosmini and Setti to complete the final business.[12]

This last step was not without its little hiccup. When Rosmini visited Pope Gregory a few days later, he found him somewhat more formal and distant. It may have been that the Pope did not want to appear to be giving special favours to the Rosminians. Rosmini was somewhat distressed at this; he felt he could no longer approach the Holy Father with the familiarity he had enjoyed hitherto. In his diary he notes: 'I could not believe that the Pope would treat me so brusquely since previously he had been happy to pass whole evenings with me.'[13] It may be Rosmini was showing himself to be a little oversensitive.

However, the Pope certainly did not spare any praise in what he wrote in the Apostolic Letter *In Sublimi*, published on 20 September and which Rosmini was able to take home with him. In it, the official document of papal approval,[14] the Pope says this about Rosmini:

... And since we know from experience that Our beloved son, the priest Antonio Rosmini, founder of this Institute, is a man endowed with singular and excellent intelligence, a soul adorned with eminent gifts, highly distinguished for his wisdom in things divine and human, conspicuous for his singular piety, religion, virtue, uprightness, prudence, and integrity, remarkable for his extraordinary love for and attachment to the Catholic religion and this holy Apostolic See; and that in the foundation of the Institute his chief object was that the charity of Christ should be more abundantly diffused in the hearts of all and should draw all into unity, and that the Catholic Church might daily reap a more abundant harvest, and the faithful be urged by a more powerful stimulus to the love of God and one another; for all these reasons We have decided to appoint the same, Our beloved son, Superior of the society for life ...[15]

Fulsome language like this is not unusual in papal documents. Nevertheless, to receive such a personal encomium in an official document was unique, and Rosmini must have been very gratified that in spite of all the thistles and brambles encountered on the way, the path to full approval had at last been safely negotiated.

Rosmini returned to Stresa where the house on the hill now became his home. Cardinal Morozzo had visited Stresa in May to lay the foundation stone for a chapel attached to the noviciate house. This building was completed in 1841. During this period Rosmini settled down to the business of governing his steadily growing family and supervising new foundations. At Domodossola, besides the care of the sanctuary at Monte Calvario, the school for boys founded by Mellerio in the town was transformed into a college under Rosminian direction. This foundation, the Collegio Mellerio, was to flourish until recent times when a fall in demand necessitated its transformation into a vocational school for the hospitality industry.

Many vocations to the Rosminian Brothers meant that a growing number of elementary schools came under the care of the Institute. They were staffed by *maestri*, trained at a College for Elementary Masters established at Intra on the other side of the lake from Stresa. The Sisters of Providence were also growing steadily and opened schools during these years at Arona, Trontano, Craveggia, Vigevano, and at Biella, an industrial town north of Turin.

Rosmini continued to send reinforcements to England. Since Gentili had fallen out with Bishop Baines, Rosmini bade him to stay on in the north of Italy. His health had not been good, so it was an opportunity for him to recuperate. Then another vehement appeal arrived from Phillips, requesting that Gentili be sent to establish a mission in Leicestershire. He had the backing of the local bishop, Dr Walsh, Vicar Apostolic of the Midlands district based in Birmingham.

Rosmini replied at once with enthusiasm, although he said there would be a short delay while Gentili's health picked up again. He had received from no lesser person than Pope Gregory a commendation of the English mission and even a warm tribute regarding the character of Bishop Walsh. Rosmini expressed a hope that Gentili's mission might lead to the establishment of a Rosminian house, which could become the English noviciate. 'May he be a new Augustine for England', Rosmini wrote prophetically.[16]

In May 1840, Gentili took up residence at Grace Dieu, Phillips' country house near Leicester, and commenced an apostolate of itinerant preaching in the neighbourhood. This was immensely fruitful and over the course of three years there were many hundreds of converts. The spiritual care of country people had often been neglected in England, so it was a vineyard ripe for the harvest. Gentili's apostolate is reminiscent of the famous 'man on a donkey', John Wesley (1703–1791), who had travelled the length and breadth of the country preaching in market squares, open fields and tiny villages, also with great success.[17]

Meanwhile relations with Bishop Baines did not improve, and eventually Pagani and the other priests were withdrawn. Some went to Oscott, near Birmingham, to help teach in Bishop Walsh's seminary. In May 1841 Pagani was sent to the market town of Loughborough, near Grace Dieu, to take over the parish; it became the first Rosminian parish in England. Soon after, Gentili succeeded him as parish priest, and it was at Loughborough that Gentili introduced various Catholic practices not seen before in England, such as the preaching of public missions.

A site for a noviciate house in England was bought between Loughborough and the city of Leicester, at Ratcliffe-on-the-Wreake. Count Mellerio, Madame Bolongaro and others contributed to the cost of this, and the famous Gothic Revival architect, Augustus Welby Pugin, was invited to design the house, whose foundation stone was blessed and laid in March 1843. It later became a school for senior students, Ratcliffe College.

Among the many converts brought into the faith by Gentili was William Lockhart, a young disciple of John Henry Newman and member of the little community at Littlemore outside Oxford which Newman had founded. Lockhart had been attracted to Catholicism for some time. He had met Gentili in Oxford in 1842 and read with delight Rosmini's *Maxims of Christian Perfection*. In August 1843 he went to visit Gentili at Loughborough, and this meeting triggered the fuse for his immediate conversion and decision to join the Rosminians.

Lockhart was later to become one of the leading Rosminian priests in England, founder of the parish at St Etheldreda's, Ely Place in London. His conversion was a huge shock to Newman, who at once resigned his position as Vicar of St Mary's in Oxford and used the defection of Lockhart as occasion to preach a memorable sermon on the *Parting of Friends*. In fact Newman followed Lockhart into the Catholic Church two years later; in spite of that sermon he and Lockhart remained good friends for the rest of Lockhart's life.

Newman became very interested in Rosmini's spirituality although, unlike Lockhart, he was never a devotee of his philosophical writing. When Newman was passing through the north of Italy in 1846 he attempted to meet Rosmini, but unfortunately Rosmini was absent from Stresa at the time, so the only connection between the two great Catholic thinkers was by correspondence – in Latin! Rosmini admired what he knew of Newman, and read and approved his famous *Essay On Development*,[18] published around this time.[19]

In 1843, Rosmini received a request from Lady Mary Arundel, a friend of Phillips and a benefactor of the Midlands mission, to send some Rosminian Sisters to start a school in Loughborough. Two Sisters were sent, arriving there in October. A school was quickly established and before long the Sisters attracted vocations and they too were able to start a noviciate. Rosmini wrote them a somewhat melodramatic Brief for the new foundation: 'Remember that you will only be able to make known what the Catholic religion really is to those souls "sitting in darkness and in the shadow of death" by the exercise of indefatigable and boundless charity.'[20]

Another successful missioner in the Midlands District at this time was the Passionist priest Blessed Dominic Barberi, who was to receive Newman into the Catholic Church in 1845. This ferment of apostolic activity attracted much popular attention – and even a satirical comment in the humorous magazine *Punch,* lampooning the Italian missioners as 'Barbarians, Pagans, and Gentiles' (a play on the names Barberi, Pagani, and Gentili)!

Another group of Rosminians that began to flourish were the Ascribed Members and Rosmini composed special Constitutions for them. In England, apart from Phillips, another distinguished Ascribed member was Msgr Nicholas Wiseman, coadjutor to Bishop Walsh and later to become the first Cardinal Archbishop of Westminster.

During 1842, two significant family events impacted on Rosmini's life. On 15 January his mother died, aged 85 years. He honoured her for her love and support and for the strong faith in which she had brought him up. In recent years he had not seen a lot of her because he was away from Rovereto, but he always ensured that she was comfortable and had all she needed in the family home. Giovanna supported her son in his life and vocation, and had become an Ascribed member of the Institute of Charity.

By coincidence his cousin and friend, Antonio Fedrigotti, lost his elderly mother during the same week. Rosmini wrote to him:

… It is good that relatives and friends should share with one another both the important troubles and joys that life brings.

I am truly with you in your sorrow, as you are with me in mine – since we have both been orphaned at almost the same time … To the eyes of faith death brings before us on the one hand the boundless mercy of God, and on the other, the excellence of both the life and death of our two dear departed ones … as they shared the same name (Giovanna) while here on earth they will also have in common the name of the Lamb written on their foreheads in heaven. There they will pray for us, my dear cousin: and they will await their sons.[21]

Rosmini had need of feminine support in his life. His sister especially had provided this during her lifetime. He grew close to Sister Giovanna Antonietti to whom he entrusted the governance of the Sisters of Providence. However, a family event later in the same year was to introduce another significant female into his circle of friendship.

At long last, in April 1842, his brother Giuseppe married Adelaide Cristani a Rallo. Rosmini came to Rovereto and presided at the wedding. Adelaide was an intelligent and gentle person and seemed to bring a little peace at last into his brother's troubled life. Sadly for them, there were no children. For Antonio it was the beginning of a warm and quite intimate friendship. Leetham notes, 'His letters to her show an easy relationship that is unique in his correspondence.'[22]

While peacefully ensconced in Stresa, Rosmini was able to find more time for writing. He wrote the *Philosophy of Right* (two large volumes) in 1841 to 1843, some political works, as well as some controversial writings. With the steady growth of the Institute in Italy and in England it might have seemed that a halcyon period was dawning; however, the peace of the Institute was suddenly shattered by a violent and apparently co-ordinated attack on the orthodoxy and integrity of its Founder.

Notes

1   Antonio Rosmini, *Maxims of Christian Perfection, Second Maxim*, 6, (edited by Antonio Belsito, IC, 2008).

2   See pp. 86–87.

3   Pagani, *The Life of Antonio Rosmini-Serbati,* p. 206.

4   Pagani, *Life,* p. 207.

5   In a letter to Rosmini (2 December 1837) Cardinal Castracane spoke of a 'gelosia' (jealousy) towards the Institute aroused by the Rosminian Constitutions when they arrived in Rome for examination. Setti noted it largely came from Jesuit Fathers, but he did not think Fr Roothaan, the Jesuit Fr General, was a party to it; indeed Setti found him helpful in negotiating problems. Setti was living in a Jesuit house in Rome (Bozzetti, *Opere Complete II,* pp. 2397–2418).

6   Pagani, *Life,* p. 206.

7   Pagani, *Life,* p. 208.

8   Pagani, *Life,* p. 210.

9   Pagani, *Life,* p. 210.

10   Pagani, *Life,* p. 211.

11   When someone seeks to become a Rosminian he goes through three stages of probation. The first (postulancy) is the inquiry stage; the second (noviciate) is the period of strict religious formation. The novice is a member of the Order. At the end of noviciate he makes simple vows (poverty, chastity and obedience) for three to six years. There is, then, a brief period of preparation called the Third Probation before taking final or coadjutor vows. If he is to be ordained priest, this happens after final vows. Later, priests may be invited to take a fourth vow of obedience to the Holy See, and become Presbyters.

12   Pagani-Rossi, ii, p. 15.

13   *Diario della carità,* 2 September 1839.

14   Apostolic Letters are official documents of the Holy See signed by the Pope and addressed to a specific entity such as a Religious Congregation.

15   Trans., Pagani, *Life,* p. 220.

16   *Ep.Compl.,* vii, 3864 and 4024.

17   John Wesley, born 1703, died 1791. Wesley was the founder of Methodism. Like Wesley, Gentili employed the itinerant approach, taking the Gospel message directly to the people.

18   John Henry Newman, *An Essay on the Development of Christian Doctrine.* London: Sheed & Ward, 1960.

19   Leetham, *Rosmini,* p. 321. Newman reported that Rosmini said he was a little shy of meeting him since his Latin was poor and he knew no English.

20   Pagani, *Life,* p. 227.

21   *Ep.Compl.,* viii, 4468.

22   Leetham, *Rosmini,* p. 275.

Chapter Fifteen

Controversy, 1841–1843

It is virtually impossible to write seriously on theological or philosophical subjects without getting embroiled in controversy. This is not necessarily a bad thing. The range and sophistication of human learning flourishes through argument and debate. A gifted man like Antonio Rosmini argued his corner with vigour and was perfectly prepared to debate with those who did not agree with him.

Rosmini sometimes himself indulges in polemical writings against authoritative writers. The list of his published works contains several examples: for instance, Melchiorre Gioia, an economist and philosopher, wrote a book on contemporary morals which Rosmini criticised vigorously. Gioia dismissed Rosmini as an 'Ostragoth'; Rosmini replied in kind calling Gioia a 'charlatan'. It was Rosmini's forthright pamphlet critical of Gioia which had made such a favourable impression on Pope Pius VIII.[1]

On the other hand there were plenty of people in Italy who disagreed with Rosmini. These controversial tussles fall into two categories: those out in the open – debates, discussions among learned commentators and in journals; and those in the shadows which came from hostile, usually anonymous, writers.

A good example of the former was his controversy with his fellow priest-philosopher, Vincenzo Gioberti (1801–1852). Gioberti was born in Turin and was an almost exact contemporary. They are often bracketed together in the list of patriots who contributed towards the *Risorgimento*, the successful movement to unify Italy. They are called 'neo-Guelphs', patriotic Catholics who desired to see Italy unified but under the presidency of the Pope.

Gioberti was much more of a political activist than Rosmini, and for that reason, like many Italian patriots of that period, he was driven into exile. While in France and Belgium, he launched into philosophical writings, and is known as an Ontologist. Ontologism proposes that the human mind is capable of direct intuitive knowledge of God. Ontologists argue that God and divine ideas are the first object of our intelligence. Rosmini on the other hand held that the first object of the human mind is the idea of being. While this primary human intuition is God-given, it is not identical with God and so Rosmini readily recognized that the human intellect is always imperfect and limited, and thus is never a direct or transparent gateway to God. It is therefore a mistake, indeed a slander, to call Rosmini an Ontologist.

Gioberti, in his earliest writings, is very respectful of Rosmini's teaching in the *New Essay on the Origin of Ideas*. Later, however, he argues vigorously that Rosmini is at fault, and in 1845 published a work of 400 pages called *The Philosophical Errors of Antonio Rosmini*. Rosmini was at first content that his allies should respond on his behalf, in particular Tommaseo. Eventually, however, he did publish a brief rebuttal: he summarises Gioberti's arguments in a series of syllogisms, then proceeds to systematically demolish each of them.

This controversy was all very gentlemanly, and both combatants declared respect for the sincerity and integrity of the other. When eventually in 1848 Gioberti returned to Piedmont and actually met Rosmini, he became once again an ardent admirer. He says: 'When once I had made Rosmini's acquaintance, I could not but lament the bitterness of what I had written: and I too, with Italy itself, began to reverence such great wisdom united with so much virtue.'[2] Later, Gioberti's philosophical writings were placed on the Index by Pope Pius IX.

Rosmini and his Adversaries

Sadly, scholars are not always as polite or charitable in their criticisms of each other. In 1839 Rosmini published his *Treatise on Moral Conscience*, and it aroused a storm. While Rosmini proposed various distinctions which were at variance with principles held by some contemporary moralists, especially some members of the Society of Jesus, it was the venom and ferocity of the attack on his orthodoxy and on his good name which brought considerable suffering on Rosmini and on his religious family. The attack was largely anonymous but it soon became evident that the chief protagonists were Jesuits.

During the process of approval of the Institute by the Holy See, strong opposition had been voiced by a Jesuit, Fr Zecchinelli.[3] At the time Rosmini wrote: 'How little did I expect to find enmity where I had looked for brotherly love.'[4] Up to this time Rosmini's dealings with the Jesuits had always been fraternal and free from controversy – hence his sense of shock and sadness. It was a presage of what was to come.

Rumours began to circulate in Rome and elsewhere that some of Rosmini's works were under examination and might be condemned by the Holy See. There was no factual evidence for this: it was simply the rumour mill generating bile. However, the assault became more tangible in April 1841 when, simultaneously in Rome, Genoa, Lucca and Turin, there appeared a scurrilous tract: *Some Affirmations of Antonio Rosmini, priest of Rovereto, with a few Reflections* by Eusebio Cristiano.

It was a private publication. *Eusebio Cristiano* was a pseudonym.[5] But the fact that the pamphlet appeared spontaneously in several different cities suggests a coordinated assault. Several of Rosmini's friends at once jumped to his defence. He himself did not manage to obtain a copy for some weeks. The pamphlet claimed to be protecting readers from Rosmini's false and heretical views, which were corrupted by the influence of Calvin, Luther, Baius, Jansenius and others. He was described as 'blind, a liar, brazen'; his words were 'perverse and deceptive'.

Rosmini wrote to Cardinal Tardini of Genoa: 'I am most willing to retract should I have erred. But if I find no errors but mere misunderstandings of my meaning as interpreted by this anonymous writer, I will spare no effort to remove any possible cause of this interpretation.'[6] And to a friend in Rome, Fr Paolo Barola, he said:

> This war is not made against me in particular but against the Institute of Charity. The secret cry of those who think themselves powerful is: 'Come, let us cunningly oppress him' [Jeremiah] ... The Lord permits this evil so as to draw from it some greater good: I thank Him with a joyful heart ... Not a single one of the accusations levelled against me is true. One after another they are a string of calumnies astutely pieced together.[7]

Rosmini decided he must reply to Eusebio, so in August he published an extensive reply, *Answer to the so-called Eusebio Cristiano*. He is scathing in his refutation, but he also takes the opportunity to restate the Catholic teaching regarding Original Sin, misrepresented in the pamphlet. His language shocked some of his friends such as Mellerio. In defence, he wrote to Mellerio:

> In my reply I followed your advice and moderated some of my expressions which were rather harsh – though I gather you still feel that the tone is too bitter ... my opponent first offended against me and wounded me in my most vulnerable spot which is the integrity of my faith.
>   ... I believe that the way I adopted is a way of doing good to my opponent. It is the way used by our Lord and all the saints ... Our Divine Master was no less meek, no less humble, when he called Herod *a fox*, or the Pharisees *blind hypocrites*, than when he prayed for those who crucified him ... There are many ways of showing charity; and sometimes it means that one has to call the blind *blind* and the fox *fox*.[8]

The anonymous opposition was not long in retaliating. Before the end of 1841 three more pamphlets appeared, reiterating the arguments of *Eusebio* and criticising the distinction between sin and guilt, which it was claimed was an invention by Rosmini.[9] Rosmini responded at once to this with an article *The Ideas of Sin and Guilt explained.*

Throughout 1842 the controversy raged. Since it had become a more general attack on everything he had written, more of Rosmini's followers were again prompted to fight back in his defence. Rosmini's philosophical works were by this time taught in seminaries and universities all over the northern part of Italy. The rumours and slanders also multiplied: his works, it was said, were due to be examined in Rome, especially the *Treatise on Conscience*. It was even hinted that a condemnation had already been issued.

There is no doubt that all this evil gossip was harmful to Rosmini's reputation and to the good standing of the Institute. Some of his most powerful supporters hesitated about him: Mellerio withdrew financial support to the College in Domodossola. In England, Ambrose Phillips and another wealthy convert, Sibthorp, stopped their donations to the building of the noviciate at Ratcliffe.

Rosmini's friends in Rome assured him that the Pope's trust in him was unwavering. Cardinal Castracane wrote: 'The Holy Father has not changed his opinion of you, whatever people may say ... he knows your high and solid faith and the purity of your doctrine which does not deserve the imputations which are made against it.'[10]

Intervention by Rome

Nevertheless, it was high time for the Holy See to intervene, and the opportunity was given by the appearance in Paris early in 1843 of a letter in the newspaper *L'Ami de Religion*, written by Fr Giuseppe Rozaven, Generalitial Assistant of the Society of Jesus. Rozaven compared Rosmini's situation with that of Père Lamennais, recently condemned by the Church:

'We know of a writer who was even more celebrated than Rosmini and who also enjoyed great esteem. What has become of him?' The inference of this remark is obvious – that Rosmini was destined to fall as Lamennais had fallen – and when Pope Gregory read it he was incensed. He at once (1 March 1843) called a meeting of cardinals to consult their opinion. As a result, he imposed silence on both parties in a letter sent directly to Fr Roothaan, the General of the Jesuits, and to Rosmini, requesting that the ban extend to all members of both Societies.[11]

Rosmini received this letter with relief. He at once withdrew some controversial writings of his own which were in the process of publication, and he communicated the papal ban to his brethren. He wrote to the Pope expressing his gratitude. He also wrote to Castracane: 'the decision which the Pope has taken is sure to produce some good, at least provisionally.'[12] That final word 'provisionally' speaks volumes: Rosmini was under no illusions that the storm was over. It was a welcome respite, but the forces which were seeking to destroy him were in remission rather than defeated. It did mean, however, that for a few years Rosmini was free to continue his philosophical and theological writing in peace.

What was it that his opponents found objectionable in his *Treatise on Conscience*? First, Rosmini was critical of the prevailing theory of *Probabilism*, which was taught by some Jesuit moralists. This school taught that you could follow a ruling of conscience if it was 'probably true': in other words as long as some moralists held it. Rosmini maintains that you must always seek the best way of acting morally. He believes that God has given us the light of reason to illumine our minds when seeking a solution to a moral dilemma. We are always obliged to follow what appears to be the optimum pathway, because that is the way Providence points us. Rosmini is anything but a laxist in his teachings.

He also makes a distinction between sin and guilt. Sin is a disorderly action contrary to truth and goodness; whereas guilt is incurred when we deliberately choose to act immorally. A guilty action is always an act of the will. The traditional teaching of the Church on Original Sin, which Rosmini supports, refers to a state which humanity inherits. There is no guilt on our part, until we choose to give in to that weakness of human nature consequent on Original Sin.

Rosmini was contributing to an ongoing debate in moral theology. If people disagreed with him, he was quite prepared to argue the point. But an anonymous campaign of denigration embracing all his teachings was a quite different matter. It was a form of persecution, and what grieved him most was that it damaged his Religious family. Vocations slowed to a trickle while his orthodoxy was in question. The works of the Institute were threatened. So he was hugely grateful for the relief afforded by the Papal decree, even though he was fearful that it would not last.

Notes

1   See above, page 86.
2   Pagani, *Life,* p. 231.
3   See above, p. 144.
4   Pagani, *Life*, p. 208.
5   Eusebio Cristiano's real name was Pie Melia (1800–1883). He entered the Society of Jesus in 1815 and left in 1853. Later he moved to live in London, where he died.
6   *Ep.Compl.*, vii, 4260.
7   *Ep.Compl.*, vii, 4268.
8   *Ep.Compl.*, vii, 4329.
9   Bessero Belti, *The Rosminian Question*, p. 13.
10 Leetham, *Rosmini,* p. 244.
11 Fr Roothaan denied that Eusebio Cristiano was a Jesuit – but only on the grounds that no Jesuit had submitted this book to him for permission to go to print (Bozzetti, *op. cit.*).
12 *Ep.Compl.*, viii, 4745.

Chapter Sixteen

Interlude, 1843–1848

The following five years were among the most tranquil of Rosmini's life. The storm had abated and his two Institutes continued to flourish and expand. The English mission especially was prospering. He was able to appoint two of his most able companions as Fathers Provincial: Giovanni Battista Pagani in England and Francesco Puecher in Italy. Relieved of some of the burden of direct rule, Rosmini launched into what was possibly the most fruitful and creative time of his life as a thinker and writer.

Nevertheless, he was still sensitive to the dangers which continued to threaten the Institute. He wrote again to Cardinal Castracane expressing his concerns (12 April 1843).[1] He quotes a letter where the head of the Jesuits, Fr Roothaan, sought to excuse himself of any responsibility for the Jesuit persecution on the grounds that some of his subjects wrote in languages he did not understand. It seems that he did not accept this excuse as valid. Rosmini also questioned whether the Pope had done enough to secure justice for the Institute:

These writers have gone beyond merely criticising me: they have in my opinion committed formal errors. The greatest threat to the world today is Rationalism and they have trespassed into it, by exalting reason to the detriment of grace.

I hope that the Holy Father will not leave the job [of silencing them] half done. The time is coming when we will not have the present Pope. Hence the urgency for the Institute to receive a complete justification.

In another letter (to Gentili in England, in reply to the latter's strong support during the controversy) Rosmini said he was convinced that *Eusebio Cristiano*'s book would be condemned and finish up on the Index.[2] Rosmini had a strong sense of truth and justice, so he was dissatisfied that the evil attacks on the Institute and on himself had not been resolved. At the same time he accepted the suffering that this was causing as part of the providence of God.

Pope Gregory continued to express his personal esteem for Rosmini and his religious family even though there was never to be any formal condemnation of those who had pilloried him. In 1845 the Pope said to Fr Luigi Passavalli, a priest from Trent: 'Rosmini is the greatest philosopher in the Catholic Church at the present day.' And he singled out the Institute of Charity for special praise at a meeting of Cardinals that same year.[3]

Rosmini did receive some heartening support from various priests of the Society of Jesus who dissociated themselves from the libellous attacks of some of their colleagues. In particular, a Fr Perrone, whose name had been associated with the 1843 letter of Rozaven in the *Ami de Religion,* came to visit him in Stresa, pleading that his name had been taken in vain and laying the blame squarely on Fr Roothaan and his Assistant, Rozaven. However, what really did serve to allay the storm came from an unexpected quarter. Gioberti published, in 1847, a book called *Il Gesuita Moderno (The Modern Jesuit)* strongly attacking the Jesuits and as a result provoking a new outbreak of persecution against Jesuit priests in various countries. A group of Jesuits was driven out of Switzerland and fled across the Simplon Pass. Rosmini hastened to give them sanctuary at Stresa. This gesture was greatly appreciated by others in the Society. In fact, Rosmini was very critical of Gioberti's book; but the vibes it created served to take the heat off him.

In June 1846, Gregory XVI died. At the ensuing conclave Cardinal Giovanni Mastai-Ferreti was elected, taking the name of Pius IX. He was fifty-four years old, and was destined to reign as Pope until 1878, thus ushering in the longest pontificate in the history of the Church. Rosmini at once wrote offering the filial obedience of the Institute of Charity to the new Pope and received a very gracious reply.[4]

Rosmini felt the death of Pope Gregory as a major blow. To Mellerio he wrote that the Institute had lost a father: 'Imagine what must be my personal sorrow at the loss of one who always gave me such proofs of special trust and affection.'[5] It was the end of an era.

Verona

Another apostolate in Northern Italy which showed great promise was prompted by the Bishop of Verona who insisted that the Institute establish a presence in that city. Verona is a beautiful place on the Adige River some 100 km south of Rovereto. It too lay in Austrian territory. Indeed the Austrians were busy at this time repairing the fortifications, so that Verona became one of the 'Quadrilateral' of forts, the military base for their army of occupation under Marshal Radetzky.[6]

This strong Army presence attracted a number of German speakers to settle, and it was this that prompted his friend Bishop Grasser to invite Rosmini in 1832 to send a German-speaking priest to look after these newcomers. Rosmini saw this invitation as a providential sign that the Institute might establish itself in Verona. He made it a condition that the chaplain must be accompanied by another priest companion and a lay brother, so that the nucleus of a stable community might be established. The bishop agreed.

This eventually bore fruit the following year when Rosmini himself came to the city to help set up a new house. The appointed chaplain was Fr Antonio Oberrauch, a novice in the house at Trent. Two other religious accompanied him. This first foundation had something of a chequered career. The Austrian authorities as usual were difficult: it was said that the Imperial government did not favour new religious congregations. The bishop, although very kindly disposed towards

Rosmini, was inclined to dither; Rosmini himself became preoccupied with the Rovereto parish and the problems at Trent, so he could not give the new foundation his best attention.

At the end of 1835, Rosmini had to close the house in Trent and he himself withdrew from the parish of Rovereto. Some of the brethren from Trent went to Verona to join the little community while their future was determined. Most of them left the Institute, but some determined to stay, and one of these was Giovanni Boselli who had completed his noviciate at Trent.

When Boselli arrived in Verona in January 1836, there was not a lot for him to do in the parish, since Oberrauch, being the German-speaker, was fully occupied with the care of the Germans. However, it was not long before Boselli found himself busily employed in the parish of San Zeno in another part of the city, teaching the faith and also caring for the sick. There had been quite a serious outbreak of cholera.

His zeal attracted the admiration of the elderly Archpriest, Fr Bartolomeo Gualtieri.[7] San Zeno was a parish of 4,600; there was a lot of poverty and it was needy. The parish church was the ancient Basilica of San Zeno. It was – and still is – one of the most beautiful mediaeval churches in Italy.

Gualtieri wanted to make provision for the care of the parish after his death, and was looking for a religious congregation to help provide it. He was prepared to leave all his money for this purpose. When he eventually suggested the Institute of Charity to Msgr Grasser, the latter was delighted and gave his approval at once. The old priest therefore made his will accordingly. For some time, Boselli and another Rosminian priest, Giacomo Mazzi (himself a Veronese), assisted Gualtieri in the parish.

A formal approach was made to Rosmini during 1837, and he saw that at last here was an opportunity to make a more stable foundation. Unfortunately the vacillations of the bishop, his death in 1839, and the constant obstruction of the Austrian authorities put this plan on hold. Grasser's successor, Msgr Aurelio Mutti, was also favourably disposed towards the Institute. But it took several years before Rosmini was able to make a proper foundation.[8]

In July 1845, Rosmini sent back two priests to assist in the parish. Again it was Boselli and Mazzi. Mazzi was a skilled negotiator, and he spent some time and energy with the Church and Imperial authorities to get them to agree to the Institute being established in the city. Finally, in December 1846, Vienna agreed to a Rosminian foundation at St Zeno's.

Early in 1847 a community of six priests was assembled, with Fr Giacomo Molinari as parish priest. Rosmini's intention was to set up a noviciate alongside the community house. The new Pope Pius IX granted the parish to the Rosminians in May; in March 1848 the diocesan Curia made it over to the Institute in perpetuity. The good work of the priests at St Zeno's gave great satisfaction both to the people and to the bishop.

However, this happy outcome was not to last. The Austrian government never gave the foundation its final sanction. After war broke out in 1848, Rosmini's part in mobilising Italian and Church opinion against the continuing Austrian presence in Northern Italy sounded the death knell for a Rosminian presence in any of the Austrian territories. The Imperial Commissary issued a decree closing the Rosminian house in October 1849, but it was not put into effect immediately. Molinari eventually departed in November 1850, followed by the other brethren two months later. They had been there barely five years.

There is a postscript to this sorry affair. In 1866 Lombardy and Venezia became part of the newly united Kingdom of Italy, and Austrian domination finally came to an end. The Bishop of Verona at the time, Msgr Luigi di Canossa, wrote to the then Father General Bertetti inviting the Rosminians to return. Sadly, the offer was turned down because Bertetti did not have the men available at the time.

The English Mission

In England both the Rosminian Fathers and the Sisters were extending their works and attracting good vocations. The Sisters established a noviciate in Loughborough and the Fathers established one at Ratcliffe. This was quickly followed by a College for boys on the same site, which opened its doors in 1847.[9]

But perhaps the most spectacular new development was the launching of parish missions. In this the indefatigable Luigi Gentili was the initiator. In May 1842 Gentili left Ambrose Phillips' house at Grace Dieu and moved to the new parish in nearby Loughborough, taking charge of it when Pagani was briefly recalled to Italy. He launched himself into this new apostolate with his usual zeal.[10]

In March 1843 Gentili, aided by the other Rosminian priests at Loughborough, initiated the first ever parish Mission in England. It lasted eight days, and the Vicar Apostolic of York, Bishop Briggs, joined the team for the final days. Sixty-three Protestants were received into the Church and many children baptised. A few weeks later the exercise was repeated at the nearby village of Shepshed, yielding a similar harvest.

This large number of conversions caused Rosmini to query whether these converts had received adequate instruction (a concern also expressed by Bishop Wiseman). Rosmini had been meticulous in his own catechesis, both to children and adults, when he was a parish priest himself. Instant conversion was something of a dubious achievement, often claimed by Methodists and other dissenting groups. However, Gentili preached his missions in established parishes where there would be plenty of opportunity for catechetical follow-up (what is now termed the *mystagogia*). The descendants of many of Gentili's converts are still to be found living in Leicestershire today.[11]

Parish missions had originated in France with St Vincent de Paul and his Congregation of the Mission in the seventeenth century, with the special aim of re-evangelising country districts where faith had languished. They were adopted with enthusiasm in the following century by St Alphonsus di Liguori, predominantly in the countryside around Naples. They consisted of daily sermons in the parish church, celebrations of the sacraments, especially Penance, processions, and solemn liturgies. This became a principal work of St Alphonsus' new congregation, the Redemptorists.

Gentili was clearly cut out for this sort of work, so in September 1844 Rosmini relieved him of all parish responsibilities to engage full time in preaching parish missions. A young English priest, Fr Moses Furlong, was appointed to be his assistant. Furlong was not only a good preacher, but was also robust enough to stand up to the rigours of almost continuous missioning.

Rosmini followed the course of his disciples' missionary endeavours with the keenest interest and support. He had published a *Manuale dell'Esercitatore* (Preacher's Manual) in 1839, and Gentili used it. All over the country he introduced devotions to Mary, especially during the month of May, and the Forty Hours Devotion before the Blessed Sacrament. He himself often spent long hours in the confessional, even throughout the night.

Initially, missions were given throughout the north of England. Gentili and Furlong were often supported in the north by the Vicar Apostolic, Bishop Briggs. Between 21 September 1845 and the end of that year they preached ten missions (of 98 days' duration overall), often concluding in one place with Mass in the morning and starting again in another town that very same evening. It was a punishing schedule, and ultimately this contributed to Gentili's early death. In 1846 and 1847 the mission field spread to London, although churches were smaller and numbers attending were fewer.

Up to the time of his death, Gentili was to preach no fewer than fifty-three public missions up and down England and Ireland, as well as retreats for clergy and religious, and many individual retreats which he directed.[12] He was often supported by the local bishop, who sometimes came to close the mission or help in its direction. This ceaseless activity around the country was greatly assisted by the rapid extension of the rail network, growing like wildfire in England during those years.

Rosmini was constant in his support and encouragement for Gentili's missionary work. Early in the piece he waxes quite lyrically: 'May God bless your labours. May he grant you an abundant harvest, descendants more numerous than the stars in heaven, the sands of the sea!'[15] His encouragement and careful counselling of this tumultuous character merit special attention:

> God does not expect of you more than you can give: and you can give only what obedience allows. To be dissatisfied over this because you would love to do more is a sort of temerity. It is presumptuous, a lack of trust in God.[16]

Trying to rein in Gentili's enthusiasm was something of a vain hope.

Gentili's activities did not always earn his Superior's unstinting support. There was a fierce exchange between the two during 1844 over whether or not a parish should be accepted in the city of Birmingham.[17] The local Ordinary, Bishop Walsh, had requested it. Gentili thought that accepting a new work there would harm the existing parish in Loughborough. But instead of putting his case to his Superior, Father Pagani, he spoke instead to Ambrose Phillips, who at once wrote to the Bishop threatening to withdraw financial support if this new parish were to take the Rosminians away from Leicestershire. He also wrote protestingly to Pagani, threatening to withdraw financial support for Ratcliffe College, even saying that he would cease being an Ascribed member.

Pagani was forced to concur. It shows how much power wealthy patrons had in those days, and how the clergy were expected to dance to their tune. When Rosmini heard about this affair he came down on Gentili like a ton of bricks: it is reminiscent of the spat they had had years previously while Gentili was still a student in Rome. Rosmini writes:

I have received your letter of 3 April in which you tell me what you have said and done with regard to the negotiations over the Birmingham mission [parish] for the discharging of your conscience, so that if I find you at fault I may give you an appropriate penance.

Unfortunately I find you very much at fault, to my immense regret. The substance of your letter is that for the good of our Institute in England you have manipulated things in such a fashion as to bring to nothing a work arranged in its entirety by your Superior ... How could your conscience allow you to fight against the work of your Superior? You reply that you acted so as to ward off a grave danger which threatened the Institute.

But had you the authority to act in this way? Why is it that you did not hold firmly to the principle of faith, which assures you that the one who obeys is never mistaken? Ah, my dear Don Luigi, open your eyes: recognise how imprudently you have acted, how you have gone against both the virtue and the spirit of your vow of obedience. Ask God's forgiveness and promise Him sincerely that you will amend your ways.

... In addition you made use of culpable means to further your intention making clear to important people your disapproval of what your Superior had decided upon, and in this way lessening his credibility and authority, and reputing him to be a man of little prudence, whereas in truth he is worthy of all respect. Good heavens! Who could have believed that the devil could deceive you under the appearance of good, to this extent?[18]

Gentili was devastated by Rosmini's letter, and on receiving it he was unable to celebrate Mass or even to pray for a couple of days. He wrote back at once apologising and acknowledging everything he had been accused of. Rosmini, of course, at once forgave him: 'Your letter took a great weight off my heart. I had been truly distressed by what had happened; but now I am fully consoled.'[19]

This episode has been treated at some length because it demonstrates how firm Rosmini could be with the follies of his subjects – but also how instantly forgiving. It was not quite the end of the affair, since Rosmini reminds him later how both Bishop Walsh and Bishop Wiseman had been offended by what he had done and therefore they too deserved an apology.

Gentili later grumbled to Rosmini that he was always finding fault with him. In fact, Rosmini was usually most encouraging. But he was careful not to appoint Gentili vice-Superior in England, giving that job to one of the Englishmen, Fr Peter Hutton. He knew his men. He understood their gifts and their shortcomings. He made his decisions accordingly

During 1848, the focus of Gentili's mission changed to Dublin, where the enthusiasm of the people was even greater, and perhaps as a result of persecution and poverty the harvest of souls was most abundant. It was there, in 1848, that he contracted typhoid fever while preaching a mission, and died after a brief illness on 26 September. He had made such an impact on the Catholic people of Dublin that his funeral was a triumph reminiscent of that of the great patriot Daniel O'Connell a few years earlier. He was buried in the patriot plot in Glesnevin cemetery, near the grave of O'Connell himself.[13] His death did not put an end to the preaching of missions, and Furlong especially continued in this apostolate, aided by Lockhart and others.

Another factor making this form of apostolate so urgent and important was the terrible famine that afflicted Ireland during these years. Successive failures of the potato harvest caused starvation on a huge scale, and hundreds of thousands of poor Irish were forced to emigrate to the industrial cities of northern Britain as well as the United States of America. It was to these northern cities that Gentili primarily went. The extraordinary and wilful inaction of the British government contributed to the disaster, which eventually cost about a million lives.

Rosmini's response to the Irish crisis was characteristic. In December 1846 he wrote to Pagani:

> *Caritas Christi urget nos.* I have read in the public press the heart-rending descriptions of the famine afflicting the poor Catholics of Ireland. My dear brother, we belong to the

Institute *of Charity,* and are we to stand aside, indifferent and sitting on our hands at the sight of the evils which oppress our Irish brothers and sisters? Is there nothing we can do for them?

It is in times of great calamity that we have to exert the full force of that charity burning in our hearts: we have to make every effort, to the limit of our powers and beyond, trusting in the providence and goodness of God ... You who are on the spot will be able to decide what is best ... if you have to go about England begging for alms, do that![14]

Rosmini himself collected a huge sum of money in Italy – over 1,000 pounds sterling – for famine relief. He was normally a prudent and moderate person, but when conditions demanded it he would throw caution to the winds. He wrote widely to drum up support in Italy for famine relief.

Writings

Of the many works which Rosmini wrote during these years prior to 1848, three stand out. In 1845 he published the *Theodicy.* It was a subject which had preoccupied him twenty years earlier – Pagani-Rossi uses the term 'inebriated' about his fascination with this subject![20] 'Theodicy' means the providential action of God in the world. The word was first coined by the German philosopher Leibniz, describing his attempt to reconcile the benevolence of God with the existence of evil.

Rosmini demonstrates how the world is ruled by an intelligence who must be God. So how can we explain evil? Moral evil is evidently caused by the wilfulness of human beings. But Rosmini asserts that the very existence of virtue and the constant promptings of conscience are evidence of the direct influence of God. Rosmini even goes so far as to say that evil actions in the world tend to reinforce the certainty of God's presence. It is God who provides hope and God who prompts repentance and change.

A little later Rosmini started work on another book, which he also had been working on and thinking about for many years: his *Psychology*, eventually published in two fat volumes in 1850. For him, it is the science of the whole human being – the science of the soul. In 1832 he had published a volume called *Anthropology in the service of Moral Science*, followed a few years later by the first volume of his *Supernatural Anthropology*. The *Psychology* is really a continuation of these earlier works.

Rosmini was interested in how the instincts and behaviour of a human being develop, and he followed the various rather primitive experiments that were already happening. He asserted that ultimately the powers and capabilities of a person are subject to his or her intelligence. You cannot chop a person up into animal and human segments. Ultimately we are all one, and it is the mind which controls all our actions. How this happens is the field of psychology.

There is a characteristic unity in Rosmini's thinking. Science, philosophy, theology, spirituality are all interrelated. The influence and benign action of God is always present. This principle is never more evident than what is perhaps the greatest of all Rosmini's philosophical explorations, his *Theosophy*. Pagani-Rossi calls it the 'summit of Rosmini's genius'.[21]

It is a huge synthesis of everything that had gone before. Rosmini divides the work in three: *Ontology*, which studies the nature of being; *Natural Theology* which affirms the actions of God in the natural world; and *Cosmology* which studies the natural world itself. Up to 1854 there were six published volumes with associated essays. It was still a work in progress at his death.

Rosmini resembles St Augustine in the sense that his speculations always lead him back to God and God's action in the physical world, especially in human society. The eighteenth century empiricists deliberately excluded the idea of God from their speculations. But for Rosmini that would be to ignore the centre of everything. Every experience of our lives eventually in faith leads back to God. Therefore it is difficult to categorise Rosmini as primarily a philosopher or a theologian. Like Augustine, he is a great and original Christian thinker.

During these years Rosmini also wrote on a host of other topics, especially on political matters. In 1841 he completed his monumental *Philosophy of Right*, in two large volumes. His political interests were not just speculative. He also produced a model *Constitution* for a united Italy. And he was emboldened by the succession of an apparently more liberal Pope to finally publish his *Five Wounds of the Church*.[22]

The variety of his interests is illustrated by three publications in 1847–48: *An Essay on Communism and Socialism*; *On the Goods of Christian Marriage*; and a reflection on the Magnificat entitled *The Canticle of the Virgin Mary proclaimed.* Sometimes Rosmini would do research for others who asked his help. He prepared material on the Koran for Cardinal Castracane, entitled *Testimony of the Koran to the Blessed Virgin Mary*.[23]

At this time he lived in the house at Stresa where the noviciate continued to flourish, to the degree that the building had to be extended to accommodate greater numbers. Many of the vocations were very able men attracted to Rosmini by the wisdom of his writings. An example is Lorenzo Gastaldi, a priest theologian in Turin who had defended Rosmini in the controversies of 1843–44. He became attracted by the idea of a vocation to the religious life and came to Stresa to try his vocation. After noviciate Rosmini sent him to strengthen the Rosminian presence in England. Gastaldi eventually chose to leave the Institute and return to the diocesan priesthood, but he always remained close. In 1867 he became bishop of Saluzzo, then Archbishop of Turin (1871–1883), as well as attending the First Vatican Council.

While concentrating his mind on study and the following of his first vocation to write for the Church, Rosmini hardly moved from Stresa except to preach the odd sermon or give a retreat. He directed the members of the Institute and the Sisters through his vast correspondence. He was especially diligent in the support he gave to Sr. Giovanna Antonietti, who often found the burden of governing the Sisters of Providence almost beyond her. He was always ready to encourage anyone in the two Institutes, irrespective of their position. One is tempted to wonder whether Rosmini had not become too settled in his life. Stresa is one of the most beautiful places on earth, a perfect place indeed for writing books. Gentili pressed him to come and visit the mission in England, but he didn't do so (though he was planning such a trip when he became ill in 1854). One could think that the fortunes of the Verona mission might have been happier if he had gone personally to direct and support by his presence.

One should not, however, begrudge Rosmini this time of comparative calm. It was not to last. 1848 dawned, the 'year of revolutions' in Europe. Rosmini received a call he felt he could not refuse, and it caused the biggest and most fateful 'revolution' to date in his personal life.

Notes

1   *Ep.Compl.,* viii, 4773.
2   *Ep.Compl.*, vii, 4379.
3   Pagani, *Life*, p. 247.
4   *Ep.Compl.*, ix, 5729.
5   *Ep.Compl.,* ix, 5626.
6   The 'Quadrilateral' were a group of four fortified towns – Mantua, Peschiera, Verona and Legnano – lying between Lombardy and Venetia.
7   Pagani, *Life*, p. 249.
8   Pagani, *Life*, pp. 249–250.
9   Pagani, *Life*, pp. 252–253.
10 Pagani, *Life*, p. 252.
11 See *Dissertation* by Cambridge history scholar Elizabeth Holt. She attributes Gentili's success in attracting new converts to Catholicism to the fact that at a time of serious poverty he went out to the poor in the countryside and the backstreets, and accompanied his preaching with active material charity. The essay is entitled *Catholic Conversions in mid-Nineteenth Century Leicestershire.* See also Leetham, *Luigi Gentili,* p. 130.
12 Belsito, *Witness* (special edition, No. 24), pp. 88–99.

13   Later, Gentili's remains were transferred to Omeath, on Carlingford Lough, where there was a Rosminian school, and there is now an impressive Calvary next to his grave, much venerated by local people.
14   *Ep.Compl.*, ix, 5775.
15   *Ep.Compl.*, vii, 4178.
16   *Ep.Compl.*, vii, 4236.
17   Belsito, *Witness,* op.cit., pp. 81–82.
18   *Ep.Compl.*, viii, 5006.
19   *Ep.Compl.*, viii, 5021.
20   Pagani-Rossi, ii, 137.
21   Pagani-Rossi, ii, 150.
22   See above pp. 108–114.
23   Published in Rome in 1904 by Desclée.

Chapter Seventeen

Mission to Rome, 1848

*'A good priest ... warm of heart
and weak of intellect'*

In October 1847 Prince Metternich, the Austrian Chancellor,
wrote this to his ambassador in Paris about the new Pope Pius
IX:

> Each day the Pope shows himself more lacking in any practical
> sense. Born and raised in a liberal family, he has been formed
> in a bad school; a good priest, he has never turned his mind
> towards matters of government.
> Warm of heart and weak of intellect, he has allowed himself
> to be ensnared, since assuming the tiara, in a net from which
> he no longer knows how to disentangle himself, and if matters
> follow their natural course he will be driven out of Rome.[1]

This devastating judgment on the part of Europe's greatest
statesman, even though bitter and exaggerated, contains
more than a grain of truth. For Metternich, the conclave of
1846 had produced the one unacceptable result – a liberal
Pope. Metternich watched on in alarm as the new Pope
proceeded on a series of policies absolutely in contrast to
those of his reactionary predecessor Gregory XVI, and which
Metternich judged to be ill-advised and dangerous.

Pius began by issuing a general amnesty, which resulted
almost at once in the return to Rome of many radicals and
revolutionaries who had been locked up or driven out by
Gregory's government. Metternich commented dryly: 'God
never grants amnesties; God pardons.'[2] Pius followed up in

quick succession with a series of reforms: a commission to build railways (forbidden by Pope Gregory on moral grounds); the provision of gas lighting in the streets of Rome; the setting up of an agricultural Institute, and the introduction of laymen into the government of the Papal States. All these moves were popular with the general public.

He also initiated a form of civic guard for the Papal territories. This at once set the alarm bells ringing for the Austrians, who responded by extending their military occupation of the town of Ferrara in the Romagna (inside Papal territory). Pius reacted strongly, even threatening to excommunicate them. Metternich was infuriated but he was forced to withdraw. There were, in his opinion, really only two parties in Italy at that time: the party of reaction and the party of revolution. There was no middle way. In acting against the party of reaction Pius was aligning himself with revolution. He would suffer the consequences.

In fact, Pius became an overnight hero with all the progressive forces in Italy and the darling of more liberal governments throughout Europe. The cry of the street mobs was 'Viva Pio Nono'; even the Master of Balliol College, Oxford, declared the new Pope to be 'a capital fellow' – praise indeed![3]

A visitor to Rome in April 1847 was the French layman Frederic Ozanam, founder of the Society of St Vincent de Paul.[4] He describes what was an almost nightly occurrence in the city streets. Pius had just announced the calling of a *Consulta*, a representative body from around the provincial areas of the Papal States. An evening procession was called in celebration.

> ... We were informed that the people were getting ready to thank the Pope for his new edict, and that there would be a beautiful *fête aux flambaux*[5] ... The rendezvous was the Piazza del Populo. Torches were being distributed and those who took them ranged themselves ten abreast ... The triumphal march opened with lines of men with lighted torches, then came the proclamation of the Secretary of State Cardinal Gizzi announcing the *Consulta*, printed on white

linen and carried aloft like a large banner; then a band of military music; then a dense column of men bearing torches – some six thousand in all.

... Nothing was more touching than to see walking side by side workmen in their blouses, priests in their soutanes, many of them with white hair, and all united in the same feeling, expressed in the same cry, *Viva Pio Nono! Viva Gizzi!* A profound silence descended on the crowd when they reached the Quirinal Palace and the Pope came out to give his blessing.

Ozanam belonged to the French liberal Catholic party, founded by Lamennais and carried on by the writer Count Charles Montalambert and the celebrated Dominican preacher Père Jean-Baptiste Lacordaire; so, naturally, he was filled with delight at this unprecedented experience.[6]

A surge of enthusiasm for the new liberal Pope spread throughout Europe and ignited reform parties in practically every country. No wonder Metternich was so alarmed, and he would have been even more so had he foreseen that this groundswell of popular opinion would eventually trigger his own downfall.

1848, Year of Revolution

The year 1848 is unique in European history. In January a revolt broke out in Palermo, Sicily, against the Neapolitan Bourbon rule.[7] It was relatively successful, and the following month in Naples King Ferdinand II was forced to grant a constitution to the whole kingdom. This local disturbance triggered the spread of revolutionary movements like wildfire across Europe, affecting some fifty states. It was a totally uncoordinated series of events not destined to bring about decisive change; eventually reaction would set in everywhere restoring old autocratic models of government.

In Paris, in March, a popular revolt finally ended the French monarchy. King Louis Phillipe abdicated, and the Second Republic was ushered in. This led to the return of the

Bonapartes in the person of Louis Napoleon, nephew of the great Emperor. He was elected President of the Assembly, and two years later he was to take on himself the title of Emperor – Napoleon III.

Across Germany there were popular demands for constitutional government in the various states, and this helped fuel pan-German nationalism. In Vienna the government of Prince Metternich was toppled. Metternich himself fled and, like many displaced and exiled political figures during the nineteenth century, took refuge in England. It was the swansong of the great Austrian after thirty years of European dominance.

In Italy also, demands for constitutional change spread across the peninsula. The presence of foreign Austrian rule in the north was again challenged. The Austrian army withdrew at once from Venice, and a republic was declared under the lawyer Daniele Manin, assisted by Rosmini's friend Niccolò Tommaseo. In Milan, after five days of popular revolt between 18 and 22 March – the celebrated *Cinque Giornate*[8] – Austrian forces under Marshal Radetzky withdrew eastward to the fortified 'Quadrilateral' of forts around the city of Verona.

There were demands for constitutional government also in Piedmont. Gioberti returned from exile to a rapturous popular acclaim. King Charles Albert hurried to grant an interim constitution known as the *Statuto*, which served as a basis for representative government. The resulting parliament became the stage for Count Camillo Benso Cavour, consummate politician and Italian statesman, who was eventually to lead Piedmont to dominance over the whole of Italy. The *Statuto*, although it fell well short of popular demands at the time, became a basis for the eventual constitution of a united Italy, and indeed remained the foundation for government up to the time of Mussolini in the twentieth century.

Aroused by this nationalistic mood, King Charles Albert declared war on Austria and led his troops into Lombardy, being welcomed in triumph in Milan. His army was supported by token forces from other Italian states, even including a detachment from the Papal States. However, the king was so incompetent as a military leader that he failed to move swiftly enough against the Austrian forces. Having been allowed to regroup and receive reinforcements from Vienna, they easily defeated the Piedmontese army at Custozza, near Verona, on 24 July. The King and his army retired chastened to Turin. He would shortly abdicate in favour of his young son, Victor Emmanuel.

Why, after all these years of apparent peace and stability, did this revolutionary movement spread so rapidly? There are many factors. The ideas of the Enlightenment demanding 'government by the people and for the people' had gradually spread among educated classes. In Italy, people resented the dominance of Austria as much as they feared the return of the French.

Aided by a literary movement led by Alessandro Manzoni, Niccolò Tommaseo and others, the Italian language began to establish itself as a *lingua franca* across most of the country. Newspapers became standard reading and provided sources of news and inspiration in the cities. Roads and railways were being built and improved, enabling people to circulate more freely. Increasing numbers of travellers from northern Europe visited Italy every year, which helped to break down insularity. A public opinion was being formed, and this tended to favour the idea of a single Italian nation.

One factor, characteristically Italian, was the influence of opera. In the cities, people of all classes patronised the opera, and the mid-nineteenth century was the golden age of Italian operatic composition. Giuseppe Verdi became something of a popular hero, and from 1840 onwards he composed a series of highly successful works. His opera *Nabucco* opened in *La Scala* opera house, Milan, in March 1842, and almost at once the famous *Chorus of the Hebrew Slaves* became a rallying song for a united Italy. Every performance was punctuated by cries of *Viva Verdi!* His name VERDI was later interpreted as an acronym for *Vittorio Emmanuele Re d'Italia* – 'Victor Emmanuel, King of Italy'.

Rosmini had always been a patriot, and this movement aroused his deeply felt nationalistic feelings. He left his mountain retreat and went to Milan immediately after the *Cinque Giornate*. There he published a political pamphlet, and met the head of the provisional government and the new Archbishop, Bartolomeo Romilli, an Italian who supported the movement for independence. He mixed again with his old literary friends like Manzoni, and this helped fuel his patriotic fervour. He wrote to a friend, Alessandro Pestalozza: 'Long live the heroic Milanese, true sons of Italy. Let us intone the canticle: *In exitu Israel de Egypto, domus Jacob de populo barbaro.*'[9]

He learnt with approval that Pope Pius was also resolved to follow the other Italian princes into constitutionalism.[10] Rosmini, however, became concerned that the Pope would simply copy other Italian states. In February he wrote to Fr Carlo Gilardi, his agent (or representative) in Rome at this time:

> I am in great anxiety about Roman affairs ... Rome should produce a work truly Roman, original, worthy of the Pontiff-king, something which might serve as a model for the whole world. I should like to propose such a constitution if asked ... Say nothing to any one unless it be to Cardinal Castracane, if God inspires you to do so.[11]

Gilardi was so inspired, and Castracane was delighted at the suggestion. Rosmini sent a draft proposal, the fruit of many years' deliberation. It sought to secure justice and the rights of property by establishing a political tribunal and proportional suffrage. The Pope expressed interest and twice said to Castracane that he would like Rosmini to come to Rome as an advisor for him. According to one biographer, Gilardi presented a bound copy of *The Five Wounds of the Church* to the Pope, who said: 'I have already read it; convey my congratulations to the Abate.'[12] On his part, Rosmini was reluctant to make a move unless he received a specific invitation from the Holy Father himself.

Summons to Turin

A summons was not long in coming, but it arrived from an unexpected source. In the chaos resulting from the April defeat of the Piedmontese army by the Austrians, the Turin government came up with a plan to solicit papal support in order to continue the war against Austria. The administration at that time was led by Gabrio Casati, a Milanese politician whom Rosmini had met following the *Cinque Giornati* in March. Casati and Gioberti, also now a member of the administration, persuaded their colleagues to entrust this mission to Rosmini.

On 31 July 1848 a letter arrived from them urging him to come to Turin. He set out at once arriving on the evening of 2 August. Next morning he met with the Council of Ministers headed by Casati. They placed before him a proposal that he should go on their behalf to ask the Pope to join an alliance of Italian states against Austria and send troops to help reinforce the Piedmontese army.

Rosmini at once protested that there was no way the Pope would agree to such a proposal. Earlier in the conflict between Piedmont and Austria the Pope had withdrawn a Papal force originally sent north to secure Papal territory. Instead he had issued an Allocution (29 April) stating: 'We are on earth the Vicar of Christ, author of peace and lover of charity', adding that the Vicar of Christ could never wage an aggressive war against a Catholic country (such as Austria).[13] Furthermore, Rosmini suggested that the papal government would surely be suspicious of the expansionist ambitions of a Piedmontese government and resentful of her anticlerical stance.[14]

Instead, Rosmini proposed that he might approach the Pope with two proposals: to negotiate a Concordat with Piedmont guaranteeing the liberty of the Church in return for certain concessions; secondly to urge the Pope to support a federal union of Italian states, with the Pope as President. There followed a heated debate.

A contemporary commentator suggests that ultimately

Rosmini was moved by his love of Italy and his ardent wish to support the unification and independence of the nation. Therefore he agreed to accept the mission, much as he suspected the motives of the Piedmontese politicians. Rosmini's plea was for some guarantee of freedom for the Church: 'a sincere liberty, a freedom for all – and therefore also for the Church – and not merely an irreligious liberty which concealed other sinister factors.'[15]

Later that day two of the Ministers, Gioberti and Rattazzi (later to become a leader of the anticlerical party in Parliament), visited him in his lodgings and put before him a threefold mandate: to seek the military cooperation of the Holy See, to work for the creation of a political league of Italian States, and to put together a Concordat. It was the first point the government was primarily after, the other two being 'sweeteners'.[16]

It was not clear how official this intervention by Gioberti and Rattazzi was. Rosmini was reassured by the receipt of a letter of commendation to King Charles Albert seeking the royal blessing on his Roman mission. He therefore set out that same evening to try to find the King. As he went towards the war zone he met hundreds of desolate and weary soldiers retreating into Piedmont. Eventually he tracked Charles Albert down in Vigevano, just over the border in Lombardy.

The King was much dispirited by the recent military defeat; nevertheless he welcomed Rosmini and over lunch he gave his approval for his Rome mission, seeming to be especially pleased with the project for a Concordat. Charles Albert was a deeply religious man, and it was he who had sought Rosmini's help some years earlier in the establishment of a royal mausoleum at the Sacra di San Michele.[17] Alluding to the anticlerical posture of the press and parliament, the King lamented: 'See how they have drawn down vengeance on us instead of God's blessing.'[18]

Rosmini departed armed with a letter of commendation to the papal government. He took with him Giuseppe Toscani as secretary and a brother assistant, Antonio Carli, and set out at once for Rome. It was to be a fateful journey. They arrived in the Eternal City on 15 August.

Rome

Rosmini's small household took up lodgings in the Villa Albano close to the papal residence in the Quirinal palace.[19] His first action was to meet the Piedmontese Ambassador, the Marchese Pareto, who had been busy in Rome negotiating a Customs Union proposed by Pius, between the Papal States, Piedmont and Tuscany. The hope was that such a union might be the first step towards some sort of confederation, which other Italian states might be encouraged to join.

An essential prerequisite for Rosmini's mission was to receive the official credentials the Casati administration had promised. They had not arrived – for the simple reason that the Turin government was on the point of being replaced by another grouping of more anticlerical ministers.

Rosmini still had the King's letter, so on 17 August he sought an audience with the Pope and presented it. He was received with great warmth. The Pope appeared to be well disposed towards both the idea of a Concordat with Piedmont and the project for a Confederation of Italian states. Then, somewhat playfully he said to Rosmini: 'You did not want to come and live in Rome near the Pope; but now Providence has brought you here. I will put you in prison and not allow you to depart any more!'[20]

Rosmini did not understand what the Pope meant by these words, but four days later his friend Cardinal Castracane made it abundantly clear. The Pope wished to make him a Cardinal, and then he would be obliged to live in Rome. Rosmini was thunderstruck. After a few days considering the implications of this move, he returned to see the Pope and explained that, as Provost General of the Institute of Charity, even though he was bound to respect the Pope's command, he could not accept such an honour without consulting his brethren because of his obligations to the Institute.

The Pope conceded that he should do this, but that nevertheless he was determined to make him a Cardinal at the next Consistory, due in December. He assured Rosmini that the Cardinalate was no longer seen as a great honour, but had now become a burden and a sign of contradiction.[21] Rosmini therefore wrote a letter to be distributed to each of the Presbyters of the Institute seeking their opinion. This took a little time, but eventually the replies came in. Ten were for his acceptance, including a warm letter of encouragement from Gentili. The only one against was his secretary Toscani.

It is significant that Toscani was the one person with Rosmini in Rome, and therefore probably in the best position to judge. Another who was appalled by the idea of Rosmini becoming a cardinal was the brother assistant, Antonio Carli. Carli even went so far as to seek a private audience with the Pope to protest against the move. It was to no avail. However, Pagani notes that the quick-witted and wise brother was more discerning than the rest. He said to Rosmini: 'Do not accept . . . you would do great harm to yourself and the Institute and the poor of Christ.'[22]

While waiting for his credentials to arrive, Rosmini pursued the project to create an Italian Confederation. He had joint meetings with the Piedmontese Minister in Rome, Domenico Pareto, the Tuscan Minister, Scipione Bargagli, and the Pope's personal representative, Msgr Giovanni Corboli-Bussi. Corboli-Bussi had been the secretary at the conclave which elected Pius IX and was much favoured by the new Pope for important missions. In 1847 he had visited various Italian states advocating the formation of a Customs Union. He was possibly the most 'Italian' member of the Pope's entourage.

After four meetings with Rosmini acting as minute secretary, a comprehensive plan was arrived at which was submitted to the Pope. The Pope was pleased with the plan and called together a council of Cardinals to examine it. The proposals were:

1. A perpetual Confederation is established between the States of the Church, the King of Sardinia and the Grand

Duke of Tuscany, in which, by means of a unity of forces and action, the territories of the same States are guaranteed, and the progressive and peaceful growth of liberties and national prosperity agreed upon are protected.

2. The august and immortal Pontiff Pius IX, the mediator and initiator of the League and Confederation, and his successors will be perpetual presidents.

3. Within the space of a month from the ratifications of the present agreement, a delegation of the three Confederating States will assemble in Rome, each of which will send three persons and they will be elected by the legislative power, and who will be authorised to discuss and establish the federal Constitution.

4. The federal Constitution will have for its aim to organize a central power, which should be exercised by a permanent Diet in Rome.

There follows a list of tasks which the central power would exercise, including authority to established a Customs Union and a common currency, to declare war and peace, and build some uniformity into the legal system. Provision was included for other Italian states to join the Confederation.[23]

Rosmini proposed that delegates to the Diet would be partly appointed by the Prince and partly elected by the people.[24] He was always a supporter of monarchy as being the best political system to maintain social stability, but he was also aware of constitutional movements in European states which included the establishment of elected parliaments. His aim was to create a balance between the rights of the princes and the aspirations of the people. The Pope's initial response to this plan was entirely favourable.

Rosmini was at his best in this sort of negotiation, establishing principles of government and working out means of putting them into effect. But was it the right time for this? The general situation both in Italy and in Rome itself was becoming increasingly chaotic and uncertain. The new administration in Turin was primarily interested in the expansion of Piedmont across the north of Italy by driving out the Austrians. On their part the Austrians were intransigent.

When his credentials eventually arrived from Turin with an exclusive emphasis on war, Rosmini saw that his official mission had become untenable, so on 30 September he sent his resignation to the Minister in Turin, Ettore Perrone. He added, however, that he was still prepared to advise whomsoever the Turin government might appoint to come to Rome.[25]

Rosmini here found himself caught between a rock and a hard place. The Piedmontese government was expansionist and bellicose. On the other hand the Curia could not accept a situation where a Confederation presided over by the Pope could be pressured into declaring war on a Catholic power. Yet without such sovereign authority this new Italian Confederation would be looked upon with contempt by other European states – or so Rosmini surmised.

Meanwhile, in Rome itself, one civil administration succeeded another, but none seemed able to keep the turbulent populace in check. A strong hand was needed, and Rosmini suggested to the Pope that the right person might be Count Pellegrino Rossi. Although a Tuscan by birth, Rossi had pursued a varied career as academic and politician in Switzerland and in France. He had come back to Rome in 1846 as French Ambassador, and soon established himself as friend and confidant of Pope Pius.

Rossi was appointed chief minister on 15 September, and at once set about trying to prevent the Papal States falling into chaos. He stabilised the finances, and used the remnants of the defeated Papal army to enforce public order. But his brusque manner and forcefulness did not please everybody. Rosmini became alarmed and proposed to the Pope that there should be a moderating figure alongside Rossi. The Pope responded by inviting Rosmini to lunch with him, when he nominated him a consultor to the Holy Office and to the Index. It appeared to be a first step towards appointing Rosmini as his Secretary of State, a move soon anticipated in the press.

Rossi and Rosmini were poles apart in their thinking. Rossi's notion of a Confederation, for instance, differed vastly from Rosmini's. Rossi convinced the Pope that instead there should be a League of Italian princes. It would be a more authoritarian and dictatorial body. Rosmini thought it madness to turn back the clock in this way and abandon the constitutionalism being won all over Italy. He said as much to Pius.[26] But there was other opposition being aroused against Rosmini within the Roman Curia. Seeds of doubt were being sowed in the Pope's mind about Rosmini's orthodoxy, specifically his apparent advocacy of the election of bishops in his recently published book *The Five Wounds of the Church*.

Meanwhile in the city streets there was growing opposition to Rossi. Since the Amnesty of 1846 there had appeared in the city a swarm of political clubs, the most extreme of which were advocates of republicanism. Some members had been followers of the revolutionary *Carbonari* movement or of Mazzini's *Giovine Italia*. Dr Pietro Sterbini belonged to the strongest of the clubs and was editor of the most influential local newspaper, *Contemporaneo*; he soon became the leader of the republican movement. The clubs stirred up the mob, once so ardent in their adulation of the Pope but now demanding much more radical changes.

It was Sterbini who eventually hatched a plot to assassinate Rossi. Rossi was due to address the Chamber of Deputies on 15 November, and Rosmini went down to the Chamber with Domenico Pareto to await his arrival. They found a seething mob outside. There were constant sounds of turmoil and much hissing. Then someone rushed into the Chamber to say that Rossi had been shot outside. As soon as Rosmini established it was true and that Rossi was dead, he hastened to the Quirinal to be at the side of the Pope.[27]

Revolution

The assassination of Rossi was the trigger needed to ignite the flames of revolt. The following day a noisy mob surrounded the Quirinal. Some shots were fired and one of the papal secretaries was killed. Tension grew as the Swiss guards attempted to keep the revolutionaries at bay. A cannon was dragged in with the idea of breaking down the door to the Palace. The Pope at first resisted these attempts to force his hand, but when he realised that the lives of the Swiss Guards could be at risk he knew he must give in to demands for a new ministry to succeed that of Rossi.

After the assassination, Rosmini had spoken with the Pope, and recommended him to summon General Zucchi who was in charge of the Papal army, from Bologna. But it was too late for that. From the nearby Villa Albano he witnessed the confusion outside the Quirinal. The Pope capitulated and acceded to a new government. To his consternation Rosmini learnt that his name was included in the new ministry as President of the Assembly with the portfolio of education.

Rosmini felt sure his nomination had been extracted from the Pope under duress. He sent Toscani to the Palace to confirm this. The Pope had believed that Rosmini would be a bulwark for him in a threatening situation, but soon realised that was a vain hope. So Rosmini at once tendered his resignation.

At this time Rosmini detected the first signs of a hostility towards him among the papal entourage. He was seen as belonging to the liberal camp, and those were the trouble-makers. However, Cardinal Antonelli, the pro-Secretary of State, passed him a message: 'The Holy Father bids me to tell you that, in case he should leave Rome, he will be pleased to see you where he takes up his abode.'[28]

During this time of pressure and danger for the Pope, many of the papal entourage abandoned him but Cardinal Antonelli remained staunch, a show of loyalty Pius was never to forget. He was also supported by the Ambassadors, and it was Count Spaur, the Bavarian Ambassador, who organised his eventual escape.

On 24 November, Pius was smuggled out of the city dressed as an ordinary priest. He arrived the following morning in Gaeta, a small town north of Naples over the border into Neapolitan territory. Being at the centre of a revolutionary event and of having his right hand man murdered by the mob was for the Pope a mind-changing experience.[29]

Pius had now become an exile in a foreign place. It gave him ample time to reflect ruefully on recent events.

Notes

1 E.E.Y. Hales, *Pio Nono*, p. 72.
2 Hales, ibid., p. 60.
3 Hales, ibid., p. 18.
4 Frederick Ozanam was beatified by Pope John Paul II at World Youth Day 1997.
5 Torchlight procession.
6 Hales, ibid., pp. 54–55.
7 See Chapter 2, endnote 11, p. 22.
8 *Cinque Giornate*: five days of popular uprising in Milan.
9 Luciano Malusa: *The Diplomatic Mission of Rosmini to Rome*, p. 3 (tr. J.A. Dewhirst). The canticle *In exitu* is sung in the Divine Office and represents the joy of the Israelites in escaping from the 'barbarian' Egyptians at the time of the Exodus.
10 Pagani, *Life*, pp. 259–261.
11 *Ep.Compl.*, x, 6113.
12 Paoli, *Vita di A. Rosmini*, p. 419.
13 Pagani-Rossi, ii, 169.
14 Pagani, *Life*, p. 265.
15 Malusa, *La Missione a Roma, Commentario*, p. 11.
16 Malusa, ibid., p. 13.
17 See above, p. 133.
18 Pagani, *Life*, p. 266.
19 The Quirinal Palace is right in the heart of the city of Rome, and since the time of the Renaissance it had been the Pope's main residence. It is now the Italian President's official home.
20 Pagani, *Life*, p. 266.
21 Pagani, *Life*, pp. 266–267.
22 Pagani, *Life*, p. 268.
23 Malusa, ibid., pp. 20–22 (tr. Dewhirst).
24 A Diet is a term used for a conference called together for a specific purpose and consisting of delegates from different places.
25 Muratore, *Rosmini per il Risorgimento*, p. 94. *Ep.Compl.*, x, 6242.
26 Muratore, ibid., pp. 94–96.
27 Pagani, ibid., pp. 271–272.
28 Pagani, ibid., p. 274.
29 Pagani, ibid., pp. 274–275.

Chapter Eighteen

Exile at Gaeta, 1848–1849

After the assassination of Minister Rossi, Rosmini went to the French Embassy where the Rossi family had taken refuge prior to escaping back to France. There he also met Cardinal Sciolla, who disclosed to him that the Pope was intending to leave the city and seek sanctuary outside Papal territory. The Pope had indicated he wished Rosmini to follow him, which meant that, much as he personally would have wished to return home to Stresa, his prior concern was to obey the express wishes of Pius. Sciolla also provided him with a papal passport. This was providential since his own was in the hands of the Roman police.[1]

He then retired outside the city to Albano to await developments. He prepared two carriages in the event of a rapid departure, leaving Antonio Carli to look after his affairs in Rome. Early in the morning of 25 November, the Pope's brother, Count Gabriello Mastai, arrived with the news that Pius had been successfully smuggled out of the city in disguise the previous night. Rosmini persuaded Mastai not to go back to the city which was no longer safe, but to accompany him along with the ex-Minister Antonio Montonari to Gaeta, where they were told the Pope had gone.

The party set out in the two carriages and arrived at Gaeta the following morning. Gaeta is a small seaside town midway between Rome and Naples. They went immediately to a plain inn where the Papal party was staying; they found Pope Pius dressed as a simple priest, accompanied by Cardinal Antonelli

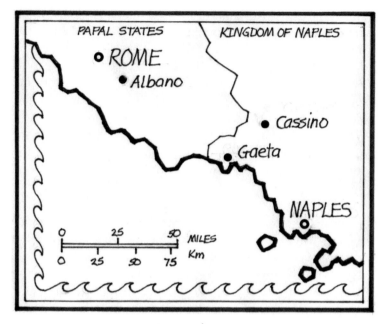

Rome and Gaeta

in lay dress. Count Spaur, the Bavarian ambassador who connived their escape from Rome, had gone ahead to announce their arrival to the King. Later that morning the King and Queen arrived from Naples by boat, and the Pope and Antonelli were conducted to the royal villa along with the Pope's brother. Rosmini and Montanari found lodgings with a Canon Orgero, a professor of philosophy and admirer of Rosmini's writings.

The warm welcome of the King of Naples solved the immediate problem of where the Pope was to spend his time in exile. Both Antonelli and Spaur were inclined to favour seeking the aid of Austria to reinstall the Pope in Rome. The biographer Pagani's judgment on Antonelli's machinations is that this was all part of a crafty plan to 'let affairs in Rome run to extremes and then call in Austria to clear the ground of every Liberal institution.'[2]

At Antonelli's suggestion Pope Pius issued a *motu proprio* appointing a Commission of seven under Cardinal Castracane to supervise the governance of the Papal States. Rosmini was critical of this plan especially as it contradicted the Constitution which Pius himself had granted to his people. He suggested instead that the Pope set up a provisional government in Bologna where the people were loyal and there was a contingent of troops under General Zucchi ready to protect him.

In the event, Castracane was most unwilling to accept the responsibility placed on him by the *motu proprio*, and the Council of Deputies rejected it outright. Instead they sent a deputation south to invite the Pope to return to Rome at once. The deputation was stopped at the frontier, and the Pope refused to receive them. From that point on the Council in Rome turned its back on the Pope and moved towards a republican form of government.

The Pope was inclined to appeal over the heads of the Council directly to the people, commanding their loyalty. Rosmini then suggested that he might move to Benevento, a town within the Papal States still loyal to the Holy Father's rule. The Pope did not respond to this idea either, but asked Rosmini's help in drawing up a manifesto to issue to his people. Rosmini produced a lengthy but conciliatory document, the gist of which is as follows:

> The Pope appeals to his people as their Pastor to return to their duty of loyalty and not listen to seditious voices. The Pope lists the many services he has performed for the people such as granting them a Constitution, appealing to them to be patient and let these reforms bear fruit. He denounces the brutal assassination of his Minister Rossi and the violence done to his own person by the revolutionaries.
>
> He reminds the people that he is the spiritual Father of 200 million Catholics all over the world and that his temporal power and authority is compromised by their recent actions. In Italy itself he has always sought peace while supporting the movement towards union of the Italian peoples.
>
> In short, he has been faithful to the Constitution he granted to his people. It is the revolutionaries who have violated it.[3]

This attempt of Rosmini to advise the Pope again came to nothing. Evidently conciliation was not what was required. Anything Rosmini suggested from that point on was ignored or perhaps blocked by Antonelli. Personally the Pope always made him welcome, but Antonelli and others in the Papal Court became increasingly hostile towards him.

Various people sought Rosmini's help in influencing the direction of the papal thinking. One was Gioberti, now Chief Minister in Turin. Rosmini did his best to satisfy these appeals, but had to plead that he was only a private person and had no real influence. He wrote in his diary: 'The Pope informs me of his decisions after the event and not before.'[4]

Rosmini was fast becoming aware of the change of atmosphere towards him at the Papal Court, so he decided he would distance himself for a while; he therefore sought the Pope's leave to go to Naples early in 1849 to oversee the publication of some spiritual works. He was also suffering from poor health, and he hoped it would enable him to recuperate. However, he wrote frequently to the Pope, who continued to act graciously towards him, even asking him to publish something against the errors of the day. Rosmini responded at once, bringing out his *Essay on Communism and Socialism.*[5]

While in Naples, he lived at first with the Vincentian Fathers, and later in very simple circumstances with the Capuchins on the edge of the city. Meanwhile in Gaeta there was no progress to resolve the political crisis. Under the influence of Antonelli the Pope also became convinced that only an appeal to a foreign power was going to bring him back to Rome. The most likely candidate would be Austria.

We can see here two incompatible political philosophies. Antonelli and the conservative party surrounding him wanted the Constitution scrapped and the Pope reinstated forcibly by a foreign army. Rosmini always favoured a more peaceful federal solution as the best way to preserve papal power, supporting moves towards Italian unity.

To achieve this a balance would be needed between the constitutional aspirations of the people and the traditional rights of princes and of inherited property. Rosmini's political thinking is demonstrated in a quotation from his own account of his Mission:

> Now that the period of princely despotism is ended, the Pontificate of Pius IX must signal a new epoch in which the Roman Pontificate picks itself up and takes up again its ancient and natural authority and also frees its temporal power from its dependency on princes. This cannot happen unless the Holy See joins itself closely to the people and draws its strength from them, as was the case in its finer days.[6]

The Pope had at first followed this line. He had flirted with liberal ideas and promoted them during the first two years of his pontificate. But his experience of the revolution of November 1848 and subsequent flight had changed his mind forever. He would not be the only Pope to change his political course radically as the result of a painful personal experience. There have been two examples in the twentieth century.[7]

When Rosmini eventually returned to Gaeta from Naples later in the year, Pius greeted him with the words: 'Dear Abate, we are no longer constitutionalists'. It was a repudiation of all that he had done politically during his first two years as Pope. Rosmini protested:

> Your Holiness, it is a serious matter to change the course you have entered upon and split your Pontificate into two halves. I am also of the opinion that the Constitution cannot be restored at once; but to let the people retain some hope of its ultimate restoration would have a good effect, for it is dangerous for a prince to move in two opposite directions.[8]

From that moment Rosmini knew that his political mission, originally accepted in Turin nearly a year earlier, was in tatters. It only remained for him to retire gracefully. Any idea that the Pope would wish to make him a cardinal seemed to have evaporated.

Meanwhile the situation in Rome itself moved away from any form of compromise. The Assembly called for an election by universal suffrage, and although only a minority of citizens voted, a new Assembly came together in February and after a noisy first session declared the temporal power of the Pope at an end to be replaced by a republic. The stage was set for the return of Mazzini, who soon took over the reins of government.

The response of Pius IX was immediate: he appealed to the Catholic powers to repudiate this illegitimate government and restore him as the rightful ruler. But the powers were not prepared to act together. France was as ever fearful of Austria. Spain was too far away. Austria was distracted by a declaration of war by Piedmont, which quickly suffered yet another overwhelming military defeat. This left the Austrians victorious and ready to move on Rome. The French therefore acted unilaterally to anticipate this and sent a small force under General Oudinet, which landed in April at Civita Vecchia just north of Rome. Their first approach to the city was repulsed by Garibaldi, who thus established himself as one of the heroes of the *Risorgimento*.

But the conflict was too one-sided. There was no way a scratch Roman army could stand up to any of the great powers, and as soon as Oudinet was reinforced he resumed an offensive against the republicans. The conflict continued throughout June until Garibaldi was forced to flee the city. The Assembly capitulated and the so-called 'Roman Republic' came to an end. Mazzini fled back to London to continue his life of exile.

As long as the French garrison stayed in Rome, which it did until 1870, the rule of the Pope, at least over his immediate territories, was guaranteed. The Pope appointed a commission of three cardinals to rule as his regents until he chose to return to the city, which did not occur until April 1850. Antonelli was confirmed as Secretary of State and remained at Pius' right hand until his death in 1876, two years before his master.

No contrast could be greater than that between Pius and his chosen lieutenant. Pius was prayerful, of aristocratic background yet simple in his lifestyle, affable and generous. Antonelli was of Neapolitan peasant stock; never ordained priest, his private life left much to be desired. He was acquisitive, and at his death he left a fortune to his relatives. His manner was brusque often to the point of rudeness. However, he was also courageous, totally loyal to his master and most able: what more could Pius wish for?

It is incorrect to think that Pius was simply a pawn in the hands of an unscrupulous and masterful Secretary of State. Pius had a mind of his own, but he was content to use the superior political skills of his lieutenant. The relationship is not unlike that between Metternich and successive Austrian Emperors. It is ironic that the absolutist rule of Prince Metternich was toppled by the tsunami of liberal revolution first released by Pio Nono. Yet after the fall of the great Austrian, a similar relationship of absolute power was established in Rome, between Pius IX and Cardinal Antonelli. Malusa sums up the political situation under Pius as follows:

> Rosmini gave way before the declared realism of Antonelli and the fears of Pius IX. His foresight, however, was confirmed soon enough with the progressive dissolution of temporal power. The tragedy of the Papacy was played out with Pius IX and his controversial Secretary of State isolated in the storm caused by the hostility of the Italians, disillusioned by anti-national politics and the Romans, by this time sceptical of the possibility of putting together a government of Cardinals and Curia with their modern liberal policies.
>
> Between 1859 and 1870 the total loss of the so-called Patrimony of St Peter, established in the Middle Ages in different times, would take place, having become an anachronistic possession compared with the development of the National Italian issue and international right itself.[9]

Condemnation and Disgrace

Alongside this total reversal in the political climate, something even more sinister was undermining Rosmini's reputation at the Papal Court. One of the most reactionary of the Cardinals, Lambruschini, had joined the Pope at Gaeta. He had been Secretary of State to Gregory XVI and had been the leading conservative candidate in the Papal election of 1846. To him is primarily attributed the move to condemn some of Rosmini's works.

Rosmini was well aware, even before the flight to Gaeta, that those hostile to him were active. But in Rome the Pope had reassured him. In the early days of their relationship the Pope seemed perfectly at ease with Rosmini's orthodoxy, and indeed he invited him to join eighteen eminent theologians who had been invited to give their opinions regarding the expediency of issuing a dogmatic definition of the Immaculate Conception of Mary. Rosmini did this willingly, and thus he contributed to the process of solemn definition, which was to happen in 1854.

One day Pius said to him, with a smile and an appropriate gesture, 'Your enemies can see just as far as this; still, as "we are debtors to the wise and the unwise," you would oblige me by writing a letter which I could publish.' Rosmini replied that he would be willing to do so if he knew what he was being accused of, so the Pope promised that he would instruct Msgr Corboli-Bussi to draw up objections to his work and suggested corrections.[10] It became clear that the problem lay in some of the assertions Rosmini had made in his recently published book *The Five Wounds of the Church*.[11]

One query was over the *First Wound*. Rosmini, it was claimed, was advocating the use of the vernacular in place of Latin in the liturgy. Rosmini later denied this, yet it is difficult not to draw this conclusion when he names the use of Latin as creating a barrier between priests and people. Most priests understood Latin, but by this time few of the laity did. Yet the liturgy is a shared event, and full understanding of the meaning of the words is a paramount condition for good liturgy. In his religious *Rule* Rosmini emphasises that his followers should strive to understand the very meaning of the words used in liturgical and communal prayer.[12]

An even bigger stumbling block was the criticism of his *Fourth Wound*, regarding the appointment of bishops. Rosmini observes that in the early Church bishops were chosen 'by clergy and people'; that the designation of bishops by princes which came in during the Middle Ages was an abuse; and that it is essential for a bishop to be acceptable to the people he is to rule over. Rosmini founded his arguments on the basic principle that it is a natural right for members of any society to elect its leaders. Not surprisingly, he was accused of proposing to introduce democracy into the Church.[13]

Rosmini found Corboli-Bussi an easy person to work with. The agreed draft was ready by mid-December, and Rosmini took it to the Pope. In it there is an attempt to disperse the clouds of suspicion which had been stirred up against him, and it concludes with an expression of warm attachment to the Holy See and a declaration of obedience to the Vicar of Christ. The Pope received it graciously.

Later however he told Rosmini that the statement about the election of bishops was still not clear enough. Rosmini replied that he had transcribed precisely what Corboli-Bussi had proposed to him. The Pope was somewhat embarrassed when he learnt this.

During the time Rosmini was in Naples the tide against him in Gaeta was rising steadily. The Pope's confessor, Msgr Stella, voiced openly that he would never have believed Rosmini to be such a consummate hypocrite, that he was a Communist, a real plague to the Church and that in his works the name of Jesus Christ was never to be found.

A book appeared by an Oratorian, Agostino Theiner, written in German but immediately translated into Italian, which bitterly attacked him especially for his teachings in the *Five Wounds*. When Rosmini wrote from Naples sending an Easter greeting, the Pope replied: 'We exhort you to reflect on the works you have printed, to modify, or retract, or correct; we have charged Cardinal Mai to examine them.'[14] This blunt command came as a shock.

When Cardinal Mai appeared in Naples, he assured Rosmini he had declined the commission as being beyond his powers as well as being distasteful to him. Nevertheless it was symptomatic of the souring of the atmosphere at the Papal Court.

The problem was that the Pope had chosen to isolate himself. He rejected Rosmini's proposals that he should move away from Naples and back into his own States, whether to Bologna or Benevento, both places where the people were well disposed towards Pius. What was lacking at Gaeta was 'a council of statesmen alongside the Pontiff which in this context should be indispensible': so wrote Rosmini.[15]

The clamour from Rome itself was becoming more and more radical and anticlerical. It was in this atmosphere that the Pope's mind changed absolutely regarding the Constitution he had given to his people. He became resolved to cease making concessions and to distance himself from liberalism.

At the same time the Pope consented to the *Congregation of the Index* examining Rosmini's two political works, the *Five Wounds of the Church* and the *Constitution according to Social Justice*, both of which he had seemed to approve in his earlier meetings with Rosmini in Rome. At an extraordinary meeting of the Congregation under Cardinal Brignole on 30 May 1849, the two works were condemned and placed on the list of prohibited works. They were to remain there almost until the time when the Index was finally abolished in the 1960s.[16]

Rosmini returned to Gaeta at the beginning of June, when the Pope indicated to him that he now rejected constitutionalism. Rosmini began to be harassed by the Neapolitan police, so that he had to return to the Pope to complain and seek protection. It was at this point that the Pope first said openly that he was receiving a lot of criticism about him: 'They fear your influence over me … Ah, if you only knew all they have told me about you! Now they are examining your works.'[17]

Rosmini at first presumed the Pope meant it was the police who were examining his political works. Later he realised that 'they' were the Curial Cardinals. He recognised that it was time for him to withdraw. He sought permission to leave Gaeta and make his way back to Stresa. The Pope granted this. But before he left he presented the Pope with a memorial explaining and justifying his actions. He did this not merely for the sake of his own good name but also as a protection for the Institute.

He left Gaeta on 19 June 1849. He would not meet Pope Pius again. When he went to make his farewells, the Pope made no mention of the fact that he had just signed a document condemning his books.

Journey Home

It should be noted that Rosmini's time in Gaeta and Naples was by no means totally negative. He had apparently failed in his original mission. Yet during all that time he continued his vast work of correspondence, teaching, instructing, counselling and directing his Sisters and Brothers. While at Naples he composed one of his most spiritual works: *A Commentary on the Prologue to the Gospel of St John*. One can well imagine how he might receive inspiration for this beautiful book as he gazed from the Capuchin house poised high above the great city and looking across the dazzling blue of the Bay of Naples and the distant Mediterranean.

During this time he made the acquaintance of a young priest, Gustavo Hohenlohe. Gustavo later rose to become a Cardinal, but retained a warm affection for Rosmini's memory until the day of his death. Another eye-witness with him at this time noted:

> I never saw him disturbed. He was never downcast, nor did he ever give a sign or hint of the trials he was enduring ... His smile revealed a profound peace, perfect interior harmony, constant self-possession – or rather the steady reign of divine grace in his soul.[18]

Surprisingly, Rosmini's journey back to Stresa was leisurely and prolonged. It may be that he was in dire need of a period of recovery after the trials of Gaeta. He needed, of course, to go to Rome to collect his property. So it took the greater part of the summer and autumn for him to reach home.

His first stop was Capua, still inside the kingdom of Naples, where he was cordially received by the Archbishop and his clergy. When he moved on from there to Caserta he was again worried by the police. Before arriving in Rome he took the opportunity of some days of quiet retreat with the Benedictines at Monte Cassino. On reaching Albano, just south of Rome, he was pressed by Cardinal Tosti, a long-time friend, to spend some weeks with him.

Tosti treated him with exquisite courtesy, which was in marked contrast with his recent experience at the Papal Court. Tosti suggested he should write a formal reply to Agostino Theiner's assault on the *Five Wounds*. He composed quite a long and thorough defence which took some time. Later, after Rosmini's death, Tosti wrote:

> The hospitality I afforded him earned me the brightest days of my life, on account of the edification I received from his heroic virtue and the wisdom he seemed to infuse into others with a simplicity and charm which reminded us of Origen in his palmy days.[19]

On 15 August a Dominican priest, Fr Boeri, arrived with a letter from the Master of the Sacred Palace, Gaeta, informing him of the decree of the Index condemning his two works. Boeri emerged, commenting on Rosmini's reaction: 'Here is another Fénelon!'[20] Rosmini wrote an immediate reply:

> With the sentiments of a most devoted and obedient son of the Holy See, which by the grace of God I have always been from my heart and have openly declared myself, I hereby state that I submit to the prohibition purely and simply and in the fullest manner possible, and beg to inform our most Holy Father and the Sacred Congregation of this.

He only asked that since the books had been published anonymously, the author's name be not published in the decree. He hoped thereby to protect the Institute from adverse publicity. This request was ignored.[21]

His immediate submission greatly satisfied Pope Pius as it

did some others at the Papal Court. His friend, the Marquis Gustavo Cavour, called it 'an act of heroism'.[22] Rosmini knew that the condemnation would come as a great shock to his brethren, but in the event it only served to gather them more closely around him. Only one decided to leave him, and even he later regretted it. On the other hand Rosmini's perceived 'fall from grace' prompted several excellent priests to join the Institute, including Lorenzo Gastaldi, later Archbishop of Turin, and Gioacchino Cappa, the fourth Rosminian Provost General.

Some regarded his submission as excessive. Others thought it was insufficient. But he pointed out that no retractation had been demanded ... 'I was simply asked to submit ... when I offered to make any retractation it was considered unnecessary.'[23]

On 8 October he left Cardinal Tosti, and after a brief visit to his faithful friend Cardinal Castracane, he arrived in Rome. To his relief he found that his property had remained untouched. It was great good fortune, but it may have been thanks to the faithful Antonio Carli. It took him only a few days to make some final arrangements and then head north.

He made a brief stopover with Manzoni's son-in-law, Professor Giorgini, at the Villa Massarosa, near Florence. Giorgini's comments are illuminating:

> Rosmini returned from Gaeta like a commander who has lost a battle, but is conscious of having done his duty and fought in a good cause. His words about the Pope were full of reverence and affection; and his judgment of the persons then in power at Court was temperate and kind. He came back without bitterness, like a man who in the failure of his plans adores the will of God, instead of attributing it to the ill-will of men ...[24]

He paused for a day or so in Genoa to write letters of thanks to Castracane and Tosti. The affirmation and support of these two Princes of the Church acted as a salutary reassurance. Castracane had written:

I foresaw this happening, knowing the unfavourable disposi-
tions of my colleagues the Cardinals towards you, their
jealousy and their displeasure at the easy access you were
given to His Holiness and their fears regarding your influence
on his mind . . .[25]

When he arrived by the lake at Stresa his first desire was to
call at Lesa nearby and salute his old friend Manzoni. Manzoni
had recently built a villa there, only a few kilometres from
Stresa and within walking distance. He was a prodigious
walker.

On 2 November 1849 Rosmini ascended once more the
hill of Stresa – home at last. It had been a tumultuous year
for him, and his brethren noted that it had taken its toll. His
hair had turned white, but his spirit was undimmed. And
there was the huge personal relief that he had escaped the
Cardinal's hat and was home once more among his beloved
religious family.

Reflection

Judgment might be passed that Rosmini's mission had been a
total failure. Yet who had failed? Rosmini remained at all times
faithful to his principles. He had been motivated by patriotism, and had valiantly sought to find a solution to the ideals
and challenges of a united Italy, yet preserving the prestige
and religious pre-eminence of the Holy See.

The failure had been on the part of the Pope and his
advisers, notably his notorious Secretary of State, Cardinal
Antonelli. The Pope was to return to Rome a few months later
– an absolute prince escorted by foreign troops. Within ten
years Cavour and Garibaldi had made Victor Emmanuel
master of all Italy apart from the much reduced Papal States.
In 1870 the final withdrawal of the French garrison left Rome
wide open to the final step in the unification of Italy. Rome
fell easily to the Piedmontese army. Victor Emmanuel took up
residence in the Quirinal Palace, and Pius IX was thrust out to

become the 'prisoner of the Vatican'. This was to be the predicament of the Papacy for the next fifty years.

What needs to be emphasised is that the condemnation of Rosmini's books was in no way a religious action. It was wholly political. It was symbolic of the Holy See's rejection of constitutionalism and liberalism, a refusal to come to terms with the times, swimming against a relentless tide sweeping Europe and the world towards a more democratic future. Pius was turning his back on the modern age, and his stance was set in stone a few years later in the infamous *Syllabus of Errors*, in 1864.[26]

The condemnation of Rosmini's works was political also in the sense that the malign and shadowy influence of Austria can be detected. The prospect of the Roveretan becoming influential or being made Secretary of State was repugnant to Vienna. While at Albano, Rosmini was informed of this by his friend Tosti, and he wrote this to the Duc d'Harcourt: '… Austria strove mightily with the Pope to prevent my being made Cardinal, an intention already broadcast widely by the Pope'.[27]

In the Decree of 1849, Rosmini's two books, The *Five Wounds* and the *Constitution*, are simply condemned. There is no indication why. The proscription is not accompanied by any statement rejecting his teachings. The books are deemed to be 'politically incorrect', in the true meaning of those words. The political nature of the condemnation is confirmed by the fact that two other works were also condemned alongside Rosmini's: one by Vincenzo Gioberti[28] and one by Gioachino Ventura. Rosmini and the others were priests, and all three belonged to the neo-Guelph group which sought to build a bridge between the rights and legitimate sphere of action of the Church and the aspirations of the modern age in favour of nationalism and more representative government. The condemnation by Pius IX of these four works signalled a determination to break down this bridge.

The consequences of this for the Catholic Church were wholly bad. Liberalism and the democratic movements, having been slighted by the Catholic Church, sought to ally themselves with anticlerical groups, while autocratic govern-ments tended to receive the support of the Church. The Church in recent times has been roundly criticised, from the Pope down, for being too sympathetic to Fascism and for propping up reactionary and oppressive regimes, especially in South America. The seeds of this unfortunate split were sown by Pius IX and his 'grey eminence', Cardinal Antonelli.

To end on a more positive note, an article appeared in a Turin journal, the *Conciliatore Torinese.*[29] The author reads into Rosmini's humble submission a sign of his pure and disinterested love for the Church. Rosmini had chosen a life of service to his neighbour, and had avoided the sort of honours and benefices that his noble Austrian origins entitled him to. It was natural that in the face of an extreme trial of obedience this adamantine charity would prevail.[30] The anonymous author was Lorenzo Gastaldi, soon on his way to becoming a member of the Institute. It is a fitting epitaph for Rosmini's ill-fated mission to Rome.

Notes

1   Malusa, *Della Missione a Rome di A.R.*, p. 88.
2   Pagani, *Life*, p. 276.
3   Malusa, ibid., pp. 113–124.
4   Muratore, *Rosmini per il Risorgimento*, p. 102.
5   Pagani, *Life*, p. 282.
6   Malusa, ibid.
7   Pius XII suffered at the hands of Communist agitators in Germany when he was first there as a papal diplomat; that experience made him afterwards tend towards the right wing National Socialists. Pope Benedict XVI's swing to the right following Vatican II appears to have been the result of his experience of the student unrest in 1968.
8   Pagani, *Life*, p. 286.
9   Malusa, p. 13 (trans. by Dewhirst).
10 Pagani, *Life*, p. 279.
11 Rosmini, *The Five Wounds of the Church,* pp. 70–73.
12 On the same principle Rosmini could never be content with the delib-erate use of archaic language in the translation of liturgical prayers. The new vernacular translations of the Mass are an example of this.
13 Muratore, *Rosmini*, p. 112.
14 Pagani, *Life*, p. 284.

15 Malusa, ibid., p. 106.
16 Pagani, *Life*, p. 286; Muratore, ibid., p. 112. Fr Denis Cleary writes: 'Cardinal Ottaviani gave permission for the republication of the *Cinque Piaghe* two months before the Index was abolished'. (Cleary, *Antonio Rosmini: An Introduction to his Life and Teaching*)
17 Pagani, *Life*, p. 289.
18 Pagani, ibid., pp. 282, 285.
19 Pagani: ibid., p. 296.
20 Francois Fénelon (1651–17150), Archbishop of Cambrai, was one of the famous French spiritual figures of his era, much admired for his humility, gentleness and wisdom.
21 Pagani, ibid., p. 292.
22 Cavour, letter to AR, 8 September 1849, quoted by Malusa, ibid., p. 451.
23 Rosmini, letter to Bertolozzi.
24 Pagani, *Life*, p. 295. Pagani-Rossi, ii, p. 261 – a letter from Giorgini to Pagani.
25 Castracane: letter to Rosmini, 4 August 1849, quoted by Malusa, ibid., p. 442.
26 The *Syllabus of Errors* denounced a series of liberal ideas and statements in current circulation, e.g. 'The Roman Pontiff can, and ought to, reconcile himself, and come to terms with progress, liberalism and modern civilization (No. 80).'
27 *Ep.Compl.* x, 6372, a letter to the Duc d'Harcourt.
28 *Il Gesuita Moderno.* See above in the text, p. 163.
29 *Concilatore Torinese,* 14 September 1849.
30 Muratore, ibid., pp. 116–117.

Chapter Nineteen

Rosmini at Stresa, 1849–1854

After a year of turmoil, Rosmini's return home to Stresa brought him a period of comparative peace. He showed little desire to move away from his sanctuary by the lake. Writing to Msgr Luigi Besi shortly after his return, Rosmini says feelingly:

> How peaceful and pleasing is my presence here at Stresa in the midst of a family of true brothers in Christ. The Lord knows the needs of my spirit, and has granted me this welcome tonic. I have come back from a world that I had entered unwillingly and where I felt like a fish out of water.[1]

To Baroness Maria Koenneritz, a German lady he had met in Gaeta, he writes in similar vein:

> Since I have returned to the bosom of this dear family of my brothers in Christ, I have rejoiced in perfect peace and tranquillity. Here sincerity and charity reign, and these are not to be found in the world: the world does not know them, because it is ignorant of the unique happiness which it is possible to have in this life.[2]

Rosmini here speaks of the 'world' in the sense found in the Gospel of John, the opposite of a graced existence. At first, Rosmini lived at the College on the hill where the noviciate was sited. However, in 1850 the Rosminians received a very generous bequest from their benefactress Madame

Bolongaro, the gift of her villa by the lake. Madame Bolongaro had died in 1848.

The Villa Bolongaro, as it is still known, is a magnificent house with beautiful gardens, situated little more than a stone's throw from the lakefront. At first Rosmini tried to rent it out to a nobleman friend, but that plan fell through. Therefore, during 1850 he resolved to move the Generalitial household to the Villa, which had the double advantage of freeing more space in the College for the expanding noviciate and also giving him more freedom to receive guests without disturbing the routine of the noviciate house.

This new community served a threefold purpose: prayer, study and hospitality – the traditional functions of a monastic house. The Villa Bolongaro has been used for various purposes since that time, such as a Scuola Media (Middle School) and for housing the Rosminian archives. For a time it passed out of the Order's hands. Since 1966 it has returned to the purpose Rosmini gave it. It is the site of the Centre for Rosminian Studies, a conference and research centre promoting Rosminian scholarship and spirituality, housing an extensive library.

Rosmini was once more able to concentrate his energy on the affairs of the two Congregations as well as his philosophical writings. But he also received many visitors, religious and lay, who came to consult him or simply to enjoy his company. During these years he enjoyed the sort of social interaction that had been denied him in his constantly busy earlier life. The most regular of these visitors was Alessandro Manzoni who came almost daily from Lesa to visit and enjoy literary and philosophical discourse with his intimate friend. The faithful friendship of these two great Italians is commemorated by a beautiful wayside shrine on a road in Stresa just below the College.

Affairs of the Institute

The Congregations enjoyed steady growth during these years. But it was also a time of some sadness for Rosmini with the final closure of the house at Verona because of the hostility of the Austrians and the untimely death of two of his most faithful followers.

Giovanni Boselli had originally been a protégé of Maddalena di Canossa.[3] He had followed Rosmini to Trent when the community was set up there, where he did his noviciate. Later Rosmini sent him to Verona, and he was responsible for the successful launch of the parish community at San Zeno's. His sickness and death in September 1848, aged only 54, deeply distressed Rosmini. He spoke of him with unusual warmth:

> His days were full of good works; he was one of those who bore the heat and the burden of the day ... his gentle serenity on his deathbed is both a pledge and a prelude to the coming reward he will receive from the Master of the vineyard ... his untiring diligence in every ministry for the salvation of souls; his upright intentions, his fervent zeal, his charity which made him all things to all people; his deep humility ... Yes, I knew him well, this dear brother of ours, who was one of the first whose spirit gave me delight.[4]

Another tragedy, equally painful, was the loss of Giuseppe Setti the following year. Setti, even when very young in years, had been a skilful negotiator on Rosmini's behalf in Rome during the time when the Institute was being approved. Latterly he too had been in the community at Verona. He had always been somewhat delicate in health; nevertheless his death at the age of 39 was sorely felt. Giacomo Molinari, who was the Superior of the Verona community, was desolated by losing two of his companions. Rosmini felt huge sympathy for Molinari, but counselled him to see the hands of Providence even in the most grievous trials.

Meanwhile the English province made steady progress under the kindly guidance of Fr Giovanni Battista Pagani, the first Provincial in England. There were parishes in the Midlands, and missions were established in South Wales, where at that time there were no diocesan clergy. The coastline along the estuary of the river Severn was given to the Rosminians and the inland areas were allotted to the Benedictines coming from Downside Abbey near Bath and Belmont Priory near Hereford. Rosminian parishes were established in Newport, an ancient town on the borders of England and Wales, and Cardiff which was growing apace because of the construction of the docks largely by imported Irish labour: it would become a thriving industrial city and eventually capital city of Wales. And, as discussed earlier, William Lockhart and Angelo Rinolfi preached parish missions all over Ireland with considerable success.

Another outreach of the growing congregation was in the south of France. Fr Emilio Belisy, one of Gentili's original companions on the English mission, had to go home to sort out some family affairs, and the local bishop used the opportunity to invite Rosmini to establish a small community in Carpentras, a little town in Provence. In 1851 two more priests were sent to join Belisy. However, this new mission did not flourish and the priests were withdrawn after a couple of years.

In spite of the bad publicity in Italy caused by the condemnation of Rosmini's books, the Institute continued to grow slowly and the existing communities became more firmly established. The Sisters were moving ahead more strongly especially around the town of Biella, in Piedmont. Many new schools and convents were founded during these years.

A Hospice, an Athenaeum and a Monastery

Rosmini's new community at the Villa Bolangaro is described by Pagani as a 'hospice, an athenaeum and a monastery.'[5] There is an interesting description of Rosmini's life and circumstances by Fr Francesco Paoli, who joined the community at this time:

This residence of ours is an abode of piety, letters, science and hospitality ... I am convinced that all who from far and near consider this monument devoted to the cultivation of piety and learning, must be edified ...

When I compare him [Rosmini] as he is here and now with what he was ten years ago, living in one of the poorest houses in Stresa, I find him completely unchanged ... Our very reverend Father prays, suffers, pardons, believes, hopes, loves and labours with a power and alacrity which is marvellous to behold ... at times we have profound and daring disputations. Our meals, recreation, walks together or with visitors – all are seasoned, thanks to him, with spiritual and learned discourses.[6]

One of those who joined the Institute at this time was an experienced priest and seminary professor, Vincenzo de Vit. He was an archaeologist and philologist. After noviciate he too joined Rosmini at the Villa Bolongaro. His intelligence was a welcome foil to Rosmini's wisdom. Later he was to have a distinguished career as a man of letters.

Religious life in the Villa was quite monastic with emphasis on daily meditation, Mass and the praying of the Divine Office, daily examen and the recitation in common of the Rosary of Our Lady and the Paters.[7]

Fr Lockhart spent a few weeks there with Rosmini in 1853 on his way back from studying in Rome. He wrote his impressions:

As I remember him, the portrait [painted for Manzoni] resembles him greatly. It shows something of the greatness of this man in the magnificent forehead, but it wants the profound calm, gentleness and sweetness of the expression of his eyes, which indeed no painting could give; and of that dignity and holiness which, in saintly men, would seem as if it were the expression of the supernatural character stamped on their soul, which one can feel in their presence, and remember but cannot describe.

As I walked with him along the lake on the day I finished my retreat, I asked him some questions about the Risen Body of Christ. I remember as he discoursed on the Resurrection of

Christ and on the Blessed Sacrament, I could not but feel that
I had realised something of what the Apostles must have experienced as they walked with Christ on the borders of the Lake
of Galilee. I have had the privilege of knowing several great
servants of God, but no one ever impressed me so deeply as
Rosmini ...

[*and at prayer*] Rosmini's grand figure, half-a-dozen
disciples round their great master, all dimly seen by the light
of his shaded lamp: the scene was enough to impress me with
a life-long conviction of the importance of daily meditation
and of the great advantage, as a general rule, of regularly
preparing for it overnight.[8]

Rosmini still spent his mornings studying and dictating. The
first thing he wrote on return to Stresa was his *Commentary
on the Mission to Rome*. It was as if he was determined that
the true course of events as he had experienced them should
be recorded while his memory was still fresh. However, the
manuscript was shown to no one, not even to his own
community. Having made his submission to the Pope after
the condemnation, he was determined not to rock the boat.
This book eventually saw the light of day for the first time
twenty-five years after Rosmini's death.[9]

Pagani has left a description of Rosmini's method of
writing:

It was his custom to invoke the Holy Spirit before beginning
to write or dictate ... he wrote rapidly and generally standing,
but when dictating he would pace up and down his chamber,
and the effort of thought was so great that perspiration stood
out on his forehead. However deep the argument on which
he was engaged, he dictated rapidly and fluently ... 'it seemed
to me', said Luigi Setti who was one of his secretaries, 'as if an
angel were suggesting the words to him or as if he were
reading from an invisible book.'[10]

He soon returned to his philosophical writings, during 1850
putting together his *Introduction to Philosophy*. This is a
summary of his earlier writings. He sets out his philosophical
ideas in a logical order and demonstrates how they constitute

a unity of thought.[11] He also continued on the great work of his *Theosophy*, which included a commentary on the thought of Aristotle, explained and examined. After his death Tommaseo wrote that it was the finest commentary on Aristotle he had ever read.

The *Introduction to Philosophy* is, for Rosmini, a comparatively brief work and is quite easy to read (apart from some sections of interminable distinctions which Rosmini seems to be overfond of). He establishes the connection between philosophical principles and ideas of God as Creator and Redeemer. The basis of morality and the notion of Providence receive strong emphasis. A third section, entitled the 'concept of wisdom', is a sublime presentation of the nature of knowledge, goodness, virtue, the gifts of the Holy Spirit, and wisdom.

In it also is to be found his famous metaphor of a pyramid, a favourite of Rosmini's, to explain how the 'idea of being' is foundational to his thinking:

> [When we reflect on ideas] what we are doing is building a pyramid, of which the base layer consists of innumerable small truths. Above are built, layer by layer, more universal truths which rest on the first, becoming fewer and fewer and more and more universal as we ascend; until we arrive at a unity and simplicity which is universal truth . . .
>
> I have many thoughts, many ideas of things, which are all different. But what these things have in common is that, like myself, they *exist*: they have *being*. This judgment, within me, that things exist is primary; it precedes any other particular judgment about what sort of beings they are. However, there is one idea that precedes this judgment: the *idea of being* itself. This precedes any ideas I may have of particular beings. I may be deceived in my ideas about particular things: I cannot be deceived about the *idea of being*, because it is pure intuition.
>
> It even precedes the idea I have of myself. I judge that a particular thing exists because I have sensations, *feelings* that tell me it exists. But this is also true of my own being: I have an intimate feeling of myself, a *fundamental feeling*. To judge that I exist, I need first to have the *idea of being*.[12]

It is noteworthy that Rosmini produced this *Introduction* not long before he died. It is like his swansong. The only other major philosophical work at this time is his *Logic* (1853). This consists of three books written between 1850 and 1853 with some assistance by his companion Vincenzo de Vit.

During 1850–53 he also wrote a series of articles for a Turin newspaper *Armonia* mostly dealing with new legislation regarding civil marriage. This legislation, named the *Siccardi Laws* after the Piedmontese Minister who framed it, was brought in by the anticlerical ministry led by Camillo Cavour, who dominated Piedmontese politics during these years. Rosmini wrote to combat this legislation.

As might be expected, Rosmini is uncompromising in defending the Catholic Church's teaching on marriage: emphasising the Church's claim to sanction the legitimacy of Catholic marriages and to legislate regarding validity and the forms to be normally used. Rosmini attacks the Piedmontese government's attempts to usurp these powers, even though he recognises the duty of the state to protect the rights of children, property rights, and also to legislate regarding non-Catholic weddings.

Rosmini is fiercely critical of the government's initiative in copying French secular legislation originating during the French Revolution. At the same time he advocates the Anglo-American system, which protects the rights of religious minorities regarding marriage. That system is basically sound, he suggests, since the state is working to protect individual and family rights founded on the nature of human society. What is objectionable to him is when the state arrogates to itself total control over civil marriage to the detriment of the Church.

These articles are singular in that they are the only writings of Rosmini which are 'popular', in the sense that they are composed in straightforward Italian for a newspaper audience. It is worth observing that even though Rosmini was suffering considerable persecution at this time, he still continued to write and to publish. He tended to regard persecution as permitted by the Providence of God as a trial for himself and for the Institute. But it should not in any way inhibit or determine their operations and their lives as religious.

The 'Stresians'

During these years there was one aspect of Rosmini's life which brought him continuous enjoyment and affirmation. His friends often visited him, and so the life of the house was constantly stimulated by discussion and debate. Foremost among his visitors was of course Alessandro Manzoni. Rosmini sometimes went to visit Manzoni in his villa at Lesa, but more frequently it was Manzoni who strode out along the lake from Lesa to Stresa or came by carriage to visit his friend. Often he would stay the night.

Others came too, of whom the most prominent was the Marquis Gustavo Cavour.[13] Gustavo was a very religious man and became a devoted friend. A young man, Ruggiero Bonghi, came to Stresa in 1850 and stayed with Rosmini for several months. Bonghi was a Neapolitan but the 1848 events had driven him into exile, and he eventually found himself in Turin where he busied himself translating Plato into Italian. In later life he became prominent both as a writer and in Italian politics. He was not a particularly religious young man, and this fact drew on Rosmini's head some negative comments from outsiders that he welcomed an unbeliever into his household. In fact, it says a lot about Rosmini's tolerance that he was happy to befriend Bonghi and provide him with a home for a few months, as well as to draw benefit from his friend's expertise in Greek and his knowledge of Aristotle. Bonghi sometimes was critical of Rosmini, saying he took a long time saying Mass – but he still liked it! It is typical of Rosmini that he was happy to have Bonghi with him without passing negative judgments about him regarding his beliefs or his lack of piety.

Bonghi has left us a fascinating account, to some extent fictitious, of the animated debates Rosmini would have with his friends on philosophical subjects. These often took place while they were walking along the lake. It is said that they would sometimes have a break in their debate to play 'ducks and drakes', skimming pebbles across the water of the lake. Another oral tradition is that Rosmini liked winning! And why not?

Bonghi's book, *Le Stresiane* – 'The Stresians'– describes four of these debates, principally between Rosmini and Manzoni, but there were other participants including Bonghi himself.[14] The subject of each debate is some abstruse philosophical point. The reader would have to be a philosopher to truly appreciate the nuances of argument and the cut and thrust of discussion.

For instance the second debate focuses on the question whether God created the world freely and, if so, would that not be contrary to the perfection of God? Initially Manzoni wants Rosmini to pronounce an answer authoritatively since he is the 'maestro'. Rosmini demurs. 'Forget the compliments', he interjects. He is content to pose the question, but he wants to hear what the others have to say. So Cavour, Manzoni and Bonghi carry on an animated discussion, with Rosmini remaining silent. However, towards the end he comes in, and there are some quite long and complex discourses from the 'maestro'. Bonghi, with some humility, portrays himself as constantly interjecting – in a way that bright young people often do.[15]

This form of intellectual debate undoubtedly delighted Rosmini and drew him out of his solitary routine of abstruse meditation and dictation. He also loved the social interaction, much in the same way as he had enjoyed the company of his young friends when he was growing up in Rovereto. It was undoubtedly a consolation to him to know that he was appreciated and loved by his friends and his religious family, at a time when his reputation was being torn to shreds by his enemies, in Rome and throughout Italy – and even in England.

Notes

1   *Ep.Compl.*, x, 6440.
2   *Ep.Compl.*, x, 6468.
3   See text above, p. 61.
4   *Ep.Compl.* x, 6239.
5   Pagani, *Life,* p. 309.
6   Pagani, *Life,* p. 310.
7   The 'Paters' are prayers for the needs of the Church, the Institute and the world. This practice has become a feature of Rosminian life ever since.
8   Lockhart, *Life,* ii, pp. 190–94.
9   Published by Paravia, Rome, in 1881.
10 Pagani, *Life,* p. 312.
11 A summary of this work will be found in Appendix 2, an outline of Rosmini's philosophical system.
12 *Introduzione alla Filosofia,* paraphrase of sections 1, 8 and 3, 13–19.
13 Brother of Camillo Benso di Cavour, the Piedmontese politician.
14 First published for the first centenary of Rosmini's birth, Milan, 1897.
15 *Le Stresiane*, published by Piemme (Casale Monferrato), 1997, pp. 83–132.

Chapter Twenty

New Persecution

Examination of Rosmini's Works and Acquittal, 1849–1854

The death of Pope Gregory and the succession of Pius IX had been the signal for a renewed assault on Rosmini's orthodoxy. Pagani notes that while the first attack by Eusebio Christiano had been theological and the condemnation of his two works in Rome had been political, this new offensive against him was theological, philosophical and political all mixed together.[1] And the methods used by his critics suggested that it was as much an attack on the Institute as on Rosmini himself.

An anonymous booklet was secretly circulated with propositions from Rosmini's works (sometimes mutilated and truncated) on one page and censorious comments on the facing page. The title given to this work was *Postille* (*Comments*). These booklets were sent to various Italian bishops but in the greatest secrecy, so that although the attack started in 1846, Rosmini did not actually lay hands on a copy until 1850. The aim was to prevent the presence of Rosminian religious in these dioceses as much as to attack their Founder.

The *Comments* used adjectives about Rosmini such as 'false', 'erroneous', 'heretical', 'offensive to pious ears', 'blasphemous', 'seditious', 'subversive', 'dangerous to souls'.[2] Most bishops rejected the booklets as calumnious, but some were taken in, such as the Bishop of Reggio Emilia who, in February 1848, wrote asking the Pope to act against Rosmini.[3]

However, some of Rosmini's supporters rallied immediately to his defence. Professor Pestalozza, who taught philosophy and theology at the Milan seminary, was given a copy of the *Postille* by his Archbishop. He was a great advocate of Rosmini's teachings, so he set about at once to write a refutation. Rosmini was very gratified by this: he himself was disinclined to spend time and energy, especially since it appeared that much of what was written against him was scurrilous.

A second book appeared in 1850, entitled the *Letters of a Bolognese Priest*. This was intended for more general circulation but the language and the general drift was much the same as the *Postille*.[4] Rosmini was described as 'ignorant', 'a plagiarist', 'inconsistent', 'a man of twisted ideas', 'a hypocrite', 'obstinate', 'dishonest', 'full of tricks and subterfuges', 'a Jansenist fox', 'an insinuator of wicked doctrines', 'a teacher of hellish ideas', 'a calumniator', 'a deceiver of the public', 'a traitor to the church'.[5]

In a letter of 31 January 1851 to Msgr Luquet, a friend who resided in Rome, Rosmini reveals his thoughts on the crisis:

> I have been and still am uncertain whether it is better simply to abandon myself to divine providence in the new and even more bitter persecution which is at present aimed against me … without defending myself; or whether it would be more pleasing to God if I arose in my own defence …
>
> Many have said to me that the animosity, the bad faith, the twisted interpretations and the sophisms of the Bolognese priest do not deserve a reply, and that the Holy See will surely see this conspiracy and punish it, especially since it is a violation of the command given by Gregory XVI. But others beg me to make a response, in view of the power my enemies exert in Rome.[6]

Rosmini was inclined to stay silent and leave it all to the providence of God. Nevertheless he asked Luquet to let him know how things stood in Rome in his regard, and whether there might be a danger – as some had suggested – of other works of his being placed on the Index.

The ripples of this new controversy spread far and wide and inevitably worked to the detriment of the work of the Institute. The most worrisome example of this was in London. Archbishop Wiseman had spent time in Rome in 1850 and had received the red hat from Pius IX. He was appointed leader of the newly constituted hierarchy for England and Wales. On his return to England he banned Rosminians from preaching in his diocese of Westminster on the grounds that their Founder had had works placed on the Index of Prohibited Books.

The Provincial, Fr Pagani, wrote an anguished letter to Rosmini on 25 December:

> You know that for some years past Cardinal Wiseman has at times been ill-disposed towards us ... Recent events show that since his return from Rome and his elevation to the cardinalate, he has openly become a powerful enemy of ours ...

He then goes on to relate what Wiseman said to Ambrose Phillips and his wife:

> Mr and Mrs Phillips enquired from His Eminence for news of the feelings in Rome concerning you ... The Cardinal replied that your affairs in Rome were in a sorry state; that your works were being examined, and that the result of this examination would be the prohibition of some works; that these works had harmed, and continued to harm, Italy very greatly; and that both you and the Institute were regarded with great suspicion, especially as regards orthodoxy ...
>
> Mrs Phillips asked His Eminence what he thought about the future fate of the Institute. He replied that when certain of your works, at present under examination, are prohibited (which he regards as sure to happen) you would be deposed from the position as Superior of the Institute, and then the Institute would be greatly modified.
>
> When Mrs Phillips alluded to the esteem in which the Holy Father had held you two years ago, the Cardinal replied that the Pope had certainly conceived a profound respect for you; that he had really been persistent over his proposal to show a public sign of his esteem, but in the end he had allowed

himself to be persuaded [against this] by the representation of others.[7]

It is quite astonishing that Wiseman should have spoken in this way – and it reflects badly on him, especially as Rosmini had generously lent him the use of some of the regalia, bought when he himself had been told by the Pope in 1848 to prepare for the cardinalate. Wiseman had paid a call to Stresa on his way home expressly in order to thank Rosmini.

On arriving back in London, however, Wiseman dramatically changed his tune, adding his own spin to the malicious gossip. When all this was reported back via Phillips, Rosmini was able to gauge for himself how seriously the rumour mill was harming his reputation in Rome and damaging the good name of the Institute.

Shortly afterwards (8 January 1851) he wrote an anguished letter to Cardinal Castracane asking him to intercede with the Pope on behalf of the Institute:

> The sophistical cavillings, the lies and the acrimony (which must already be spread about Rome) go beyond all limits. Unfortunately everything is permissible for my adversaries. I put up with this in peace and thank God for these crosses, but at the same time I have the duty to do what I can to defend the Institute, the destruction of which is the aim of these persecutions.
>
> I hope Your Eminence will not abandon us in this terrible predicament ... Please, for charity's sake, go to the Pope, speak to him freely and tell him all about this conspiracy ...[8]

Rosmini then quotes the long section of Pagani's letter regarding the actions and statements of Cardinal Wiseman (see above). More or less at the same time, a petition was sent directly to the Holy See from Pagani in London countersigned by Frs Domenico Ceroni and Peter Hutton, protesting at the calumnies written against Rosmini and the damage these were doing to their Rosminian brethren and their work. They pointed out to the Holy Father that Rosmini was their Superior precisely because he had been appointed as such directly by Pope Gregory XVI.

Examination of Rosmini's Works

There was a prompt response. Rosmini received on 13 March 1851 an official letter from Fr Vincenzo Santucci on behalf of the Holy See, stating that Pope Pius had decided to renew the precept of silence on both parties issued by Gregory XVI in 1843. The letter continues:

> Various writings have been published which, though anonymous, had as their author or authors members of the Society of Jesus – this cannot be doubted, rather there is every reason to believe it; and so the Holy Father has decided to renew the aforementioned prescriptions.
>
> Today, such an injunction is all the more necessary and proper since the Holy See proposes to make a very thorough examination of the controverted opinions … I have informed the General of the Jesuits … By this letter I apprise you also of them, so that you will execute the Pope's decree in so far as it concerns you.[9]

Pius entrusted this examination to the Congregation of the Index. He also chose six independent consultors to do the necessary work. Rosmini was very pleased to receive this decision from Rome. He decided to send a competent person to act as his Procurator in Rome, choosing Fr Luigi Bertetti for the task.[10]

Pagani notes that Bertetti was a man of mature judgment, well versed in Rosminian teaching. He was kindly received by the Pope. He proceeded at once to provide the consultors with the necessary documents including a list of 82 published works of Rosmini. He was also at hand early in 1852 to attend the deathbed of Rosmini's great champion, Cardinal Castracane, ministering the last rites of the Church to him.

The consulters laboured away through 1852 and had their decision ready by September of that year. Only one of the six, a Canon Fazzini, was critical. The others were completely favourable towards Rosmini. One said: 'the works of Rosmini are not only free from any doctrine worthy of censure, but his

teaching is most useful for the refutation of modern philosophical, irreligious ideas'.[11]

The enemies of Rosmini continued to be active especially
in Rome, and this caused Pius to be doubly cautious, so he
appointed two more new consulters: an Augustinian, Fr
Caiazza, and a Franciscan, Fr Trullet. Finally, in March 1854,
their votes were ready. Both voted emphatically in favour of
Rosmini. Trullet's commentary is worth quoting:

> I am not exaggerating when I assert that when I came to
> comprehend the entirety of Rosmini's teachings … I found
> myself faced with a world of thought incomparably grander,
> more noble and more beautiful, speaking forth more splen-
> didly the supreme wisdom, glory and goodness of God, than
> these material and corporeal heavens of ours.[12]

Reading such an encomium it is little wonder that some
scholars who have studied Rosmini in depth do not hesitate
to rank him with Augustine and Aquinas as the greatest of
Catholic luminaries. It remained only for the Congregation of
the Index to pronounce its verdict. At a preparatory session
on 26 April 1854 three votes were taken:

- To the question was there anything in Rosmini's writings
  worthy of censure the unanimous vote was NO.
- Should this decision be made public? Again, a unanimous
  YES. Rosmini's good name needed to be cleared.
- Finally, should the accusers be condemned, specifically the
  authors of the *Postille* and the Bolognese priest? This time
  a majority voted YES, but a minority thought a milder
  sentence should be passed.

When this news was conveyed to Stresa, Rosmini was
naturally overjoyed, but he still had to wait for the full
Congregation to meet and confirm these decisions. This took
place on 3 July. Eight cardinals attended along with the Pope
himself, an unprecedented event. The full congregation
unanimously confirmed the first vote. However, whether this
should be expressed publicly by means of a Brief was left to
the discretion of the Holy Father.

Rosmini had waited a very long time for the vindication that he constantly hoped for. Sometimes he had become discouraged, and even spoke of retiring voluntarily from leadership. However, as the day drew near he bade his brethren, the Sisters and his friends to pray before the Blessed Sacrament for a favourable outcome. On the day itself he accompanied his community in a long prayer vigil. Thousands of Masses were celebrated for the one intention.

It seems that strong pressure was brought to bear on the Pope not to issue a public Brief because this would be to the detriment of the Jesuits' reputation. A plea was made that the 'Bolognese priest', identified as Fr Antonio Ballerini, a prominent Jesuit writer, teacher and theologian, had written his book without the permission of the Jesuit authorities: therefore it would be wrong to dishonour, by association, an Order which always had been, and was still, a bulwark of orthodoxy.[13]

It seems that Pius' judgment was swayed by this consideration. He is quoted as saying that 'Justice is the right thing, but prudence also is one of the cardinal virtues; we must take the middle course'.[14] The Decree *Dimittantur* was communicated to Bertetti on 10 August 1854, to be passed on privately to Rosmini (as it was to the General of the Jesuits). Bertetti protested that there should be a Papal Brief published, but he was told that 'reasons of prudence prevented the Holy Father from doing more'.[15]

The Decree *Dimittantur* (translated into Italian by Fr Remo Bessero Belti, and into English by Fr John Morris) states:

> The Sacred Congregation of the Index decrees that all the works of Antonio Rosmini-Serbati which were recently submitted to examination are to be exonerated (from the accusations which have been brought against them), and the fact that this examination has taken place must in no way be allowed to detract from the good name of either the author or the religious society founded by him, or from the praise due to his life and singular good services towards the Church. And, so that no further dissensions or accusations (new or old) shall arise and be spread about, by order of the

Holy Father silence is for the third time enjoined on both parties.[16]

Aftermath

Following the issue of the Decree, during the short time he had yet to live, Rosmini was able to rest content that his orthodoxy had been vindicated. The attacks ceased and the Institute enjoyed a period of peace. However, the fact that there had been no public declaration left people somewhat mystified. Rumours regarding his orthodoxy would continue to circulate and there was no published text to appeal to, to 'confirm or deny', so to speak. Justice had been done – but justice was not seen to have been done.

In the years following Rosmini's death in 1855 his critics periodically returned to the fray. The wording of the Decree was sometimes given a negative interpretation. Thus there appeared in the Jesuit Journal *Civiltà Cattolica* in 1856:

> The Sacred Congregation, by using this word (*dimittantur*), did not intend to issue a real judgment, whether for or against. It *dismissed* the case, leaving it ... for free discussion by the learned.[17]

Many years later, in 1876, there was a more open attack. Both the *Osservatore Romano*, in Rome, and the *Osservatore Cattolico*, in Milan, simply dismissed the *Decree* as having settled nothing. Pope Pius, although by this time a very old man, confirmed the correct interpretation of the *Dimittantur*, insisting that both newspapers retract – which they were forced to do.

Pius IX died in 1878 and he was succeeded by Pope Leo XIII, who also reigned as Pontiff for a very long time. It was a new era. Pope Leo was determined to re-establish orthodox theology in the seminaries, and he strove to do this by making the study of St Thomas Aquinas the universal basis for seminary study. His Encyclical *Aeterni Patris* (1879) promulgated this. There was no overt criticism of Rosminian philosophy in it, but it opened the door to the suggestion that those who followed the Rosminian method were no longer fully orthodox. Rosmini had written in the language of the nineteenth century and had not employed Thomist categories.

A more articulated attack on his work took place in 1881 with the publication of a book by a Jesuit scholar, Fr Giovanni Maria Cornoldi.[18] It was entitled *Rosminianism: a Synthesis of Ontologism and Pantheism*. This was very influential, but it drew a carefully reasoned response from the Franciscan Fr Trullet, the same scholar who had been one of the consultors in 1853 and had thoroughly studied Rosmini's writings at the time.

These writings evoked a storm of debate and discussion between anti- and pro-Rosminians, a debate which took on a political complexion because Rosmini was also hailed as being a 'conciliator' who had worked for the unification of Italy and reconciliation between the Holy See and the secular forces seeking unification. As opposed to this school were the 'intransigents' who strove to defend the temporal power of the Papacy at all costs and were completely hostile to the new Italy of King Victor Emmanuel. Politics always adds a dash of salt to a debate.

This atmosphere of dissension inevitably invited an intervention by authority.[19] This came like a bombshell at the beginning of 1888 with the issuing of the Decree *Post Obitum* condemning forty Propositions taken from Rosmini's writings. Thirty of these statements were from two books still unfinished at Rosmini's death and published posthumously: the *Theosophy* and the *Commentary on the Prologue to the Gospel of John*. The others were from various works published during his lifetime, and therefore officially freed from censure by the *Dimittantur* Decree of 1854.

There was no consultation of Rosminian scholars prior to the issuing of *Post Obitum*, no opportunity to defend his name or teachings; indeed the Decree came totally unexpectedly. The Superior General of that time, Fr Lanzoni, at once wrote a letter of total submission, following the example of his Founder after the condemnation of the *Five Wounds* and the *Constitution* in 1849.

The impact of this new Decree on the two Rosminian Institutes was devastating. Fr Bessero Belti observes that it resulted in a 'contraction' of the Order, a slowing of ordinations to the priesthood, a 'wariness over taking on new works of charity'.[20] Rosminians learnt to keep their heads below the parapet, so that eventually they came to be accepted in the Church on their own merits – in spite of having a Founder who was deemed to be a heretic. Some other religious who had supported Rosminian teachings were also reined in.[21] The two works placed on the *Index of Forbidden Books* in 1849 stayed there for over 100 years, virtually until the *Index* was abolished by Pope Paul VI in 1966. The 'Forty Propositions' remained officially censured by the Catholic Church for 114 years until, on behalf of the *Congregation for the Doctrine of the Faith*, Cardinal Ratzinger announced in 2001 that 'the condemnation of the Forty Propositions taken from the works of Antonio Rosmini can now be considered superseded.'[22] This cleared the way for the Beatification of Rosmini which took place at Novara, north Italy, on 18 November 2007. After a century and a half in the wilderness Rosminians could at last hold up their heads and rejoice in a Founder who was acclaimed by the Church.

Why this persecution? Isn't the Church of Jesus Christ supposed to be founded on the two commandments of love? Anyone reading the story of what Rosmini suffered as told above is inevitably left with many questions. How was it, for instance, that some Jesuits appeared to be so hostile to him and his Institute?

First, one must insist that it was by no means all Jesuits who felt and wrote against Rosmini. At most it could be said that there was a faction or a 'school' in the Society of Jesus who disagreed and criticised him, and this continued over many years. There is no evidence to suggest that the Fr General of the Jesuits in Rosmini's time, Jan Roothaan, or his immediate successor actively supported the machinations of this anti-Rosmini school. However, they apparently did little to stop it, which is surprising considering what value the Society of Jesus has always placed on the virtue of obedience.[23]

There were many Jesuits who were embarrassed by the attacks on Rosmini from within their ranks. There were others who would consider themselves as disciples of some of his teachings. This could be said of members of many other religious Institutes at the time. A good example of an alternative Jesuit view is described in William Lockhart's *Life of Rosmini*:

> One day, I think in April (1854), I was sitting in my room in the Via del Gesu, when I heard a knock at the door, and on going to open it, I introduced two Fathers, whom I knew at once as Jesuits. At that time the Jesuits were again in Rome after the restoration of the Pope, and still wore that well-known venerable habit now never seen in Italy. The senior introduced himself as Fr Etheridge, a much-respected English Jesuit, at this time Father-Assistant to the newly-elected General.
>
> ... After the usual friendly salutations and conversations on general topics, Fr Etheridge said: 'Reverend Father, you are perhaps surprised at my visit, as we are personally strangers.' I replied, of course, that 'good Fr Etheridge could be no stranger to me, and that I was always glad to meet any of the Society, for which I had always felt the greatest respect and affection.'
>
> He continued: 'I have come, sent expressly by my Father General, to say to you, and through you to your Superiors of the Institute of Charity, that the Father General regrets the opposition to your venerated Founder, Rosmini, and he wishes it to be understood that this is not the work of the Society of Jesus but of a school of opinion in the Society.' I expressed my satisfaction at this assurance, which I promised to convey to my General, Fr Rosmini.[24]

It has also to be remembered that the Jesuits themselves were in the process of recovery from a persecution which had seen them suppressed, with the approval of the Holy See, for forty years at the end of the eighteenth century. They had survived largely in Eastern Europe where the Empress Catherine the Great of Russia did not accept the religious dictates of Rome in her territories. Hence there was a strong Polish influence in the restoration.

Fr Jan Roothaan, Superior General from 1829 to 1853, was Dutch by birth but had received his early education as a Jesuit in Russia. He was a vigorous and effective leader, and the Jesuits recovered much of their strength and influence under him. But he had no sympathy with the political liberalism spreading inexorably through Europe, especially in Italy. As a philosopher he was a traditional follower of Aquinas, and in that sense too he had little in common with Rosmini.[25]

Rosmini himself, in his *Treatise on Conscience*, had been critical of some of the sixteenth and seventeenth century casuists in the Society, who did not go back to the fundamentals of morality: regarding original sin, New Testament teaching and obedience to conscience. He was, however, of the opinion that the basis for the attack had little to do with his teachings, but rather was a form of institutional jealousy: the Rosminians, having adopted some Jesuit institutions and structures and aspects of the Ignatian rule, were seen as a new reformed version of the Jesuits, in competition with the revival that was in fact in progress within the Society under Roothaan.

However, the spirit and essence of the two Congregations are quite distinct, and this allegation of collective jealousy is pure speculation. At that time there were many new Congregations for men and women religious springing up in the Church. Rosmini himself was a friend of St John Bosco and supported him financially in the foundation of the Salesians. Rosmini would often visit their houses in Turin. He was also a friend of the Barnabites, also a new Congregation, some of whose members were strong supporters of Rosminian teaching.

He found the animosity towards him from other religious hard to comprehend. He sometimes excused it as excessive zeal among people who wished to defend what they held to be religious orthodoxy. At least they seemed to be concerned to defend the truth, even if it was in a misguided way. An article in the *Civiltà Catholica*[26] stated: 'We [Jesuits] are the watchdogs in the house of God ... Rosmini's writings cast an evil shadow, so it is our job to make a noise'.[27]

In general terms it can be said that the persecution Rosmini and his Institute suffered was simply an example of the disease *odium theologicum*, which has persistently affected the Catholic Church, and other churches, throughout history. The term literally means 'theological animus, or hatred'. The author personally observed it in Rome during the 1960s, when a group of theologians centred on the Lateran University, carried on a vendetta against some biblical scholars, influential in major changes in the Church's theology before and during the Second Vatican Council.

To understand how virulent and vicious it can be, you have to experience it first-hand. Rosmini experienced it. He suffered greatly because of it. It possibly shortened his life.

Notes

1   Pagani, *Life*, p. 319.
2   Bessero Belti, *The Rosminian Question*, p. 24.
3   Bessero Belti, ibid., p. 39.
4   Fr Roothaan did not support this sort of polemic; nevertheless he continued to criticise the language and ideas of Rosmini, which he thought were deserving of examination by church authority (Bozzetti, op.cit.).
5   Bessero Belti, ibid., p. 27.
6   *Ep.Compl.*, xi, 6739.
7   Bessero Belti, ibid., pp. 32–34.
8   Bessero Belti, ibid., pp. 36–37. This letter is not published in the *Epistolario Completo.*
9   Bessero Belti, ibid., p. 42.
10   Bertetti was a highly competent Rosminian priest. Born in 1814, he went on to be the third Fr General of the Institute, dying at Stresa in 1874.
11   Pagani, *Life*, p. 326.
12   Bessero Belti, ibid., p. 44.
13   Antonio Ballerini (1805–1881) was one of the most important Roman

Catholic moral theologians of the nineteenth century. Apparently he was a very gracious man, but he had an overreaching zeal for what he called purity of doctrine, and he could be of a quite impulsive temperament that sometimes led him to offensive language. For example in his *Principe della Scuola Rosminiana* ('Principles of the Rosminian School') he used offensive terminology. Fr Roothaan was unhappy about the book; but Pius IX said it was all right to publish it, so Roothaan insisted that it should be published anonymously and that there would be no personal attacks in it. Unfortunately, in the two volumes that were published the attacks seemed all too evident. So Roothaan forbade the publication of the third volume of that work.

14   Pagani, *Life,* p. 329.

15   Bessero Belti, ibid., p. 53.

16   Bessero Belti, ibid., pp. 52–53.

17   Bessero Belti, ibid., p. 60.

18   Giovanni Cornoldi (1822–1892) was an ardent proponent of Thomistic philosophy all his life long. He was for many years a regular member of the staff of the *Civiltà Cattolica* and wrote a good number of articles on philosophy. He obviously was delighted when Leo XIII published *Aeterni Patris* virtually establishing Thomism as the official philosophy and theology of the Church. Leo XIII called Cornoldi to Rome and over several years the two of them established a great personal friendship. From 1879 to 1881 he published a series of articles in *Civiltà Cattolica* on ontologism and on pantheism, and they came out as a book in 1881. That work and his friendship with Leo XIII probably contributed to the 1887 condemnation of the forty Propositions, taken from the works of Rosmini by the Holy Office. Cornoldi was one of those 'intransigent Catholics' against just about everything that was in any way directly or even remotely connected with the new 'liberal' Italian state set up after the Italian government took Rome in 1870.

19   Pagani-Rossi, ii, pp. 709–710.

20   Bessero Belti, ibid., p. 79.

21   An article at the time of Rosmini's beatification in 2007 by Giovanni Scalese, CRSP notes that many Barnabites had been enthusiastic followers of Rosmini's teachings. After 1887 they were reined in by the Holy See, which went so far as to change the leadership of the congregation in order to tighten up doctrinal orthodoxy. A similar fate was suffered by a Venetian congregation, the *Istituto Cavanis*. These incidents are related by Fr Eduino Menestrina in his book *Rosmini: L'uomo e il santo*, vol. 1, pp. 235, 261–273.

22   Decree issued by the *Congregation for the Doctrine of the Faith*, 1 July 2001.

23   Fr Ballerini was never reprimanded for his polemics against Rosmini by either Roothaan or the Jesuit Provincial (Bozzetti, op.cit.).

24   Lockhart, *Life*, ii, p. 314.
25   There seem to be different opinions regarding Roothaan's part in the persecution. Rosmini himself never suggests that he was hostile, and he is sometimes described as a 'friend of Rosmini'. However, Fr Bozzetti quotes Bertetti saying that Roothaan 'non stava in un letto di rosa' ('did not stand in a bed of roses'; Bozzetti, op.cit.).
26   *Civiltà Catholica* was a religious review under the direction of members of the Society of Jesus. Since it was founded by Pius IX, it was seen as the semi-official voice of the Holy See.
27   Fr Bozzetti, op.cit.

Chapter Twenty-One

Final Years, 1854–1855

Rosmini believed that religious should look after their physical well-being. That is clear especially in letters he writes to his own religious. The Rosminian vocation is an apostolic one, and to be able to respond vigorously to calls of charity means you have to be fit. For this reason there is little emphasis in his Rule on physical self-denial. Working hard for others is sufficient mortification.

The early death of Luigi Gentili, who did not look after himself properly and submitted himself to a heroic regime of prayer and labour, had been a salutary lesson to Rosmini. Perhaps for this reason he is more insistent in the advice he gives to the later missioners in England. In a letter to Rinolfi at Rugby in April 1853, he underlines the need of care for 'our two zealous workers Furlong and Lockhart'.

> After three weeks of work, or a month at the most, there should be a period of a week or ten days of complete rest before they undertake another mission. Secondly, there should be one day of rest every week.
>
> They must absolutely cut down their hours in the confessional, so as to leave themselves with at least seven hours' sleep. It is true that those who are robust and rich in spirit can survive better, but for the less robust one must take greater care.[1]

These are wise and compassionate words. And there is no reason to think he did not look after his own health too.

When he became sick, he usually took time off. During the final year of his life he was treated by various physicians, but in those days there was little they could do for mysterious diseases like cancer. They took their inexorable course.

So what *did* he die of? We can only speculate. His health problems, which came and went from about the age of thirty, seemed to be primarily digestive. The fashionable thing in Italy has been, and still is, to ascribe most maladies to the liver. *Mal de fegato* (liver trouble) could be described as the national disease.

A diet which often includes wine and highly spiced dishes can affect digestion by increasing the output of stomach acid and causing reflux. Longstanding reflux may lead to oesophageal cancer, which usually results in death within five years.[2] Fr Leetham, in his biography of Rosmini, speculates that he may have died as a result of a stomach ulcer becoming malignant, although the course of that illness would have been quicker.[3]

There are two factors which made matters worse for him. One was his habitual overwork over a very long period – his output of writing had been prodigious, and when he was pacing up and down dictating to a secretary he could become quite overwrought. The other, probably graver, influence was the stress he was under over many years due to the constant persecution he suffered. He often makes light of this, but when he allows his guard to slip it is obvious that it affected him, especially his sleep and probably his general health. He certainly worried deeply about the effect the constant bad press was having on the good estate of the Institute.

There are two other incidents which occurred during that period which cast a more sinister shadow over Rosmini's time of sickness and decline. The first is reported in his diary for 25 February 1852:

> Ash Wednesday. There entered the garden at Stresa a well-dressed man, in black with a blue topcoat. There he met Antonio Carli and asked him if he was the servant of the Abate Rosmini. When Carli responded 'yes', he said he had a favour to ask – a little thing but for which he was prepared to hand

over a considerable sum of money. He took out of his pocket a small flask and asked Carli if he would pour the contents into the Abate Rosmini's morning coffee or chocolate.

Carli was horrified at this suggestion and at once refused. At which the visitor told him not to disturb himself, and quietly turned on his heel and left the garden. He went straight down to the lakeshore, where he got into a boat anchored there with three or four boatmen in it. No sooner was he aboard than they moved off and disappeared.[4]

It is certain that Carli, who was no fool, would have seen this as an attempt to poison Rosmini; the fact that Rosmini records it in his personal diary would suggest that he too saw it as highly suspicious.

The second incident took place on Rosmini's last visit to Rovereto during late August and September 1854. One evening, just before he was due to return to Stresa, he was invited out to dine by a local family. On his return home he felt ill and spent a restless night. When he failed to appear in the morning his sister-in-law, the Baroness Adelaide, went to his room and found him in some distress and trying to walk with the aid of a stick. She enquired anxiously how he was feeling. He replied simply: 'I am poisoned ... at dinner yesterday, no sooner had I taken the soup than I perceived the poison.' He named the person who had brought it to him. At the time the Baroness never mentioned this to anyone. Rosmini declined the offer to call a doctor, but treated himself before returning to Stresa.[5]

Whether or not poison played any part in Rosmini's sickness, the fact remains that while he was on holiday in Rovereto he had appeared to be well, but from October onwards his health started to decline.

Last Days

During the final year of Rosmini's life, the affairs of the Institute went ahead satisfactorily enough. In England, in spite of the negativity of Cardinal Wiseman, there was steady progress. The public missions in Ireland had been highly successful even though Rinolfi and Lockhart had once narrowly escaped being lynched by some Orangemen![6] A new parish mission was being negotiated in Cardiff, the forerunner of a great apostolate in South Wales. There had been an invitation to establish communities of both Rosminian Fathers and Sisters in London. A steady flow of vocations came to both Institutes so that the English mission was becoming self-supporting.

In Italy too vocations continued to come, although more slowly, and the news of the happy outcome of the examination of Rosmini's writings, even though not published, inevitably leaked out and this worked for the good. The only major concern was the threat on the part of the anticlerical government in Turin to suppress some religious congregations, and Rosmini had some fears that that could include the Institute.[7] This, of course, never happened.

Rosmini was still entertaining the idea of a visit to the brethren and Sisters in England even as late as February 1855, but the deterioration of his own health soon put paid to that idea. As the weeks passed Rosmini's intestinal problems grew steadily more acute, until eventually he ceased to go out and became confined to his room.

His writings ceased. Even his letter-writing diminished to a trickle. His final letter in his own hand was to Pagani in England, nominating him Vicar-General in the event of his own death.[8]

The news of Rosmini's mortal illness soon got out and his friends arrived to see him from far and wide. One of the first to come, during March, was Niccolò Tommaseo, whom Rosmini had not seen for some twenty years, although they had always kept in touch by letter. Tommaseo was nearly blind, but he greeted his old friend with great affection. It is interesting to note that Rosmini did not hesitate to gently reprimand him for an omission in his translation of the psalms where he had exercised a form of censorship by leaving out certain phrases speaking of the wrath of God. Tommaseo pleaded that the mercy of God must be seen to prevail, but Rosmini insisted that justice was no less a divine attribute than mercy. One must translate what is there, not what one may wish to be there. Tommaseo, however, was not in the least offended by this mild rebuke and leaves us an eloquent testimony of how he found his old friend:

> After a lapse of more than a quarter of a century I saw him once again during his illness before he was in immediate danger. The comparison, which the mind makes after a long interval of separation from a friend, often tends to lessen esteem and affection, but in this case it did not detract from either.
>
> In the philosopher admired by the learned men of Europe, the founder of a religious Order, a man destined for the Cardinalate, I saw still the former student of the University of Padua, the young ecclesiastic, the faithful and indulgent friend. There was the same ingenuous and innocent smile; he was cheerful under suffering, his spirit still vigorous under prostration, and I felt the invincible youthfulness of his soul.
>
> His hair was white, less from the weight of years than from long meditation combined with afflictions of body and mind; it reminded one of the modest locks which in his youth only served to enhance the lofty serenity of his brow. His voice still echoed from deep within his chest with accents both strong and sweet.[9]

During May the disease progressed to the point where Rosmini was confined to bed. News of his illness spread all over Italy and to England. Prayers rose to heaven from religious and lay admirers alike. There were even public novenas offered before the Blessed Sacrament exposed.

Fr Bertetti, now the Provincial in Piedmont, came regularly to see him, and Rosmini entrusted him with a copy of the *Constitutions* of the Institute, written during the Lent of 1828 but subsequently amended. He insisted to Bertetti that even the most minute details had been the fruit of long meditation on his part and if they were studied carefully their full meaning would emerge. He bade him to be faithful to them.

Sr Maria Giovanna Antonietti, Superior of the Sisters of Providence, came to visit for the last time. She was greatly distressed. Rosmini said to her:

> Don't be afraid, my daughter, don't be afraid! If we are separated, it is only for a moment and we will remain united in spirit. Here on earth I am little use to your Sisters for as long as I remain; indeed I may do you harm. In heaven I can be of so much greater help, certainly when I am with God.
>
> Believe in God; trust him, for the Institute is God's work and will receive all the help it needs. Be sure of this: the Sisters of Providence will prosper insofar as they are faithful to the spirit of poverty and simplicity.[10]

As he neared his end, his old friend Alessandro Manzoni was constantly at his bedside. It was to him that Rosmini confided what may justly be called his final testament. Manzoni had expressed the prayer that the Lord would keep Rosmini here on earth with his friends. Rosmini said: 'No, no; no one is necessary to God. The work which God has begun, God will complete ...' At which Manzoni cried: 'For heaven's sake, do not say that. What are we to do?'

'Adorare, tacere, godere!' came the reply. And holding Manzoni's hand he took it to his lips and kissed it. *Adore, be silent, rejoice.* These words in Italian are engraved on Rosmini's tomb, and they remain a final precious offering to all his disciples.

Death

Rosmini gradually grew weaker and he became unable to take food. He lingered during the month of June, his relatively robust constitution resisting the ravages of the disease. There was a constant procession of fellow-Rosminians, family and friends coming to sustain him. Eventually, at the end of the month, he sank into a coma and died early in the morning of 1 July 1855. He was fifty-eight years old. The day of his death was the Feast of the Precious Blood of Christ. It was a devotion he had long practised and recommended to his sons and daughters of the Institute of Charity.

His body lay in state in his bedroom for a day so that the brethren and close friends could come and watch and pray. The funeral took place on 3 July in the nearby parish church. Afterwards the coffin was borne in procession up the hill to the chapel, built on the south end of the College. Later a burial chamber was excavated where his tomb remains. Directly above in the chapel itself there is a marble life-size figure of him kneeling in prayer.

As the news of his death spread, tributes flowed in. The doughty Bishop Ullathorne, bishop of Birmingham in central England, someone who had been generally supportive of the Rosminians although often quite critical of Rosmini's writings, wrote:

> He was the restorer of that deep and profound philosophy which seeks to harmonise revelation and reason, and treats of the supernatural order at the same time as the natural – in the tradition of St Augustine, St Anselm and St Thomas. Though his writings were abstruse and difficult for ordinary minds, I think that is due to the sublimity of the subjects he treats and the height from which he contemplates them.
>
> There was a moment in his life when his virtue was put to the test. The way in which he made his submission to the Holy See and the spirit with which he invited his brethren to show their constant faith in the Rock of Peter will stay as a glorious memory and inspiration. It proved how sound was his heart and how thoroughly his intellect was made subject to his faith.[11]

John Henry Newman also wrote to Pagani:

> The news reached me unexpectedly and profoundly moved me, for although he belonged in a special way to your Institute, a man like him as long as he lived was the property of the whole Church. I fear that the tribulations he suffered have shortened his life ... I hope he will not forget me as soon as he reaches heaven, in fact we may believe he has already arrived there.[12]

Many of the Italian tributes tend to be overly sententious. One, however, well worth noting, is that of the redoubtable brother, Antonio Carli:

> I see Rosmini as another Francis of Sales for his affability and zeal for souls; as a Vincent de Paul for his universal charity; as a Gregory the Great for his greatness and generosity while remaining apart from this world ... like one of the early Fathers for his steadfastness in upholding truth and justice ... like Job in his patient acceptance of the will of God.[13]

ᐩᕱᣝᣟ

If you visit any modern Italian city you will see many monuments of the *Risorgimento*, which gained momentum during Rosmini's life and came to its climax in 1870. Nationhood for the Italians is a recent phenomenon, so it continues to be justly celebrated. The great heroes of that movement to unify Italy are commemorated by monuments, statues, street names or at least by busts in civic gardens.

King Victor Emmanuel, the first Prime Minister Cavour, Garibaldi and Mazzini are the most frequently honoured by the name of a street or a piazza; and sometimes you will come across a side street – the *Via Rosmini*. Indeed in Turin the *Via Rosmini* is a main thoroughfare. As you might expect, in Rovereto his birthplace, and Stresa where he died, his memory is especially celebrated. Among all these great historical figures, Rosmini is virtually the only churchman of that period to be so honoured by the state.

As a patriot, therefore, Rosmini figures prominently in recent Italian history. In the Italian academic world he continues to be well known because of his philosophical writings, with annual conferences dedicated to his thought as well as regular lectures or articles. Up to a dozen publications concerning his thought appear in Italian each year. All this keeps his name in the public eye. Across continental Europe he is also celebrated in academic circles, but in the English-speaking world that is not the case. Even among philosophers he is largely ignored.[14] There has been an attempt in recent times to remedy this by systematically translating his major philosophical works into English.[15]

As a religious figure he lives on primarily in the lives and tradition of his many followers across the globe. His spirituality is read and quoted, especially his little masterpiece, the *Maxims of Christian Perfection*, now translated into many languages. His educational method is regarded favourably in Italy and beyond, and has of course been appreciated by many generations of students in the schools founded by his religious Institutes.

As a churchman his fortunes have been more mixed. Initially he was grieved over and prayed for in churches all over Italy and England. Nevertheless, his critics continued to steadily undermine his reputation. After all, he had works placed on the Index of forbidden books. After the condemnation of the 'Forty Propositions' in 1887, his name effectively became mud for generations of students of theology. Until very recent times his works appeared in theological manuals among the *errori* – those 'in error'. Rosminians were defined as religious whose founder was a heretic.

There is little doubt that a lot of this had to do with the fact that, from the ecclesiastical viewpoint, Rosmini was seen, under Pius IX, as having backed the wrong horse. He was a political liberal; the Church had become reactionary, ruled over by the Prisoner of the Vatican, out of kilter with the modern world. This was to remain the case until well into the twentieth century.

The Beatification in 2007 has dramatically changed all this. An article written at the time by the ex-President of Italy, Francesco Cossiga, states emphatically that 'the quarrel between the Italian nation and the Church which opened in 1848 was effectively closed only with the beatification of Antonio Rosmini'.[16] Now he is bracketed with Newman as one of the great Catholic prophets of the nineteenth century, whose words heralded a new age for Catholicism destined to dawn at the Second Vatican Council.

Perhaps in these days we can look forward to an extended period when the memory of Antonio Rosmini will be honoured, his philosophy and spirituality made better known, and that the Catholic Church will acclaim him as one of its greatest and most loyal sons.

Notes

1   *Ep.Compl.*, xii, 7386.
2   The author is grateful for the opinion of an experienced medical practitioner, Dr Anna Holmes, who kindly offered her opinion on possible causes of Rosmini's final illness.
3   Leetham, *Rosmini*, pp. 466–467. This speculation regarding Rosmini's fatal illness was also based on the opinion of a medical general practitioner.
4   *Diario Della Carità* 1852; this is the final entry in Rosmini's diary.
5   Pagani, *Life*, p. 341.
6   Schofield, *Lockhart*, p. 86.
7   *Ep.Compl.*, xii, 7818, letter to Belisy, 20 October.
8   The Vicar General is responsible for governing the Institute *sede vacante* and organizing the election of another Provost General.
9   Pagani, *Life*, p. 344. Pagani-Rossi, ii, p. 490.
10   Pagani-Rossi, ii, p. 512.
11   Pagani-Rossi, p. 556; letter to Pagani, 12 August 1855.
12   Leetham, *Rosmini*, p. 481; letter to Pagani, 10 July 1855.
13   Menestrina, *Rosmini: L'Uomo e il Santo*, p. 28.
14   The contemporary Catholic philosopher, Alasdair MacIntyre, for example, dismisses Rosmini's efforts to respond to contemporary ratonalism as 'inadequate' and 'ineffective' (*God, Philosophy and Universities*, pp. 133, 151).
15   The late Fathers Denis Cleary and Terry Watson laboured for many years at Durham translating Rosmini's works, principally philosophical, into English, and distributing them throughout the world to English-speaking colleges and dioceses. This work is now being continued by Fr Antonio Belsito, IC.
16   In a special edition of the Italian Catholic journal *30 Giorni*, p. 31 (September 2007).

Afterword

Rosmini's life was one of extraordinary achievement: as patriot, as philosopher, as religious founder and spiritual guide.

He is justly honoured in his own country as one of the architects of Italy as we know it today. He ardently believed in a united Italy, heir to the glorious past of the Renaissance and ancient Rome. He believed that Italian, the language of the great Dante, should be spoken throughout the whole peninsula. He loved and esteemed the rich heritage of his country's art and culture.

He saw unification as a religious as well as a political process. He wanted the temporal power of the Popes preserved. He could not see, as some were already suggesting, that the temporal power was seriously compromising the religious integrity of the Papacy as well as standing in the way of political unification. Separation of Church and State was for him a step too far. In that sense, Rosmini was not prophetic.

His philosophical writings remain a hugely impressive legacy. He has always had his disciples in Italy and in other continental countries. That is as true now as it was then. The problem of translating his thought to communicate with the English-speaking world remains. What is needed is a mind of the highest calibre, which will not merely translate his words but also develop his thinking so as to converse with the contemporary world. Even better, there needs to be an English-language Rosminian academy in London or in New

York or in Dublin, to bring his philosophical ideas to a new incarnation.

However, the greatest heritage of Rosmini is in the realm of the spirit, and this still flourishes in the lives of his followers. In so far as they live and profess his spiritual principles, especially his *Maxims*, they keep Rosmini alive and well. In spite of his great intellectual achievements, Rosmini remained a humble, prayerful man. Like St Thomas, he valued his philosophy as so much straw in comparison with the vision of God. Rosmini is justly acclaimed for his holiness. Successive Popes have esteemed him and quoted him. It is to be hoped that one day quite soon he will be canonised and presented as a saint, a prophet and a doctor of the universal Church.

Yet when we look back on Rosmini's life, we have to view it with a sense of sadness for what might have been. We see it as a tragedy. Perhaps that is always the way with saints. They invite misunderstanding and persecution. Politically, his apparent failure was inevitable: he was born in the wrong place at the wrong time. The long shadow of Austrian power was destined to haunt him to his grave.

A greater tragedy was his eventual rejection and condemnation by the Catholic Church. In today's jargon we might say that Rosmini thought 'outside the box', something that too many of his Church contemporaries would not tolerate. A huge injustice was done to him, not yet adequately acknowledged. His reputation was torn to shreds, and his disciples were denied any right of reply. The placing of his books on the Index was an arbitrary political act. It had no connection with faith.

This injustice will never be fully healed until the Church changes its systems so that such things can never happen again. Catholicism espouses orthodoxy as one of its central pillars. For the official authority of the Church, it is a bounden duty to proclaim the truth as it sees it and condemn error when it finds it. But for justice to be done, what the Church condemns must be seen as truly in conflict with faith or morals, not just an alternative viewpoint which happens to conflict with the fashion of the time.

The manner in which the *Congregation for the Doctrine of the Faith* deals with writers judged to stray from doctrinal orthodoxy belongs to the Dark Ages. There is no transparency. There is no due process. A counsel for the defence is usually lacking. There is no Court of Appeal. Many have been condemned unheard.

It may be argued that you cannot simply transfer secular processes and apply them to ecclesial structures. But it can equally be argued that where there is a pattern of injustice, we could do a lot worse than look to the secular world for models to help set it right. This may become part of the agenda of a reforming Pope or of an Ecumenical Council.

Rosmini accepted the judgment of the Church even when he did not agree with it. He was a totally loyal and obedient Catholic. But that very subservience can become a factor which helps sustain tyranny. The fact is that all human beings make mistakes and can act high-handedly, especially when vested with absolute power. Religious leaders, no less than politicians and pundits, sometimes need to be challenged.

Clerics need to listen to the voice of the laity. Bishops need to heed the voice of their priests. The Church as a whole needs to hear the concerns of women. The Roman Curia needs to consult the bishops. And the Pope himself must set the example by becoming *par excellence* one who listens. If Jesus listened to the Syro-Phoenician woman and changed tack, it is an example for all to follow – from the Pope down.

So perhaps the final legacy that Rosmini has bequeathed to the Catholic Church is a lesson how *not* to treat its loyal servants. Once upon a time religious powers, Catholics and Protestants alike, burnt and bludgeoned those who thought differently. With the passage of time we have learned better. A paramount need for the Church of our age is to listen to the modern world, to new scholarship, to today's prophets: to listen and to learn from them. And not to demonise and destroy them.

Appendix 1

Rosmini the Writer

When Rosmini visited Rome in 1829 to seek the first approval of the Institute, he received an explicit commission from Pope Pius VIII. The Pope said to him:

> It is the will of God that you employ yourself in writing books: that is your vocation. The Church in these times has a great need of writers, of really solid writers, of whom we have a real scarcity.[1]

Rosmini always remembered this exhortation, took it to heart and often referred back to it. His vocation as a priest and religious centred on his daily labours at his desk. Broadly speaking we can divide his activities as a writer into three: his books on politics and spirituality; his letters; and the vast corpus of his philosophical works.

His works comprise over 100 publications, some of them little more than pamphlets but others 300–400 pages in length. He employed at least one secretary to record these, but he also had to spend quite a bit of time revising proofs. At the same time he kept several diaries, which were strictly utilitarian records of events. He rarely wrote anything in them which one could describe as personal.

He is not regarded as a great Italian stylist. In his early years he employed a somewhat artificial and complex style, but his friendship with Manzoni and other literary figures made him moderate his way of writing, and he became easier to read. He spent up to four hours every morning working at his books. He was extremely disciplined and seemed to have an encyclopaedic knowledge derived from his early reading. If he was interrupted in dictating by a visitor, he was able to carry on exactly where he left off without pause.

Rosmini's Letters

He devoted a couple of hours every evening to correspondence, sometimes dictated to a secretary but more usually written in his own hand. They are an important aspect of his charitable labours. His letters are collected in the *Epistolario Completo*: there are some 8,000 letters surviving, collected in thirteen volumes.[2] Some are brief but many are several pages long. An Italian writer, Michele Dossi, comments critically:

> Rosmini's style can at times be rather precious, with its obsolete terms and complex, over-elaborate constructions, the often excessive extent of his arguments ... [which makes it] tiring for the modern reader.[3]

Translator John Morris, English Rosminian, is unsparing in his praise about the content and impact of Rosmini's letters, especially when he is giving spiritual counsel. He responds to Dossi:

> ... these [comments on Rosmini's style] are trifling matters compared with the great value of the ascetical content of his letters, the profound faith and spiritual insight they reveal, as well as the delicate skill with which he adapts his approach to his very varied correspondents ... he spent just as much time and care in writing with advice to a laybrother or a novice as he did when addressing a cardinal or a pope.
>
>   I cannot forbear from remarking how striking is his insistence again and again, not only on such virtues as humility and obedience, but on gentleness and cheerfulness ... [Moreover] Rosmini urges on his brethren that they should act not childishly but in a *manly* fashion. Magnanimous himself in the true sense of the word, he wished all members of the Society of

Charity to be so, always *generous* [a favourite word of his along with *gentle*] with both God and neighbour . . .

A striking feature of Rosmini is his ability to 'think big' and to go into minute detail. What he recommended to others he practised himself. He regarded a religious vocation as a most sacred thing, and he was at pains, with endless patience, to help his brethren and Sisters when they had problems in fulfilling the pledges they had made to God.[4]

Fr Morris also notes how Rosmini constantly returns to certain key themes:

Abandonment to divine providence, the Church, indifference, humility, prudence and so on form an integrated theological whole – which of course is summarised in the *Maxims of Christian Perfection*.[5]

As regards individuals, Rosmini was discreet in the way he tempered his advice to fit the needs and capacity of the person he was guiding. He was especially careful in his letters to the brethren in England, who were a long way from home and learning to live in a strange country. For example, it is interesting to compare how he dealt with Pagani and Gentili, the two leaders among the first missionaries.

Gentili, pioneer and first superior, was something of a firebrand and often upset his subjects. As soon as possible Rosmini replaced him as superior with Pagani, who seems to have had good people skills. Gentili was never again given authority over a community, although Rosmini had the highest respect for his zeal and skill as a religious and a missioner as well as of his profound knowledge of the English Church.

Pagani was an entirely different character. Fr Leetham notes that Pagani was 'an ascetic, essentially a ruler of his brethren, very receptive, open-hearted, reliable, rather diffident about his capabilities, learned in theology and a good philosopher.'[6] Sometimes he tended to become depressed, and Rosmini was very gentle in encouraging him. But he could also be firm and directive as we may note in the following letter from Rosmini in April 1843:

We need to repose an unlimited trust in God's goodness and this must never be lessened, not even in the midst of miseries. We must take it as certain that God is ready to forgive us seventy times seven times . . .

You say you want to make a retreat in order to gain compunction of spirit; but I want you to make it in order to gain joyfulness of spirit . . . I command you to use your time in contemplating things which are cheerful and uplifting to the spirit . . .

We must not obstinately persist in judging ourselves, but leaving everything to do with ourselves in the hands of God. So take courage . . .[7]

Eventually Rosmini had to recall Pagani for an extended leave in Italy so that he could regain his equanimity. Pagani was a good man and a sound religious; the break restored him to a better frame of mind. But Rosmini was careful not to put Gentili in charge while Pagani was away. We have already seen how fierce, but also how supportive, Rosmini could be towards Gentili.

When Rosmini was approached in 1847 by Cardinal Franzoni to nominate someone in England for a project of the highest importance for the Church in England (in fact, it was to provide confidential information in preparation for the full restoration of the hierarchy), the question arose whether Gentili or Pagani was the right person.

Rosmini left the final choice to Franzoni, pointing out however that while Gentili 'had many external gifts, social manners, eloquence and energy', Pagani 'had prudence, learning and every other interior gift.'[8] Moreover, it was important that if he chose Gentili – which he did – it should be under the supervision of his Superior, Pagani. Gentili was to send a series of illuminating reports and recommendations of possible candidates as bishops. Pagani's name is included on the list.

Rosmini did not hesitate to send some of his most talented priests to the English mission. Another was Pietro Bertetti, who had been a seminary rector before coming to the Institute. He sought Rosmini's advice regarding methods of pastoral ministry; Rosmini wrote him a long letter in January 1850, in which he makes an interesting distinction between the virtues of simplicity and prudence. Rosmini concludes:

> You will see, my dear Pietro, that there is nothing contradictory between prudence and simplicity. They are mutually compatible. Simplicity consists in loving and prudence in thinking. Love is simple; the intelligence is prudent. Love prays; the intelligence watches. *Watch and pray* ... here is the reconciliation of prudence and simplicity.
>
> Love is like the dove which coos; the working intelligence is like the serpent which never falls to the ground, never collides with anything, because it goes along detecting with its head all the irregularities in its path.[9]

Rosmini's letters of guidance and spiritual direction were equally detailed and careful to ordinary religious as much as to their leaders. One Sister whom he wrote to frequently both before and after her entry into the Sisters of Providence was his cousin Catterina. He seems to have been especially fond of this cousin, even addressing her in his early letters by her chosen nickname 'Nina'.

When he first hears from her that she is thinking of a religious vocation he is careful not to push the idea of becoming a Rosminian. However, eventually he does say to her:

> God inspires you that you must consecrate yourself wholly to him in the service of your neighbour; I conclude unhesitatingly that, as you say, you have a vocation to the Institute of Providence. These Sisters do just what you propose to do.[10]

He insists however that she is completely open with her father, whose judgment regarding her maturity to take this step must be honoured. In the course of time she follows her illustrious cousin in making the journey to Domodossola to become a Rosminian. She is eventually professed, as Sr Maria Bonaventura.

She has the usual ups and downs living in a community and beginning a teaching career. Their correspondence continues regularly up to shortly before his death. Here are a few excerpts:

> Confidence; yes, at all times without limits: confidence when things are calm; the same confidence when storms arise, when you are well, when you are ill; when things are going well, when things are amiss ...[11]
>
> I wish the Sisters to feel in their hearts only forgetfulness of self, gentleness and love for others, zeal, indifference to all things, the love of God and perfection. In this way they will enjoy the wonderful fruits of the Holy Spirit – peace, joy, courage in doing good, trust and abandonment to God ...[12]
>
> I am glad you are happy over the school. Keep in mind when you are teaching the girls that you are exercising charity towards Jesus Christ ...[13]
>
> Whenever we become conscious of any contradiction or clash with anyone, for whatever reason, we must not lose a minute before placing ourselves before God and praying until we have recovered a feeling of humility ... Be cheerful, my dear, and all will be well.[14]

Rosmini writes many letters to the Sisters and brethren encouraging them in their work and their vocations. He seems to be unsparing in this, even at times when he is greatly stressed (as during the Mission to Rome). He did however sometimes excuse himself for brevity when he was having trouble with his eyes, an increasing burden during his later years.

It has to be said that Rosmini's letters tend to be very serious and often didactic. However, especially when writing to his religious, he is constantly guided by the ideal of apostolic charity. There is little humour and no idle chatter. Sometimes he shows considerable warmth. When he was young this was evident in his letters to his beloved sister. Later it appears in what he writes to his sister-in-law, Adelaide. He writes to her (in December 1847):

> Here we are full of compassion for so many good religious who have been forced to flee from Switzerland, and also for many Catholic families. You cannot imagine how much this

matter afflicts my heart ... I am glad to hear how generous Giuseppe [Rosmini's brother] has been to the poor Irish people. Tell him he will never regret being liberal to so many wretched people ...

However, Rosmini cannot resist preaching her a little sermon:

Money is worth nothing as long as it is kept in the safe, but it begins to have value when it reaches the hands of others through charity. My dear Adelaide, I hope you will always be a good dispenser of charity, given your prudence and kindness.[15]

Later, he thanks her for her charity in serving the country people of Sant'Ilario, a village near Rovereto; this was a favourite charity of Rosmini himself. He calls Adelaide 'a shepherdess in the Lord'.[16]

Rosmini spent many hours in his letter-writing. He saw it as a work of charity, which it was. His correspondents were many and varied. Sometimes he is engaged in special issues. Nevertheless the ultimate purpose in all his correspondence was to help the person to whom he was writing to come closer to God. It unifies his letter writing with all his other works.

Notes

1   See page p. 86.
2   Fr John Morris did an excellent job translating many of the ascetical letters into English, a task completed after Fr Morris' death by Fr Donal Sullivan.
3   Published in *Trentino,* January 1997.
4   *Ascetical Letters,* vol. 8, tr. D. O'Sullivan, pp. iii-iv.
5   *Ascetical Letters,* vol. 1, tr. J. Morris, p. 2.
6   Leetham, *Rosmini,* p. 331.
7   *Ep.Compl.*, viii, 4777.
8   Leetham, *Rosmini,* p. 330.
9   *Ep.Compl.*, x, 6477.
10   *Ep.Compl.*, viii, 4646.
11   *Ep.Compl.*, viii, 4884.
12   *Ep.Compl.*, x, 6471.

13   *Ep.Compl.*, x, 6522.
14   *Epistolario Ascetico,* no. 1444.
15   *Ep.Compl.*, xiii, 8198.
16   *Ep.Compl.*, x, 6534.

Appendix 2

Rosmini the Philosopher

At least in Italy, Rosmini is best known as a philosopher. His aim was to provide a Catholic response to contemporary Rationalism. Both the Empiricism of the English philosophical school of the eighteenth century and the Idealism of thinkers such as Kant and Hegel seemed to undermine the religious basis of European society. Rosmini sought to counter this.

It was a huge task, but one for which he was well equipped. From the time Fr Pietro Orsi took over as his tutor Rosmini had been fascinated by philosophy. He was interested in all branches of knowledge and was also a very competent mathematician. Being good at maths and having a calling towards philosophy often seem to go together. Descartes, Leibniz and Bertrand Russell were all fine mathematicians.

An upbringing in a rural backwater like Rovereto was of no disadvantage to his academic formation. The Austrian government, especially under the Empress Maria Theresa, had promoted good, sound popular education, and this was the case in Rosmini's native town. Italian was understood and spoken by many of its leading families, like the Rosminis.

The town had its *Accademia degli Agiati* – the academy of those 'of independent means' – whose leader was modestly known as the 'most independent' (*agiatissimo*). In spite of its pretentious title this literary-cum-philosophical society flourished during the latter half of the eighteenth century and the young Rosmini was welcomed into its ranks as a teenager. He contributed enthusiastically to its proceedings.

Rosmini's voracious early reading encompassed all the modern philosophers. He was especially interested in the English empiricists such as Locke, Hume and Berkeley. He realised that the scientific movement from the time of Galileo and Newton had caused an explosion of human knowledge as well as being the basis for much technological progress. He recognised that knowledge comes to us through the senses, and therefore it was basically correct to explore the origin of human thinking by starting with sense perceptions.

However, he was also aware that 'Sensism', as it was called, easily leads to a disregard of God. This was anathema to Rosmini. For him, it was like trying to solve a puzzle and leave out the most important piece. For Rosmini, all knowledge is one, and centres on God. Therefore his philosophy, his political thought and his faith journey were all one. They were all part of the pursuit of truth – and truth is one.

෧෧෨

In 1852 Rosmini published a comparatively short book, *An Introduction to Philosophy*. It brings together all his philosophical teaching. The following is a summary of parts of this book, section by section:

Introduction: Foundation of Philosophy

Rosmini defines philosophy as the 'science of ultimate truths'. God is of course the ultimate ground for the existence of everything. Under God we find the 'first created causes'. To penetrate these is as far as philosophy can go. In the eighteenth century Sensism and Empiricism permeated European philosophy with claims to be able to define and explain all knowledge. Like a barbarian invasion this led to negative consequences for European culture with ethics, law, politics, teaching, medicine, literature all severed from their foundations in the truth of God.[1]

To counter this, and with the approval of, first, his mentor

Cardinal Cappellari and then of Pope Pius VIII, Rosmini wrote the *New Essay on the Origin of Ideas*.[2] With the encouragement of the Pope he set himself this task: first to reform philosophy and, in consequence, to put right the other dependent sciences.[3]

Sensism, says Rosmini, undermines morality because it removes its essential base, which is *being*. If a thing exists, *why* and *how* it exists becomes the basis for morality. For Rosmini, morality is therefore natural to being; an objective part of human existence. Sensism on the other hand proposes a purely subjective base (what I feel or what you feel: 'My way of acting is valid because I feel it to be so').[4]

Likewise, there needs to be a sound basis for evaluating political rights. Sensism, being subjective, cannot recognise the true existence of either rights or duties. Politics without a proper moral base will degenerate into brutality and cruelty, and that gives rise to widespread hatred and resentment within society. Justice, however, demands a much sounder basis for society and basic human rights.

We have to ask the ultimate questions: *what is civil society – and what is the basis for its government?* Its basis must be respect for the rights of others; society must thus determine and regulate the rights of its members. It is the only buffer against despotism. This despotism can masquerade as democracy, like the fickle 'tyranny of the majority' that flourished during the French Revolution – and since. Rights depend on the integrity of their innate value, not on a majority vote. They arise from the intrinsic dignity of the human person.[5]

Rosmini rejects the theory of *homo economicus* – 'economic man' – which sees in man nothing beyond what one can feel and acquire. His system, on the other hand, is founded on the intuitive knowledge of *being*, from which is derived true morality and the laws of humanity guaranteeing justice.[6] It is also the basis of religion because clearly this *idea of being* is a transcendent gift. It connects us to God.[7]

The alternative to Rosmini's system is Materialism, which accepts nothing beyond what is sensible and tangible. It denies freedom, implying that human beings are simply automata. When the notion of *spiritual freedom* is abstracted, we are left with *licence* – living a life governed by passion. This was illustrated in the writings of many authors contemporary to Rosmini, from Lord Byron to Victor Hugo.[8]

The Gospel, being part of Divine Revelation, gives us access to certainty, which does not depend on any philosophy. Nevertheless a sane philosophy provides a natural preparation for human faith. Religion completes and perfects science. There need be no conflict since both are aspects of the one truth. A concerted effort is, therefore, needed to provide the world once more with a coherent philosophy, the handmaid of theology. This is what Rosmini sets out to do.[9]

Rosmini's Philosophical System

Philosophy is the *science of ultimate causes*. Some causes are general and refer to everything; others pertain only to a particular field of knowledge, e.g. the philosophy of science or of history. The philosopher *reasons* and pursues a line of thought about those things which are 'necessary'; he or she is also open to *persuasion*, but this is a much freer activity, dealing with contingencies, not necessities – things which may or may not be so.

The philosopher has to go beyond what is merely practical and useful for life, because he seeks ultimate causes, and this demands *reflection*. The question he asks himself is: *how can I be sure that I am not being deceived in my reasoning?* In other words, *what is the status of my ideas?* Logic and dialectic become a necessary part of the task.[10]

Rosmini's philosophical system is founded on two fundamental principles. First, the *idea of being,* which illuminates the human mind from the beginning of life and renders human beings intelligent. From this objective truth in our minds we learn to affirm the reality of the world around us including our own being.

The second principle explains how we interpret sensations.

We are endowed from birth with a *fundamental feeling* whereby we 'feel' our bodies and subjectively interpret the input of our senses. All our sensations are simply modifications of this fundamental feeling, so that we can come to know the outside world.

Therefore the human being discovers a certain dualism within himself (or herself): he has an intelligence founded on the objective *idea of being*, the primal intuition of the mind; and he or she senses the real world because the *fundamental feeling* is moderated by sensations. He (or she) is both an intelligent being and a sensing being.[11]

Intuition

Human intuition is foundational to Rosmini's philosophy. He believes that it comes from God. For this reason a deeply optimistic view of human intelligence permeates his attempts to understand and explain philosophy.

I have many thoughts, many ideas about things, which are all different. But what these things have in common is that, like myself, they exist: they have *being*. This judgment, within me, that things exist, is primary; it precedes any other particular judgment about them.

However, there is one idea that precedes even this judgment: the *idea of being* itself. This precedes any ideas I may have of particular beings. I may be deceived in my ideas about particular things: I cannot be deceived about the *idea of being,* because it is pure intuition and does not depend on any of my senses.

The *idea of being* even precedes the idea I have of myself. I judge that a particular thing exists because I have sensations that tell me it exists. But this is also true of my own being. I have an intimate feeling of myself, a *fundamental feeling.* To judge that I exist, I need first to have the *idea of being,* which is a necessary and certain intuition.[12]

As regards external things, we perceive them through our senses, we judge they exist because they affect us through our senses, and we acknowledge that there is something universal in the experience because, insofar as they are beings, they have *existence*.

When we come to know things we come to know their *essence*, which we can apply even to things existing only in our imagination. *Essence* is something which we intuit. It has a certain universality, which is realised only when we actually perceive the thing in question with our senses. Until we recognise something perceived through our senses, its essence remains unknown to us. The act of recognition involves both the sensing of the thing and the judgment we make that it really *is* such-and-such. We affirm its essence, and this is more than merely *ideal being* (which could be simply us imagining something).

The first experiences of an infant are through the senses. They become aware of things external to them; reflexively, they become aware of themselves. They come to know that things exist and that they themselves exist. This is something a child intuits because they already have the *idea of being* within their minds. Rosmini calls this idea of being the *light of reason*, because through it we come to know all things we experience.

The word 'light' is a useful metaphor because it implies that there is an outside source, just as sunlight implies the existence of the sun. Rosmini asserts that this source is God. But the light is distinct from God, otherwise Rosmini could be – and indeed was – accused of being an ontologist. The term *light of reason* is found among early Christian philosophers from Augustine to Bonaventure; Rosmini did not invent it.[13]

The *idea of being* is innate and is the *form* of our intelligence. What is form? It is the *raison d'être* of something. The form of a branding iron is fire/intense heat. Form is not something subjective, as Kant proposes. It is objective and is a wondrous gift with which we can arrive at truths about God and the purpose of human existence. A fruit of this insight of Rosmini's is preserved in his spiritual writing, in the sixth maxim of Christian perfection: 'to direct all the activities of one's life with a spirit of intelligence'.

Perception

Rosmini distinguishes between *intellect* which intuits and *reason* which first perceives and then reflects. Perception means coming to know the outside world. It consists of two sciences: Psychology and Cosmology.[14]

Psychology

Psychology is the science of the human mind: its essence, its development and its purpose. For the outside world to be understood it has first to be perceived via the senses; it has to be felt. The human mind does not only feel, it also perceives intellectually – and then, reflexively, it perceives itself.

But first it feels. This feeling principle of the mind we call the Ego. Initially, it is a *fundamental feeling*. It is 'simple' in the sense that it is independent of space or time. It gives life to the body; indeed it *is* the life of the body and *in se* it is immortal. (Only God can create the human Ego and only God can annihilate it. But such an annihilation would be repugnant to the goodness of God.)

God also gives the Ego a body to feel with and a world to feel. Through its feelings the mind can begin an intellectual life: it can know and understand things. Moreover it can begin to understand things without knowing how. It can distinguish between its own body, which is always present, and other bodies whose presence is transient.

The Ego moves and controls its own body, but at the same time it becomes aware of alien bodies by bumping into them. It recognises that other bodies have colour, smell, taste, etc., which it also recognises in its own body. It learns to distinguish qualities. It can move through space in such a way as to discover more and more space. The Ego then comes to realise that space is potentially limitless.

Human beings also reason, so that the Ego not only feels its body but understands it. Feeling and knowing are in close union, yet remain distinct. Only in death are these two principles separated.[15]

Human nature consists of intellect and will: the intellect is directed towards truth, the will towards virtue. Humans are moved to behave virtuously because therein lies the truth. This quest for truth and instinct for goodness is what makes human beings happy.

In fact, life is not always like that, and humans are also subject to ignorance, vice and suffering. They become unhappy. But God is not disposed to leave humans in this predicament. God intends for us a higher destiny, another life beyond comprehension by the laws of psychology. Rosmini here anticipates the coming of Christ in the Incarnation.[16]

Cosmology

Cosmology is the knowledge of the world. We place it among the sciences of perception, because as well as perceiving our own selves we also perceive the world we live in. But in the great scheme of creation we must also acknowledge beings that are beyond sense experience: we can deduce their existence (or they are revealed to us. Angels, suggests Rosmini, belong to this category).[17]

Cosmology treats of all contingent beings and their causes. Contingent beings do not exist of themselves and therefore must have a cause. We cannot perceive them unless we perceive them as being identified with the idea we have of their being. Because they are contingent they must therefore be created. We ourselves feel our subsistence, but we do not feel the cause of our subsistence. That means that we too must be created.[18]

The possibility of created things must first exist in the mind of God, otherwise how could they come to exist outside God? Why God should be moved to create them – and us – is beyond our understanding. We interpret it as part of the goodness of God.[19]

Cosmology also treats of the various beings in the universe, the laws that govern them and of their goodness. Clearly, one cannot treat of cosmology without including the sciences on which it depends, namely ontology and theology. For how can we understand the *contingent* without reference to the *necessary*? How can we treat of creation without reference to the Creator? How can we speak of things temporal without a sense of things eternal? Cosmology cannot stand alone. It depends on a higher science which deals with the nature of being itself.[20]

The power of reasoning depends on intuition and perception to provide its raw material, but by means of reflection the reason discovers new truths and can even argue the existence of things beyond the power of perception.[21] Reason works in two ways: *ontologically* – treating things as they are; *de-ontologically* – treating things as they might be.[22]

Reason divides things into *ideal* beings, *real* beings and *moral* beings. The *ideal* is how a thing is conceived in the mind; the *real* is how it is found to be in fact. *Moral* being connects the other two: it is a judgment on the fittingness or beauty of a thing, how closely the real conforms to the ideal.

An example here may help. I wish to acquire a dog. I have an idea of the sort of dog I would like (*ideal being*). I buy such an animal and call him Toby. Toby is a *real* dog. I become fond of Toby and carefully look after him. My love for Toby and my care of him belong to the sphere of *moral being*.[23]

Natural theology deals with that exercise of reason which goes beyond what can be sensed, and seeks to penetrate into what a thing really is in itself, in its transcendence – and here we are entering into the mind of God.[24] Natural theology deals with the grounds for believing in the existence of God:

- the essence of things is eternal: the infinite leads us to God.
- the 'light' illumining intelligence has no limit: it is infinite Wisdom. God is Infinite Wisdom.
- the mind in its pursuit of knowledge climbs to what is not contingent but is necessary – it leads us to God.

- moral being seeks the perfect, the beautiful: this search too must lead to God.

God cannot be 'sensed' nor intuited by us, so any knowledge of God has to be through reason or through revelation. Beyond asserting the existence of God as the source of the light of reason, etc. any other knowledge of God will be negative (this reasoning is termed 'apophatic', in effect, asserting what God isn't).

We cannot apply to God the defects or limitations of other beings. Any gifts we might esteem in other beings cannot apply to God in their contingent or limited state; only by analogy and if multiplied to an infinite degree. Even those who would argue that the affirmation of the Trinity of Persons is open to reason, must accept that this argument is only possible through a *via negativa.*[25]

What does eminently fall within the scope of Natural Theology is the *Providence of God,* whereby all things are subject to God's infinite power. The conservation and government of the Universe, therefore, are controlled by God. Without compromising the freedom given to humans by God, God wills that the concerns of people are subject to the utmost goodness, beauty and holiness.[26]

Rosmini here considers '*perfection*' (which he classes as *de-ontological* – that is, something which might be). The good is possible to us but is often rejected. In fact, we can always do better! One could say therefore that perfection is unattainable. God wills that humans avoid evil and pursue the good, which means that perfection is something we strive for but never reach.

Where does evil come from? Moral perfection is dependent on the human will, which is a central attribute of the human person. The will chooses to obey or not, whereas the laws of physics do not admit of such choice. The apple has to fall. Adam did not have to fall, he chose to.[27]

Moral perfection is a real challenge to human beings because of the Fall.[28] However, humanity is given an archetypical boost in the person of Jesus Christ, whose life presents an example for us to follow 'if we wish to be perfect' (Mt. 5,48). Christ shows us how to behave in order to become better human beings: that is, to follow the Law of Christ. In practical terms humans have to work out their own 'perfection' by making ethical choices. They have to apply the Law of Christ in particular situations. For a start, humans are obliged to recognise the laws of their own being, e.g. self-preservation. Rosmini expresses this universal obligation as 'to recognise being in its order'. This means to acknowledge that some things are more important, more just, more noble than others. A higher being – so to speak – requires greater care and emphasis. Caring for humans comes ahead of caring for pets. The nobler the being, the more it should be loved.

The highest of all beings is God, who is therefore deserving of the highest reverence and love. It is from this first law that the other obligations of the natural law flow: to love and respect the creatures and the earth that God has created for us. This moral law embraces all created things in their entirety.

Conscience is our guide in specific actions, which follow from this law. If we are in doubt as to a specific law – whether or not it applies – then we are not bound by it; but we still need to avoid evil consequences, e.g. giving scandal. Rosmini emphasises that humans must respect one another, despite cultural differences.

Finally, there is a degree of excellence towards which all should strive – and a degree of turpitude, which all must eschew. There is a dignity and joy in striving for the best, and it will receive its reward, just as vice will receive its punishment. Rosmini notes that the philosopher can only take the enquirer so far along the road to human perfection. The rest must come through the Revelation of God.[29]

Human Rights

The common good confers on people certain rights which protect them from being harmed by others. These rights exist, whether recognised or not. They govern a person's freedom and property.

A person may claim something as his or her property, but the claim has to be rationally substantiated before they can be said to have a *right* to it. All rights give rise to *duties,* whereby others must respect their rights and they must respect the rights of others. Rights are individual (those belonging to me personally) or social (those belonging to us socially).[30]

Rosmini's Political Thought

The survey of Rosmini's principles up to this point summarises much of what he wrote in his final philosophical work, *An Introduction to Philosophy.* However, it is inadequate for anyone who really wants to know about his system in any depth. It is intended for the casual reader. The specialist needs to pursue enquiries elsewhere.

It also says little or nothing about how he developed his political ideas. Rosmini was a man of his times and was intensely interested in what was happening in the European world. Even though Rovereto was under Austrian government, and had been for more than 100 years, Rosmini grew up an Italian patriot. Over the business of Pope Pius VII's *Panegyric*, he had already shown his colours and put himself offside with the Austrian authorities long before he started to write seriously on philosophy.

The political system in the Austrian Empire under Prince Metternich was totally autocratic. The word of the Emperor was law. The *Divine Right of Kings* may not have been preached, but it was certainly practised. On the other hand, Rosmini inclined to the sort of constitutional government which had been practised in England since the Revolution of 1688 and which was becoming influential in Piedmontese government circles. Rosmini would have some sympathy with Camillo Benso Cavour.

The British system was based on a balance between king and parliament, and the parliamentary system became steadily stronger with the passage of time. The Westminster Parliament already offered a template for all European constitutionalists. During Rosmini's lifetime the great Reform legislation was passed as well as the abolition of the slave trade in 1807, and then, in 1833, the total abolition of slavery as an institution.

William Wilberforce, the principal architect of this revolution, was slightly senior in age to Rosmini.[31] He was the greatest parliamentary orator of his age. For forty years he was an exemplary constituency MP for the largest electorate in England. His ceaseless campaigning steadily changed the mindset of a political generation, and sounded the death knell to the slave trade, one of humankind's most scandalous institutions.

It is worthy of note that, like Rosmini, Wilberforce was a very religious man. Unusual among politicians, he spent an hour in personal prayer every morning. He was a regular churchgoer; his family grew up mostly devout Anglicans and some entered the ministry.

In his writings Rosmini says little about the institution of slavery, but he was a great admirer of the English parliamentary system, and it influenced him later in composing his projected Constitution for a United Italy. The brand of democracy he advocated gave the vote to all people with property. He seemed to have mixed feelings about universal suffrage – but that was usual in the days before universal education.

In fact, the germ of a more universal democracy can be found in Rosmini's writings. He proposes two layers of representation. The first safeguards the rights of property. It exists to administer the goods of the state and tends to reflect the power of wealth. It is utilitarian, and resembles what was already present in the English parliament. But he also proposes a parallel 'parliament' which is based on principles of justice for all, irrespective of wealth and status. It protects human rights, especially the rights of the minority, easily infringed upon by powerful secular interests or even by the state itself.

Rosmini is prophetic in this second proposal. It anticipates the advent of universal suffrage. It is also being realised today in the judicial bodies spawned by the EU and UN, such as the International Court of Justice, which deal with questions of international importance such as nuclear or chemical weapons, pollution, drug trafficking, the rights of refugees and immigrants. All these involve the infringement of basic human rights.

Rosmini proclaims the equality of all human beings before God. Every human person is imbued with the idea of being from the first moment of existence, and therefore basic human rights belong to all members of the human race. The notion of the fundamental dignity of the human person, as proclaimed in Vatican II documents (*Gaudium et Spes*), is a very Rosminian idea.

Charity stands at the heart of Rosmini's vision in all his writing. He does not neglect to apply this imperative of the gospel also to politics. Charity, or love ordered towards God and always exercised in truth, is for Rosmini not just a virtue to be practised in favour of individuals but is a practical means of ongoing reform and development of civil society.[32]

Citizens animated by charity, he argued, will work to ensure that society is based on justice, and tempered by the reconciliation of opinions and particular interests through mutual esteem, reciprocal concessions and reasonable dealings. Rosmini insisted that civil society is the servant not the master of the family and should respect and serve it.[33]

Rosmini follows the English philosopher John Locke[34] in defending the right to own property; property owners became, to use a modern term, the principal stake-holders in representative government. Like Locke, Rosmini fully accepts the hereditary principle. Both were monarchists. Locke saw this as simply an extension of the principle of inheritance. The monarch inherits the governance of the state, just as the head of the family inherits the family property.

In this respect Rosmini was a child of his age and upbringing. He frequently used his inherited wealth on behalf of the poor, especially in his hometown of Rovereto. We saw this practically when he was parish priest in Rovereto. He was a philanthropist. Nevertheless, it cannot be said that Rosmini embraced social justice in the way a modern social reformer might. He did not question the right of the privileged classes to inherit wealth, nor did he see any connection between disparity of wealth and the plight of the poor. In this respect too he resembles Wilberforce, who was scorned as a hypocrite by the social reformer William Cobbett[35] because he put all his efforts into improving the lot of African slaves but appeared to do nothing for the poor of his native England, especially the peasantry. The Catholic Church too had to wait till the end of the nineteenth century for *Rerum Novarum*.[36]

Rosmini poured his energy into the reform of society through the renewal of religion. His first priority from 1828 onwards was the foundation of two religious Institutes as well as the Ascribed membership of lay Catholics who would live the Rosminian ideal in civil society. The decisive moment of Rosmini's contribution towards a more just society came when he climbed the hill to Monte Calvario in February 1828.

Is Rosmini's Philosophy Relevant Today?

Every great thinker belongs to a certain age. It is unjust to condemn Plato because he did not understand or anticipate the exigencies of modern life. Rosmini must be judged according to his own age, and his virtue was that he truly strove to meet the needs of his native Italy in the nineteenth century.

He wanted the Catholic Church to be part of the process of the unification of Italy. He provided ideas for a constitution, which embraced both the just ambitions of Italian nationalists and constitutionalists and yet preserved the rights of the Church and of princes. He was not listened to, and the placing of his two books on the Index was part of Pius IX's rejection of the modern political system.

Rosmini, however, failed to see that the structures of the new economic system contained seeds of inequality which were intrinsically unjust. He was not ahead of his time in this respect. But then there are many people even today who cannot recognise it either.

Rosmini lived before the time of Freud and Jung. Therefore his philosophy also lacks the huge emphasis on interpersonal relations, which form the foundation of many modern systems. For instance, the contemporary philosopher Emmanuel Levinas says that to understand the way society works we need to acknowledge that the primary ethical moment is in acknowledging the 'face of the other'.[37] This form of altruism is very close to the ethics of the New Testament, but no one in Rosmini's day spoke like that.

These criticisms do not take away the immense value that Rosmini's teachings have even today. In Italy and in other continental countries philosophers think Rosmini has a lot to offer to our times. It is in the Anglo-Saxon world that his philosophy is practically unknown or misunderstood, and that is a tragedy.

How might we put his contribution to philosophy in a nutshell? In his own words: 'if only we were zealous enough in our love of knowledge and our passion for truth!'[38] Love of truth for Rosmini was no abstract exercise. If human beings are called to the truth and made by God for truth, then their philosophical studies become a labour of love for humanity. These studies become what Rosmini called 'intellectual charity'.

That is why he so vehemently opposed Sensism and Empiricism, decrying those godless ideologies which 'tempt and deceive by disguising falsehood and presenting it, dressed up as truth, to the young or unsophisticated mind.'[39] To counter forces he saw as destructive of men and women's sublime calling to truth, he worked tirelessly to protect 'the flame of genius' which 'can only be kindled in the fire of truth, morality and religions which are ignored by the sense, but kept alight in the inner sanctuary of the intelligence.'[40]

In a world characterised by an exploding gap between rich

and poor as well as by moral relativism and subjectivism, to pursue truth as a way of loving society and protecting the common good is very appealing, something which contemporary Anglo-Saxon culture would do well to take more seriously.

Notes

1   *Introduzione alla Filosofia*, i, 9–10.
2   *A New Essay on the Origin of Ideas* (*Nuovo Saggio*) first published in Rome 1830.
3   *Introduzione alla Filosofia*, i, 11.
4   Ibid., i, 12.
5   Ibid., i, 14.
6   In the text, Rosmini's emphasis on the *idea of being* as the fundamental idea of his system has already been referred to in Chapter 5 (p. 44) and in Chapter 19 (p. 215).
7   Ibid., i, 15.
8   Ibid., i, 16–17.
9   Ibid., i, 18.
10   *Introduzione alla Filosofia*, iii, 1–9.
11   Muratore, *Conoscere Rosmini*, p. 85.
12   *Introduzione alla Filosofia*, iii, 10–19.
13   Ibid., iii, 20–34.
14   Ibid., iii, 115–117.
15   Ibid., iii,118–132.
16   Ibid., iii,144–151.
17   Ibid., iii,152.
18   Ibid., iii,153–157.
19   Ibid., iii,158–159.
20   Ibid., iii,160–162.
21   A contemporary example of this is Higgs' Boson. This is one of the fundamental particles, whose existence was proposed many years ago by the the physicist Higgs but not proved empirically until in 2012 when it was discovered at CERN.
22   Ibid., iii, 163–165.
23   Ibid., iii, 166–170.
24   Ibid., iii, 176–177.
25   Ibid., iii, 178–186.
26   Ibid., iii, 187–188.
27   Ibid., iii, 203–206.
28   The dogma of the Fall of humanity and the sin of Adam is generally challenged in our times because of the acceptance of Evolution which

extends to human origins. What is indisputable is that humans sin, that evil exists. However we choose to explain sin and evil, we cannot deny them or ignore them.

29   Ibid., iii, 211–225.

30   Ibid., iii, 226–231.

31   William Wilberforce (1759–1833) was an English politician, Member of Parliament first for Hull and then for Yorkshire, close friend of William Pitt the Younger. Early in life he underwent a conversion to evangelical Methodism, and through the influence of Thomas Clarkson, he became an impassioned campaigner against slavery. He was responsible for legislation abolishing the slave trade in the British Empire (1807) and the final abolition of slavery as an institution in 1833.

32   *Introduzione alla Filosofia*, iii, 104, 106.

33   *Introduzione alla Filosofia*, iii, 109.

34   John Locke (1632–1704) is a father of English liberalism and a seminal thinker of the Enlightenment. Unlike Rosmini, he believed that we are born with a mind without ideas (*tabula rasa*) and that all ideas come through the senses. He is the founder of English empiricism.

35   William Cobbett (1763–1835) was a political reformer, pamphleteer and advocate of the poor, especially the rural poor. Although not a Catholic, he also fought for Catholic Emancipation. He is regarded as mentor of the great Reform legislation of 1832.

36   *Rerum Novarum* was the first great papal encyclical on social justice, issued by Pope Leo XIII in 1891.

37   Emmanuel Levinas (1906–1995) was born of Jewish parents in Lithuania but lived and was brought up largely in France. He is responsible for the *Ethics of the Other*. The encounter with the Other is the prime experience from which all ethics are derived.

38   *Introduzione alla Filosofia*, iii, 2.

39   Ibid., iii, 3.

40   Ibid., iii, 17.

Appendix 3

Rosmini the Countryman

Rosmini never felt at home in big cities. He was born in a remote town in the mountains near the border with Austria. He lived half his life there. When he founded the Institute of Charity, he chose for his centre of operations Monte Calvario, a mountaintop near Domodossola, in Piedmont. He later moved to live in Stresa – now a luxury resort on Lake Maggiore, but in those days it was a rustic place. If you looked at a print of that time, you would see Stresa as quite a small village of fishermen and farmers. Traffic consisted of carriages carrying post and goods, and a few people travelling between Milan and the Simplon Pass using the new road Napoleon had made.

It is true that the mansion Rosmini lived in, the Villa Bolongaro, was probably the richest and largest house in Stresa: but his daily life there was most simple. One must imagine, as his secretary Paoli puts it, a small community of loving brethren, a few friends (such as Cavour, Manzoni and Bonghi) and many visitors.

Rosmini, then, was essentially a countryman, a man of the mountains. When Pope Pius VII, on his first visit to Rome, tried to persuade him to stay on in the city, his response was typical. The Pope said: 'There are important occupations in which you could do much good'. Rosmini replied: 'Your Holiness, I'm a simple country man. I love retirement, silence, prayer, meditation and constant occupation. But for God, if He wills it, I will leave my enjoyment of God'. In this short dialogue we may see already what will become a consistent attitude in his life.

In fact, he had to spend considerable periods of his life in cities: Padua, Milan, Rome, Turin, Naples, so he was able to feel within himself the tension between the two ways of life. What he always missed in the city was the simplicity, sincerity and closeness of a familiar neighbourhood – the friendship of the village.

His childhood experience had been idyllic. He had a loving family, the stimulating presence of his uncle Ambrogio, his sister and brother, his cousins Fedrigotti and Rosmini, and a circle of friends of the same age and similar interests. So his early years were passed in a most happy environment: prayer, study, outings, games. These influences all helped to shape the man.

It is to be noted that when later he stayed in towns he carefully avoided hotels, preferring always the fraternal atmosphere of a religious house or monastery – Jesuits, Franciscans, Passionists and others. He did accept having to living in a 'palazzo' (Villa Albano) when he was in Rome as plenipotentiary of King Charles Albert to Pope Pius IX, but it was only for a short period.

When he visited Turin for the first time in 1836, he voiced his unease to a few close friends (see p. 135). To his mother he wrote, 'The people of Turin are gracious and gentle to me … yet I find their flattery unbearable. I have had a bellyful of their praise, so that it issues forth from my nostrils! I seem to myself to be such a simpleton – a country bumpkin! But I have no time for their sort of empty rhetoric. I cannot be other than I am' (17 July 1836).*

It is not surprising therefore that he failed to cope satisfactorily with the Piedmontese politicians in 1848, who tried to manipulate him in their attempts to persuade Pius IX to take their side against Austria. Rosmini was out of his depth dealing with those wily men.

It was really no better when he found himself at the Pope's side, having to deal with Cardinal Antonelli and others at the Papal Court. While it in no way excuses the cunning and

malice of those who sought his disgrace and downfall, it has
to be recognized that he was like a fish out of water, especially
after the Pope himself changed sides and renounced constitutionalism. Rosmini's great mistake was to stay around too
long, thinking that Pope Pius still wanted him and needed
him.

When one reflects on the various processes which caused
Rosmini to lose favour and eventually to suffer grave persecution, these personal factors need to be borne in mind.

(This appendix is based on a piece written by Fr Luigi Cerana,
IC. Like Rosmini, Fr Luigi also is a countryman from the
Trentino. He shares Rosmini's preference for life away from
cities, even though his Rosminian apostolate has taken him
far from his native home to Africa and to India.)

Note

*   (*Ep.Compl.*, v, 2814)

Principal Works of Antonio Rosmini

(by date of publication)

Original works in Italian and Latin	Date of Publication
Della Educazione Cristiana (three volumes)	1821
Panegirico alla Santa e Gloriosa Memoria di Pio VII	1823
Sulla Divina Providenza nel Governo dei Beni dei Mali Temporali	1825
Constitutiones Instituti a Charitate	1828
Massime di Perfezione Cristiana	1825–30
Nuovo Saggio sull'Origine delle Idee (four vols)	1828–30
Principi della Scienza Morale	1830
Descrizione dell'Istituto della Carità (two parts)	1830
Antropologia in servizio della Scienza Morale	1831–32
Antropologia Soprannaturale	1832–36
Discorsi Parrocchiali in S Marco a Rovereto	1834–35
Catechesi dette in S Marco a Rovereto	1834–35
Regole della Dottrina Cristiana	1835
Regole dell'Istituto della Carità (in Latin and in Italian)	1837
Catechismo secondo l'Ordine delle Idee	1838
Conferenze sui Doveri Ecclesiastici	1838–47
La Società e il suo Fine	1838
Discorsi Parrocchiali	1834–35
Manuale dell'Esercitatore	1839
Trattato della Coscienza	1839
Filosofia del Diritto (two vols)	1841
Della Naturale Costituzione della Società Civile	not given
Risposta al finto Eusebio Cristiano	1841
Sistema Filosofica di Antonio Rosmini	1844
Compendio di Etica	1845
Teodicea (three vols)	1845
Psicologia (two vols)	1846–50

278   *Antonio Rosmini: Persecuted Prophet*

Saggio sul Comunismo e Socialismo	1847
La Costituzione Civile secondo la Giustitia Sociale	1848
Delle Cinque Piaghe della Santa Chiesa	1832–48
Operette Spirituali (two vols)	1849
Introduzione al Vangelo secondo S Giovanni	
Commentata	1849
Della Missione a Roma di A. Rosmini negli anni	
1848 e 1849	1850–51
Dottrina dell Carità	1851
Logica	1854
Teosofia (in nine vols)	1846–54
Epistolario Completo (over 8,300 letters in 13 vols)	1887

Many of these books have appeared in recent years in the National Edition of Rosmini's works, produced by Città Nuova Editrice, Rome.

English Translations

Title	Publisher	Date
Constitutions of the Institute of Charity	Rosmini House, Durham	1969
Maxims of Christian Perfection	Quorn	1992
The Origin of Ideas (Part One)	Fowler Wright	1987
The Origin of Ideas (Part Two)	Durham	1991
Principles of Moral Science	Fowler Wright	1988
Anthropology as an aid to Moral Science	Durham	1991
Philosophy of Politics (two vols)	Durham	1994
Philosophy of Right (six vols)	Durham	1993–96
Treatise on Conscience	Durham	1989
The Five Wounds of the Church	Fowler Wright	1987
Introduction to Philosophy	Durham	2004
Introduction to Psychology (three vols)	Kegan, Paul, Trench	1884–88
Introduction to Theodicy (three vols)	Longman, Green	1912

Most of the recent translations of Rosmini's books were the work of the late Frs Dennis Cleary and Terry Watson, at Rosmini House, Pity Me, Durham.

Select Bibliography

Rosmini, A., *The Ascetical Letters* (8 vols), translated and edited by John Morris, IC and Donal Sullivan, IC. Loughborough: John Morris, 1993–2012.

Rosmini, A., *Conscience*, translated by Denis Cleary, IC and Terence Watson, IC. Durham: Rosmini House, 1989.

Rosmini, A., *The Constitutions of the Society of Charity*, translated by Denis Cleary, IC and Terence Watson, IC. Durham: Rosmini House.

Rosmini, A., *Delle Cinque Piaghe della Santa Chiesa*. Roma: Città Nuova, 1981.

Rosmini, A., *Della Missione a Roma*, (commentary by Luciano Malusa). Stresa: Sodalitas, 1998.

Rosmini, A., *Epistolario Completo*, (complete letters in 13 vols). Casale Monferrato: Giovanni Pane, 1892.

Rosmini, A., *The Five Wounds of the Church*, translated by Denis Cleary, IC and Terence Watson, IC. Leominster: Fowler Wright Books, 1987.

Rosmini, A., *Introduzione Alla Filosofia*. Roma: Città Nuova, 1979.

Rosmini, A., *Massime di Perfezione Cristiana*. Roma: Città Nuova, 1976.

Rosmini, A., *A New Essay Concerning the Origin of Ideas* (3 vols), translated by Denis Cleary, IC and Terence Watson, IC. Durham: Rosmini House, 2001.

Rosmini, A., *Scritti Politici*, (ed. Umberto Muratore). Stresa: Sodalitas, 1997.

Leetham, C.R., *Rosmini, Priest, Philosopher and Patriot.*
Baltimore: Helicon Press, 1958.

Pagani, G.-B., *Life of Antonio Rosmini-Serbati.* London:
George Routledge and Sons, 1906.

Pagani-Rossi, *La Vita di Antonio Rosmini* (2 vols). Rovereto:
Manfrini, 1959.
('Pagani-Rossi' is the name commonly given to the definitive Italian
biography of Rosmini, first written in the nineteenth century by G.-B.
Pagani; revised in 1959 by Professor Guido Rossi.)

Pusineri, G., *Rosmini*, (ed. by Remo Bessero Belti, IC). Stresa:
Sodalitas, 1989.

Bessero Belti, R., *The Rosminian Question,* translated by
John Morris, IC. Loughborough: John Morris, 1992.

Davidson, T., *The Philosophical System of Antonio Rosmini-
Serbati.* London: Kegan Paul, Trench, Trübner, 1891.

Menestrina, E., *Rosmini l'uomo e il santo* (2 vols). Verona:
Fede & Cultura, 2009, 2010.

Muratore, U., *Conoscere Rosmini.* Stresa: Sodalitas, 2008.

Muratore, U., *Rosmini per il Risorgimento.* Stresa: Sodalitas,
2010.

Muratore, U., *Una 'Lettura' Di Rosmini.* Roma: Città Nuova,
1981.

Bonghi, R., *Le Stresiane.* Casale Monferrato: Piemme, 1997.

Cronin, V., *Napoleon.* London: Collins, 1971.

Daniel-Rops, H., *The Church in the Eighteenth Century.*
London: J.M. Dent, 1964.

De Ruggiero, G., *The History of European Liberalism.*
London: R.G. Collingwood, 1959.

Doyle, W., *The Oxford History of the French Revolution.*
Oxford: Clarendon Press, 1989.

Duggan, C., *The Force of Destiny: A History of Italy since
1796.* London: Allen Lane, 2007.

Ferretti, M.B., *The Rosminian Sisters of Providence.*
Domodossola, 2000.

Field, C. and Kauffman, R., *The Hill Towns of Italy.* San
Francisco: Chronicle Books, 1996.

Gaddo, G., *Giorni Antichi,* vol. 2. Stresa: Sodalitas, 1989.

Goethe, J.W., *Goethe's Travels in Italy,* translated by A.J.W. Morrison and E. Nisbet. London: George Bell & Sons, 1892.

Hales, D., *La Bella Lingua.* London: HarperCollins, 2010.

Hales, E.E.Y., *Pio Nono.* New York: Image Books, 1962.

Hearder, H., *Europe in the Nineteenth Century.* London: Longmans, 1988.

Leetham, C.R., *Luigi Gentili, A Sower for the Second Spring.* London: Burns & Oates, 1965.

MacIntyre, A., *God, Philosophy and the Universities.* Lanham, Maryland: Rowman and Littlefield, 2009.

Newman, J.H., *Apologia Pro Vita Sua.* London: Oxford University Press, 1913.

Newman, J.H., *An Essay on the Development of Christian Doctrine.* London: Sheed and Ward, 1960.

Palmer, A., *Metternich.* London: Weidenfeld and Nicholson, 1972.

Puecher, F., *The Last Days of Felice Robol.* Turin: Marietti, 1837.

Valle, A., *Rosmini e Rovereto 1834–1835.* Rovereto: Longo, 1985.

Index